Parties and Pressure Groups

DOCUMENTS IN AMERICAN GOVERNMENT

John P. Roche · *Leonard W. Levy*

BRANDEIS UNIVERSITY

PARTIES
AND
PRESSURE
GROUPS

HARCOURT, BRACE & WORLD, INC. NEW YORK · BURLINGAME

To CONSTANCE

CONTENTS

THE PARTY SYSTEM EVALUATED

Part Two: PRESSURE GROUPS

THE ROLE OF LOBBIES IN A DEMOCRACY

THE LOBBYING ACT OF 1946

THE CASE HISTORY OF A LOBBY

DEMOCRACY'S DILEMMA

Parties and Pressure Groups

INTRODUCTION

For obvious reasons of space, the authors of standard texts in the field of American government are unable to provide material in depth on the various areas and problems they examine. If they did, their works would begin to resemble the Corpus Juris Secundum, which, when last seen, was growing through the roofs of law libraries. Yet, with all due respect to the twin demons of time and space, there is a sense in which a course in American government taught without reference to the primary sources lying so close at hand is like a course on Hellenic archeology taught from slides at the University of Athens. Many instructors have, of course, introduced primary materials on their own, but often the best documents are not available in sufficient quantity for class use.

Documents in American Government is designed to provide a solid body of source documentation in specific areas of American government. This volume of the series is concerned with parties and pressure groups; others will deal with Congress, the Presidency, the judicial process, and so forth. Every effort has been made in the course of editing to maintain the continuity and logic of a document even at the cost of brevity. The natural consequence of this policy is more limited coverage, but we are convinced that more can be gained by the use of fewer, longer selections than from the "seed catalogue" approach. A great deal depends upon the quality of the selections, and we hope that the materials presented here in adequate fullness meet the standards to which we have aspired.

Perhaps because the American party system is so loose and heterogeneous, there is an enormous amount of primary literature on the subject but no one document that provides a matrix, such as the program of a British party.

American party politics almost defy rational generalization. There are state and local politics fought on one level and almost totally concerned with parochial issues, there are Congressional politics where national issues play an important part, particularly in Presidential years, but where there is also heavy emphasis on matters of local concern; and finally there are Presidential politics, the quadrennial battle at the top between the champions of the two coalitions, a joust in which the personality of the contenders is surely as crucial to the outcome as is their disposition of specific issues.

In short, we do not have a national "party system" in any meaningful sense of the term. We have fifty states with two-party systems in varying stages of vitality or disrepair, and the variations between state parties employing the same general label—Democratic or Republican —are marvelous to behold. Compare for instance the New York Republicans (Rockefeller, Javits, and Keating) with the Goldwater Republicans of Arizona. Or, on the other side of the fence, contrast the California Democrats with those of Alabama. And this variety exists not just between states but also within any one state. It is possible in California for a liberal Republican to run for Congress in one district while a John Bircher wearing the same party label contends for office in the next. A Democratic Congressman from Queens County, New York, may be far more conservative than a Republican from Manhattan, just across the East River.

To some degree, every American candidate, every county and city organization, every state committee, is in business for itself. In one state, local candidates will eagerly attach themselves to the coattails of a Presidential candidate: bumper stickers will advertise the cause of Kennedy and Jones or Eisenhower and Smith. In other areas, candidates will pretend that the top of the ticket does not exist: there were no Stevenson-Kennedy bumper stickers in Massachusetts in 1952, for example. John F. Kennedy, running for a Senate seat in what his advisers warned him was a devastatingly Republican year, disassociated his campaign from the Democratic slate and salvaged a narrow victory. Conversely, in the same year, Republicans—even solid Taft men who were convinced that Ike was a bit of a socialist—rushed to have their pictures taken with the candidate in hopes that some of his appeal would stick to them. Democratic state organizations have even supported GOP candidates for President, and in 1936 the North Dakota Republicans plugged for Franklin D. Roosevelt.

Curiously, despite the sound and fury that engulfs the nation each November, competition in American politics is much less effective than is generally realized. In less than a quarter of all Congressional districts is there a real fight—that is, does the underdog candidate have a significant chance of winning. The Republicans, the Southern Democrats, and the urban Democrats (to a lesser extent) each have their substantial bloc of safe seats. As for the Presidency, between 1860 and 1910 the Democrats held the White House for eight years; in the past half-century the odds have been better—the GOP has controlled the executive branch for twenty years—but since 1932 the Republicans have been fighting against what appears to be a permanent Democratic electoral majority and have only succeeded with the aid of a national hero, General Eisenhower.

But the survival power of state political organizations is enormous, precisely because of the looseness and lack of ideological rigidity that makes our "party system" so difficult to describe. The New York Republicans make a superb adaptation to the imperatives of urban

2

life and not only live to fight another day but in recent years have also held both Senate seats and the governorship. The Democrats in California, destroyed for a generation by factionalism, gerrymandering, and fine GOP leadership, emerged from hiding in the late 1950's to capture—and redistrict—the state. Ironically, it is the "one-party-ism" of large areas of the country which makes this condition possible: no matter what goes on at the state or national level, there are bastions that are absolutely safe, that can serve as rallying points for the future and provide training grounds for new leadership and patronage to help build an organization. The national administration has little patronage to hand out—when the Eisenhower Administration took office, the hungry Republicans discovered only about 5,000 positions that could be used to reward the faithful—but state, county, and municipal governments are still largely dominated by the "spoils system." When William Scranton defeated the Democratic candidate for governor of Pennsylvania in 1962 and brought a change of administration to Harrisburg, all Democratic state officeholders braced themselves for the same complete purge that George Leader had administered to Republicans in 1954 as incoming Democratic governor. Throughout the lean years at the state level, the Pennsylvania Republicans had retained control of most of the counties in the state, and their organization had remained intact. By the same token, the state's Democrats in 1963 were anything but shattered by defeat: they still held the two major city administrations and were nursing plans for future revenge.

The fragmentation of political power and the incredible variety that one can find in political outlook from one state to the next, indeed from one county to the next, have led some critics to argue that American parties do not "stand for anything," that "there is no difference between voting for a tweedledee Democrat and a tweedledum Republican." There is some truth to this; in many elections the voter is not offered any vivid alternatives. Yet there is plenty of raw ideology in American politics: Montgomery County, Maryland, had a contest in 1962 between liberals and reactionaries that featured everything but barricades; many a school board has been raided by Birch Society guerrillas; in Wisconsin in 1962 liberal Democrats slugged it out with right-wing Republicans for control of the governorship; and in a number of Congressional districts avowed Goldwater Republicans have assailed liberal Democrats as "com-symps," or worse.

General divisions, while blurred by personality factors, emerge at the level of Presidential elections as well. No serious Republican candidate for President can afford to insult the cities, but it is clear that Democratic candidates have a far stronger urban orientation. No Democratic candidate will affront the business community, but it is equally clear that GOP nominees put a higher value on the virtues of the entrepreneur than on the goals of trade-unionists. Democrats emphasize economic growth and full employment, Republicans fiscal responsibility and the balanced budget. Perhaps the best way to summarize this elusive but nonetheless pervasive distinction is to suggest that Democratic spokesmen trust the state and look to government for the attainment of vital goals, while Republicans treat it with suspicion, as a necessary evil that must be put under constant checks to prevent a withering away of individual initiative and the growth of serfdom.

In Congress one finds a very clear line between the liberal Democrats (with a handful of Republican allies) and the "conservative coalition" on precisely this issue. This creates an ideological paradox at times: the Southern Democrats vigorously oppose state action (national) to desegregate but militantly favor state action (by the "sovereign states") to maintain white supremacy. Their opposition to national state action, however, tends to show up in Congressional voting where Southern Democrats line up with the Republicans to defeat such urban-oriented legislation as the creation of a Department of Urban Affairs, education bills, and, of course, civil-rights measures.

The fascinating thing about this system is that it works at all, particularly when one discovers—by reading the relevant documents—the eccentric character of the nominating process and the unnerving potentialities of the Electoral College. One sometimes tends to agree with the distinguished British observer James Bryce that "Divine Providence has under its special protection drunks, small children, and the United States of America." Yet somehow the American people's fundamental commitment to free institutions seems to dominate the scene. For example, after five months of squabbling and litigation, the courts ruled that Democratic candidate Carl Rolvaag was in fact the winner of Minnesota's November 1962 gubernatorial election—by 91 votes! The Republican incumbent had remained in authority awaiting the outcome—initial rulings had favored him—but an office in the capitol was also provided for the Democratic challenger. Although the stakes were anything but small and the cry "we wuz robbed" is easy when one loses 619,751 to 619,842, Rolvaag quietly took over as chief executive. Similarly, fervid claims that the Democrats had "stolen" the Presidency in 1960 by vote frauds in key states trailed off in a few weeks—though in many nations revolutions have arisen from less combustible issues.

To say this is not to suggest that Bryce had the clue to American survival—that since nothing serious has gone wrong since 1876, when a political minority put Rutherford B. Hayes into the White House (or perhaps since 1884, when Grover Cleveland with a popular majority lost in the Electoral College), we should leave the machinery alone. Several documents in this volume are concerned with the question of reform, and the reader is left with the task of reaching his own viewpoint on the merits of the existing system and the suggested reforms.

4

In addition to materials on political parties, we have included a number of selections on pressure groups, the so-called fourth branch of government. Senator Henry Jackson of the state of Washington was referred to in 1963 as the "Senator from Boeing" because of his efforts to discover why a huge contract for TFX fighter aircraft had been awarded by the Defense Department to the General Dynamics Corporation instead of to the Boeing Company. Congressman Harold Cooley of North Carolina has been designated "sugar daddy" because of the authority he has exercised over the allocation of foreign sugar quotas and his close political connections with the sugar lobby. Congressmen from the big cities are notably sensitive to the demands of constituents that restrictive immigration laws be loosened. Some critics have even gone so far as to suggest that the United States is dominated by a "power elite"—an industrial-military complex that manages Congress like a puppet show.

Our concern in this volume is not to provide the reader with authoritative answers; the documents we have included do, however, provide a solid point of departure for further exploration. It is perhaps important to note that the power of pressure groups, or "lobbies," in the United States is a function of the weakness of the political party system. Senator Jackson, Congressman Cooley, and their colleagues on Capitol Hill are not members of disciplined political machines; they do not respond to the party "whip" as British M.P.'s do. They are responsible first and foremost to their own constituents, and efforts of Presidents to control their own party contingents in Congress have met with limited success. Few politicians anywhere are prepared to commit hara-kiri on the altar of party loyalty—note the earlier reference to John F. Kennedy's strategy in the 1952 election.

Since no party organization worth the name exists at the national level, and since Congress operates by coalition politics, the individual or group that wants to obtain a favorable climate of public policy for its objectives moves naturally to the locus of decision: to the individual members of Congress or, for Administrative succor, to the President and his principal administrators. In the case of the TFX experimental fighter aircraft mentioned above, Boeing naturally protested to the legislators from the areas of its major activity: one rumor had it that Kansas—where the Boeing factory was hoping to process the order— was being "punished," but that since Kansas is hopelessly Republican, Senator Jackson, a Democrat from a state where Boeing has huge enterprises, had taken up the case. The same rumor—and Washington is par excellence the city of rumor—said that Texas, where the General Dynamics–Grumman subsidiary has its plants, was marshaling its forces to withstand the assault. In the midst of all this furor, the President and Secretary of Defense have the task of developing a coherent policy on contracts!

Pressure groups are obviously a permanent feature on any democratic landscape; they exist in all free societies as an expression of the views of various segments of the populace. Are there limits which properly can be established on the work of these groups? At one extreme, the answer must be "yes": it is a crime to attempt to bribe a legislator. At the other extreme, a "no" seems equally appropriate: one of the earmarks of a totalitarian society is its elimination of "factions," parties, and other autonomous expressions of public opinion. Somewhere between these extremes the citizens of a democratic society must draw lines; several documents in this volume are concerned with efforts that have been made to prevent abuse of private power without limiting freedom of expression.

Finally we might add that specific questions relating to the work of Congress and the President have been arbitrarily excluded from this volume. While government is a seamless web, convenience has dictated that problems focusing on these institutions be reserved for treatment in other volumes in this series.

Brandeis University
June 1963

JOHN P. ROCHE
LEONARD W. LEVY

POLITICAL PARTIES

THE NATIONAL PARTY COMMITTEES

DOCUMENT 1 MEMBERSHIP AND DUTIES

Once every four years the United States undergoes a frenetic and intense national convulsion: the Presidential election. For a period of about six months in years divisible by four, the political pressure builds up to the decision on the first Tuesday after the first Monday in November. Ad hoc groups of all sorts sprout from the earth like mushrooms: Artists for Kennedy, Independent Citizens for Nixon, Democrats for Eisenhower, Women for Stevenson, and the like, ad infinitum. Handbooks are prepared and special materials are designed for coping with the eccentricities of every sector of the electorate.

The first Wednesday after the first Monday in November, however, brings a profound calm broken only by the bickerings of the defeated. All these special organizations, established at prodigious cost (see Document 8), vanish from the scene, leaving behind them peeling billboards and huge debts. The President-elect braces himself for the upcoming tussles with Congress, and the locus of party organization reverts for three-and-a-half years to the state and local arenas.

All that remains to indicate that American political parties have national functions are the two national party committees. In fact, these committees rarely meet between Presidential contests—what continuing authority they have is vested in a national chairman who supervises the Washington headquarters, makes speeches from time to time (particularly if his party was defeated), and organizes the immense campaign to pay the bills incurred in the last election. The national committees also have the responsibility for organizing the Presidential nominating conventions, and occasionally—for example, in the Taft-Eisenhower fight in 1952—control of the committee becomes a factor in the struggle between aspiring candidates. In addition, the national committees would presumably be in charge of designating a replacement for a Presidential candidate who died in the period between the convention and election day. Fortunately, this has never occurred, although Horace Greeley, Liberal Republican candidate in 1872,

9

passed away after his defeat at the polls but before the electoral count.

In real terms, however, the committees have no significant power over their sovereign constituencies, the state party organizations. The selection that follows must be understood as a formal statement of committee membership and responsibility—membership in fact is generally bestowed either directly or indirectly (depending upon state law) upon elderly notables as a token of esteem rather than as a grant of power.

THE DEMOCRATIC NATIONAL COMMITTEE

The Democratic National Committee is an agency of the Democratic Party, established at each Democratic National Convention, with authority to take all appropriate action to promote the principles and programs of the Democratic Party in the interval prior to the next succeeding national convention.

The principal duties and powers of the national committee include the following:

a. To maintain national headquarters of the Democratic Party in Washington, D.C., at all times and in the national convention city before and during the sessions of the national convention;

b. To conduct the national campaign for the election of the presidential and vice presidential nominees of the national convention;

c. To promote, and aid and assist in, the election of all candidates for public office on the ticket of the Democratic Party in all general elections in each State, Territory, and District;

d. To promote, encourage, and sponsor: Party organization at every level; an adequate system of political research; preparation, distribution and communication of party information in and through all available media; development and maintenance of proper public relations for the party; cooperation and coordination among all party committees, organizations, groups, public officials, and members; enlistment and assignment of party members as speakers for party, nonpartisan and other meetings or programs; the performance of party mandates; and the discharge and fulfillment by the party of its platform pledges and other commitments publicly made;

e. Under such rules and regulations as may be prescribed by the national committee, to encourage and assist groups of party members in the organization of Democratic clubs to promote and further principles, programs,

FROM: *Nomination and Election of the President and Vice President of the United States, Including the Manner of Selecting Delegates to National Political Conventions,* House Document Number 332, Eighty-Sixth Congress, Second Session (Washington, D.C., Government Printing Office, 1960), pp. 25–27, 40–41.

THE NATIONAL PARTY COMMITTEES

and nominees of the Democratic Party and to issue certificates of recognition to any such Democratic clubs so formed or heretofore organized and now existing, provided that the authority to prescribe such rules and regulations shall not be delegated;

f. To devise and execute ways and means of financing all activities, the performance of all duties and the exercise of all powers by it and to co-operate and work with other segments of party organization at State and local levels in the development of an integrated and coordinated finance plan for the party, and to define, prescribe, and fix quotas of money to be raised for the national committee in each State, Territory, and District by the party organizations within such areas;

g. To plan, arrange, manage, and conduct the national convention quadrennially, including:

1. Fixing the time and site thereof;

2. Authorization of the call for the national convention;

3. Determination and apportionment within authority granted by last national convention of number of delegates and alternates for States, Territories, and Districts;

4. Preparation of temporary roll of delegates and alternates accepted as prima facie correct pending action on contests reported by the Committee on Credentials for disposition by the national convention, including judging of contests for listing on temporary rolls;

5. All physical arrangements, including hotel reservations, convention offices, staff headquarters, granting of concessions, adjustment of auditorium and other facilities to requirements, installation of telephone, telegraph, radio, television, press, and motion picture facilities;

6. Arrangements for seating of delegates, alternates, press, radio, and television representatives and visitors;

7. Appointment of temporary officers, including the temporary chairman, subject to the approval of the national convention;

8. Creation and designation of such committees, and the exercise of such further powers as may be necessary to the planning and production of a well organized and efficiently managed national convention;

h. To adopt such resolutions and memorials as it may deem to be required to implement the platform of the national convention;

i. To establish, maintain, and sponsor such committees, groups, staffs, or councils for the formulation of party policy not inconsistent with the platform of the last national convention as the national committee may consider wise and beneficial to the party;

j. To inaugurate, maintain, and operate an organized plan of sustaining memberships in the Democratic Party;

k. To do any and all other things reasonably incidental to the performance and exercise of the duties imposed and powers conferred by the national convention and in promoting the principles and programs of the Democratic Party.

The resolution presented by Hon. William S. Potter, of Delaware, and adopted by the 1956 Democratic National Convention provides that the Democratic National Committee shall consist of one man and one woman from each State, District, and Territory—

the members of said committee to be selected in the manner prescribed by the laws of the respective States and Territories; and where there shall be no statutory provision, that method of selection shall be pursued which conforms to the established party rules and regulations. All such selections, except where contests shall exist, shall be acted upon by the Democratic National Convention, and the members of the committee, when so ratified and confirmed, shall hold office until the adjournment of the next succeeding national convention wherein their successors are chosen.

Where a vacancy occurs, the vacancy shall be filled upon the nomination of the State, Territory, or District committee. No person not a resident of the State, Territory, or District from which he or she is elected or appointed, shall be eligible to hold such office; and be it further

Resolved, That said national committee be and it is hereby authorized to elect a chairman, not more than six vice chairmen, a secretary, and a treasurer, and that the chairman so elected be and he is hereby authorized to appoint such assistants and committees as may be considered necessary for the efficient conduct of the business and affairs of the said committee.

++++

REPUBLICAN NATIONAL COMMITTEE

RULE NO. 19

a. A National Committee shall be elected by each National Convention, called to nominate candidates for the President and Vice President, and shall consist of two (2) members from each State, Territory, Territorial Possession, and the District of Columbia, and an additional member as hereinafter provided.

b. The State Chairman of each State that casts its electoral votes for the Republican candidate for President at the preceding Presidential election, or in which State a majority of the representatives in Congress and members of the United States Senate (in computing the majority the total membership of the House of Representatives from such State shall be added to the membership in the United States Senate from such State) are Republicans, or in which State there is a Republican Governor, shall be a member of the Republican National Committee by virtue of his office as State Chairman. The Territory Chairman of each Territory having a Republican Delegate to Congress shall be a member of the National Committee by virtue of his office.

c. In case during the period between National Conventions a State or

Territory should no longer be entitled to a third member on the National Committee, then the Chairman of the State or Territory that has lost its right to membership through failure to qualify under this rule shall at once cease to be a member of the National Committee.

d. In case during the period between National Conventions a State or Territory shall become entitled to a third member of the Republican National Committee, the then duly elected and acting Chairman of such state or Territory shall automatically become a member of the National Committee.

e. Such additional member of the National Committee as above provided for shall have full voting rights as a member of the National Committee while a member of said Committee.

RULE NO. 20

The roll shall be called and the Delegation from each State, Territory, Territorial Possession, and the District of Columbia shall nominate, through its Chairman, one (1) man and one (1) woman to act as members of the National Committee.

RULE NO. 21

When the law of any State, Territory, Territorial Possession, or District of Columbia provides a method for the selection of members of the National Committee of political parties, the nomination of the members of the Republican National Committee in accordance with the provisions of such law shall be considered nominations to be carried into effect by the Delegation from such State, Territory, Territorial Possession, or District of Columbia, provided, however, that this rule shall not apply to the membership on the National Committee by the State Chairman in case the Chairman of such State is entitled to membership on the National Committee.

RULE NO. 22

Where the laws of a State, Territory, Territorial Possession, or District of Columbia do not provide a method for the selection of members of the National Committee of political parties, instructions by State or Territory and District Conventions to Delegates to the National Convention as to nominations for membership in the National Committee shall be obeyed by such delegates; and if not obeyed, may be made operative by a vote of the National Convention or referred to the National Committee with full power to act. It is provided, however, that this rule shall not apply to a Chairman of a State or Territory that is entitled to membership under Rule 19.

RULE NO. 23

When a majority of the Delegates from each State, Territory, Territorial Possession, and the District of Columbia shall have so nominated a member of the National Committee, the Convention shall thereupon elect the person so nominated to serve as a member of the Committee until the meeting of the National Committee elected by the next National Convention.

When a State or Territory is entitled to a third member of the National Committee as heretofore set forth in Rule 19, the then elected and acting Chairman of such State or Territory as is entitled to a third member of the National Committee shall be certified as a member of the National Committee.

RULE NO. 24

The National Committee shall issue the call for the next National Convention to nominate candidates for President and Vice President of the United States at least four (4) months before the time fixed for said Convention; and Delegates and Alternates to such Convention shall be chosen in such manner, and the call shall be issued and promulgated in such manner as the National Committee shall provide, but not, however, in a manner inconsistent with these Rules.

RULE NO. 25

The Officers of the National Committee shall consist of a Chairman; four (4) Vice Chairmen, who shall be two (2) men and two (2) women; a Secretary, a Treasurer, and such other officers as the Committee shall deem necessary, all to be elected by the National Committee. The Chairman shall appoint a General Counsel for the Committee and an Assistant Chairman, who shall be a woman and who shall be director of women's activities.

RULE NO. 26

The National Committee is authorized and empowered to select an Executive Committee, to consist of fifteen (15) members, in addition to which the Chairman, the Assistant Chairman, the Vice Chairman, the Secretary, the Treasurer, the General Counsel, the President of the National Federation of Republican Women, and the Chairman of the Young Republican National Federation shall be ex officio members and the Chairman, with the consent of the National Committee, may appoint such other committees and assistants as he may deem necessary; whenever such committees are appointed they shall consist of a chairman, and an equal number of men and women.

RULE NO. 27

Vacancies in the National Committee shall be filled by the Committee upon the nomination of the Republican State Committee in and for the State, Territory, Territorial Possession, or District of Columbia in which the vacancy occurs; the National Committee shall, however, have power to declare vacant the seat of any member who refuses to support the nominees of the Convention, which elected such National Committee, and to fill such vacancy.

RULE NO. 28

The first meeting of the National Committee shall take place within fifteen (15) days after the convening of the National Convention electing such Committee, upon the call of the member oldest in time of service upon the previous National Committee; and thereafter upon call of the Chairman, or, in case of vacancy in the Chairmanship, upon call of the Vice Chairman, senior in time of service as a member of the National Committee, but such call shall be issued at least ten (10) days in advance of the date of the proposed meeting. Upon written petition of sixteen (16) or more members of the National Committee, representing not less than sixteen (16) States, filed jointly or separately with the Chairman, asking for a meeting of the National Committee, it shall be the duty of the Chairman within ten (10) days from receipt of said petition to issue a call for a meeting of the National Committee, to be held in a city to be designated by the Chairman, the date of such called meeting to be not later than twenty (20) days or earlier than ten (10) days from the date of the call.

RULE NO. 29

The rules of the House of Representatives of the United States shall govern in all meetings of the National Committee insofar as they are applicable and not inconsistent with these Rules. The Committee shall make its own rules governing the use of proxies at any meeting.

THE NATIONAL PARTY CONVENTIONS

DOCUMENT 2   APPORTIONMENT OF
DELEGATES AND VOTES

The President of the United States is clearly the most powerful democratic chief executive in the world. Yet the two nominees who present themselves to the people for that office each election year are designated by bodies with roughly the same legal standing as the annual convention of the American Political Science Association. But although the national conventions are unregulated by national law, both parties have evolved standardized procedures for nominating their respective candidates. The first problem is deciding how many delegates to the convention should be apportioned to each state. The relative weight of each state's influence, of course, differs with each party. It would, for example, be patently absurd if the Republicans gave their Southern state organizations the same weight that Southern Democrats have at Democratic conventions. Consequently, each party has worked out an elaborate system of bonuses for good performance, with additional delegates authorized to states where the party workers have demonstrated their ability by winning statewide office or carrying the state in the preceding Presidential election.

Since the national convention occurs only once in four years and since loyal party functionaries look forward to attendance as a sort of pilgrimage, it is easy to understand why half-votes are employed. One hundred and sixty delegates can share eighty votes—and in addition a slate of alternates can turn up to participate in the festivities. As television viewers of past conventions will recall with anguish, a roll-call vote of a large delegation may thus seem interminable. Efforts have been made to short-cut the recount when a state's vote is challenged, but two factors block reform: first, the determination of dogged partisans that "all the Indians must wear their war paint," that is, stand up and be counted in public; and, second, the hope of various delegates that their vote will be recorded on the television screens of their envious friends and neighbors back in Waltham, Massachusetts, Anchorage, Alaska, or Eagle Pass, Texas. It is also pointed out that *great progress has been made since the days when quarter-votes and eighth-votes were permissible!*

This selection sets forth the principles applied by the Democratic and Republican parties to the allocation of delegate strength to the various state party organizations.

POLITICAL PARTY RULES AND BASES OF APPORTIONMENT AT NATIONAL CONVENTIONS

The national committees of the Democratic and Republican Parties usually announce the appointment of delegates to the national convention. This apportionment or distribution of delegates among the States is made pursuant to party rules, the actual determination being a duty of the national committees of their respective parties. It is based not only on [the] number of Senators and Representatives in Congress to which a State is entitled but also, to some extent, on the success of the party in the particular State or a congressional district at the preceding election. The methods of apportionment used by the two major parties differ somewhat, but . . . both parties make use of the congressional apportionment in determining the apportionment of district delegates. . . .

APPORTIONMENT OF DELEGATES TO THE 1960 DEMOCRATIC NATIONAL CONVENTION

The Democratic National Committee by resolution on September 16, 1959, apportioned the 1,521 votes in the 1960 national convention among the 50 States, the District of Columbia, Canal Zone, Puerto Rico, and Virgin Islands. At the same time the national committee fixed the maximum number of delegates and the maximum number of alternates for each State or Territory. Each State was given one-half vote for its national committeeman, and one-half vote for its national committeewoman.

The national committee has not prescribed how the votes or delegates shall be designated, whether "at large" or "district" votes. The

FROM: *Nomination and Election of the President and Vice President of the United States, Including the Manner of Selecting Delegates to National Political Conventions,* House Document Number 332, Eighty-Sixth Congress, Second Session (Washington, D.C., Government Printing Office, 1960), pp. 1–4, 25.

State committee or State convention or any other person or committee prescribed by State law or party rules may determine whether all of the State's votes and delegates are to be at large (that is, on a state-wide basis) or whether the votes and delegates based upon the United States Senate seats shall be at large and the votes and delegates based upon the U.S. House of Representative seats shall be district.

A State is not required to halve its votes and it is not permitted to fractionalize below one-half votes. The State is entitled to have only one alternate for each full vote, excepting the one vote divided between the national committee members. The problem created by having two and one-half votes for each Member of the House of Representatives (if the State decides to allocate such votes on a district basis) and requiring an alternate to be chosen to represent the one-half vote of the district can be solved by having two districts combine in selecting one alternate to be available to represent the one-half votes of the two districts.

No alternates are to be chosen for the national committee members. Each Democratic National Committee member has the right, under the resolution of the national committee, to "designate in writing to the chairman of the delegation a person to vote and act in said convention" for and on his or her behalf, in the event of absence during any session of the convention. Members of the national committee are to be members of the delegation and each is entitled to one-half vote.

The following action by the Democratic National Committee, apparently pursuant to authority granted by the 1956 national convention, explains the apportionment of votes and delegates to the 1960 national convention:

[Resolution adopted by the Democratic National Committee, September 16, 1959]

Be it resolved by the Democratic National Committee, That the distribution of votes for the 1960 Democratic National Convention shall be on the following basis:

1. Each state shall have two and one-half (2½) votes for each of its United States Senators and each of its Members of the United States House of Representatives. Wherever this distribution results in a fractional vote for any state, the next highest number shall be used, and the extra one-half vote shall be classed as an at-large one-half vote for the state.

2. There shall be 8 votes for the District of Columbia, 6 votes for Puerto Rico, and 3 votes each for the Virgin Islands and the Canal Zone.

3. In the event the total number of votes had by any state under paragraphs (1) and (2) hereinabove is less than the number of votes had by any

state in the 1956 Democratic National Convention, such total vote hereunder shall be increased for such state to the total number of votes had by such state in the 1956 National Convention and such additional vote or votes shall be classed as an at-large vote or votes for such state.

4. Each state, the District of Columbia, and each territory shall have one additional vote for its two members of the Democratic National Committee, each to be a member of the state's delegation and to have one-half vote. In the event that any member of the National Committee is unable to attend any session of the Convention, such National Committee member shall designate in writing to the chairman of the delegation a person to vote and act in said Convention for and on behalf of such member.

5. The states may elect either delegate with one vote or two delegates each with one-half vote for each of the votes hereinabove provided, except the votes of the National Committee members.

6. One alternate is to be elected for each full vote, except those of the National Committee members.

APPORTIONMENT OF DELEGATES
TO THE 1960 REPUBLICAN NATIONAL CONVENTION

MEMBERSHIP IN THE NATIONAL CONVENTION

RULE NO. 30

The membership of the next National Convention shall consist of:

A. Delegates at Large

1. Four Delegates at Large from each State.

2. Two additional Delegates at Large for each Representative at Large in Congress from each State.

3. Four Delegates at Large from Territory of Alaska, eight Delegates at Large for District of Columbia and six Delegates at Large for the Territory of Hawaii, and four additional Delegates if the Delegate to Congress elected at the last preceding election was the Republican nominee. Three Delegates at Large for Puerto Rico and one for the Virgin Islands.

4. Six additional Delegates at Large from each State casting its electoral vote, or a majority thereof, for the Republican nominee for President in the last preceding Presidential election. If any State does not cast its electoral vote or a majority thereof for the Republican nominee in the last preceding Presidential election, but at that election or at a subsequent election held prior to the next Republican National Convention elects a Republican United States Senator or a Republican Governor then in such event such State shall be entitled to such additional Delegates at Large.

B. District Delegates

1. One District Delegate from each Congressional District casting two thousand (2,000) votes or more for the Republican nominee for President or for any elector pledged to vote for the Republican nominee for President in the last preceding Presidential election, or for the Republican nominee for Congress in the last preceding Congressional election.

2. One additional District Delegate for each Congressional District casting ten thousand (10,000) votes or more for the Republican nominee for President or for any elector pledged to vote for the Republican nominee for President in the last preceding Presidential election, or for the Republican nominee for Congress in the last preceding Congressional election.

C. Alternate Delegates

One Alternate Delegate to each Delegate to the National Convention.

ELECTION OF DELEGATES TO NATIONAL CONVENTION

RULE NO. 31

Delegates at Large to the National Convention and their Alternates and Delegates from Congressional Districts to the National Convention and their Alternates shall be elected in the following manner:

a. By primary election, in accordance with the laws of the State, Territory, or District of Columbia in which the election occurs, in such of these as require by law the election of Delegates to National Conventions of political parties by district primary; provided, that in any of these in which Republican representation upon the Board of Judges or Inspectors of Elections for such primary election is denied by law, Delegates and Alternates shall be elected as hereinafter provided.

b. By Congressional District or State Conventions, as the case may be, to be called by the Congressional District or State Committees, respectively. Notice of the Call for any such Convention shall be published in a newspaper or newspapers of general circulation in the Congressional District, State or Territory, as the case may be, not less than fifteen (15) days prior to the date of said Convention; provided, however, that in selecting Delegates and Alternates to the National Convention no State or Territorial law shall be observed which hinders, abridges, or denies to any citizen of the United States, eligible under the Constitution of the United States to the office of President or Vice President, the right or privilege of being a candidate under such State law for the nomination for the President or Vice President; or which authorizes the election of a number of Delegates or Alternates from any State to the National Convention different from that fixed in these Rules.

c. By the Republican State Committee or Governing Committee in any State in which the law of such State specifically authorizes the election of Delegates in such manner.

d. In a Congressional District where there is no Republican Congressional Committee, the Republican State Committee shall issue the Call and make said publication.

e. All Delegates from any State may be chosen from the State at Large, in the event that the laws of the State in which the election occurs, so provide.

f. Alternate Delegates shall be elected to said National Convention for each unit of representation equal in number to the number of Delegates elected therein and shall be chosen in the same manner and at the same time the Delegates are chosen; provided, however, that if the law of any State shall prescribe the method of choosing Alternates they shall be chosen in accordance with the provisions of the law of the State in which the election occurs.

g. The election of Delegates and Alternates from [the] Territory of Alaska, Territory of Hawaii, Puerto Rico, Virgin Islands and the District of Columbia shall be held under the direction of the respective recognized Republican Governing Committee therein in conformity with the Rules of the Republican National Committee or the laws of the Territory, Territorial Possession or District of Columbia.

h. Election of Delegates shall be certified in every case where they are elected by Conventions, by the Chairman and Secretary of such Conventions respectively and in case of election by primary, they shall be certified by the proper official, and all certificates shall be forwarded by said duly elected Delegates and Alternates in the manner herein provided.

i. All Delegates or Alternates shall be elected not later than thirty (30) days before the date of the meeting of said National Convention, unless otherwise provided by the laws of the State in which the election occurs.

j. Delegates and Alternates at Large to the National Convention shall be duly qualified voters of their respective States, Territories and Territorial Possessions, and in the case of the District of Columbia, shall be residents therein.

k. Delegates and Alternates to the National Convention, representing Congressional Districts, shall be residents and qualified voters in said districts respectively.

ELECTION OF DELEGATES TO DISTRICT AND STATE CONVENTIONS

Delegates to Congressional District and State Conventions shall be elected under the following rules:

l. Only legal and qualified voters shall participate in a Republican primary, caucus, mass meeting, or mass convention held for the purpose of selecting delegates to a County, District, or State Convention, and only such legal and qualified voters shall be elected as delegates to County, District and State Conventions; provided, however, that in addition to the qualifications provided herein the governing Republican Committee of each State or Territory shall have the authority to prescribe additional qualifications not inconsistent with law. Such additional qualifications shall be adopted and published in at least one daily newspaper having a general circulation throughout the State or Territory; such publication to be at least ninety days before such qualifications shall become effective.

m. No Delegates shall be deemed eligible to participate in any convention to elect Delegates to the said National Convention, who were elected prior to the date of the issuance of the Call for such National Convention.

n. District conventions shall be composed of Delegates who are legal and qualified voters therein, and Delegates to State Conventions shall be qualified voters of the respective districts which they represent in said State Conventions. Such delegates shall be apportioned among the counties, parishes, and cities of the State or District having regard to the Republican vote therein.

RULE NO. 32

No State, Territory, Territorial Possession, or the District of Columbia shall elect a greater number of persons to act as Delegates and Alternates than the actual number of Delegates and Alternates respectively to which they are entitled under the Call, and no unit of representation may elect any Delegate or Delegates, or their Alternates, with permission to cast a fractional vote.

DOCUMENT 3 SELECTION OF DELEGATES

Once the national committees have determined how many delegates to the party conventions each state will have, each state is free to determine its method of selecting delegates. These delegates, once chosen in the variety of ways set forth in the following document, are virtually autonomous. In practical terms, of course, they are subjected to restraint: a Massachusetts delegate who had the temerity to vote for

Lyndon Johnson at the 1960 Democratic convention would hardly have returned to a bright political future in the Commonwealth. But delegates have deserted their political suzerains and done very well by it—when they switched to the winner. During recent years a number of Midwestern post offices have been under the contented jurisdiction of onetime Taft enthusiasts who transcended petty loyalties and supported Eisenhower at the 1952 Republican convention.

In a number of states there are so-called Presidential primaries. Some are mere expressions of public sentiment, while others theoretically "bind" delegates to the will of the people. However, the essentially fictitious character of such "binding" designations is revealed by the case of the California delegates to the 1960 Democratic convention, who came pledged to a "favorite son," Governor Edmund (Pat) Brown. Senator Kennedy, out of "courtesy" to Brown, had refused to enter his name in the state's Presidential primary to avoid an expensive primary brawl with a strong potential supporter who was not himself a serious candidate. The California delegates voted for Brown until he released them. They then chose between the front-runners in terms of their own appreciation of political realities.

The selection that follows provides a vivid insight into the variety and the lack of a national pattern that is characteristic of the American party system while demonstrating the authority of the state party organizations over the process of delegate selection.

The method of selecting delegates to the national convention varies. Some States regulate the selection by statute. Methods presently used are election of delegates at the primary election or selection by the State conventions or State committees of the party. In some States where the primary is used to elect the delegates, the voter is given a chance to express his choice as to presidential and vice presidential candidates. In such cases the ballots are prepared so the voter may indicate his preference. This method is termed the "preferential presidential primary." The methods employed by the various States are shown in [the following] Table . . . .

✦✦✦✦

FROM: *Nomination and Election of the President and Vice President of the United States, Including the Manner of Selecting Delegates to National Political Conventions,* House Document Number 332, Eighty-Sixth Congress, Second Session (Washington, D.C., Government Printing Office, 1960), pp. 23, 30–31, 42–43.

SELECTION OF DELEGATES   23

STATE	1. *Delegates selected at State or district conventions or by State executive committee*	2. *Delegates elected at primary with no presidential candidate involved*
Alabama	Democrats at primary Republicans at State and district conventions.	Democrats only and only in event of a contest among delegates.
Alaska	State convention	
Arizona	State executive committee	
Arkansas	State committee	
California		
Colorado	District delegates elected at district conventions and delegates-at-large elected at State convention.	
Connecticut	State convention	
Delaware	State convention	
District of Columbia		
Florida		
Georgia	Republicans at State convention; Democrats by State committee.	
Hawaii	State convention	
Idaho	State convention	
Illinois	State convention selects delegates-at-large only.	

3. Delegates elected at preferential presidential primary where choice for President is expressed by voters			4. Delegates elected at State convention but separate preferential presidential primary where choice for President is expressed by voters at Presidential candidate's request with vote binding on delegates.
a. Yes or no	b. Is vote binding on delegates, viz., are delegates pledged?	c. Is consent of presidential candidate required?	
No			
No			
No			
Optional. (A preferential primary must be held by a presidential candidate's party if such candidate so petitions the State committee 6 months prior to the national convention.)			
Yes	Yes	Yes	
No			
No			
No			
Yes	Yes		
Yes	No	No	
(It is optional with delegate as to whether presidential candidate's name is printed on ballot along with his name.)			
No			
No			
No			
Yes; district delegates only.	No	No; candidate's name must go on ballot if he so files with secretary of state.	

STATE	1. *Delegates selected at State or district conventions or by State executive committee*	2. *Delegates elected at primary with no presidential candidate involved*
Indiana	State convention	
Iowa	State convention	
Kansas	State convention (party council)	
Kentucky	State convention	
Louisiana	Delegates-at-large by State convention; district delegates by district conventions.	
Maine	Republicans at district conventions so authorized by State convention; Democrats at State convention.	
Maryland	State convention	
Massachusetts		
Michigan	State delegate convention	
Minnesota	Delegates-at-large by State convention, district delegates by district convention.	
Mississippi	State convention	
Missouri	State convention	
Montana. (New law effective in 1960.)	State convention	

3. Delegates elected at preferential presidential primary where choice for President is expressed by voters			4. Delegates elected at State convention but separate preferential presidential primary where choice for President is expressed by voters at Presidential candidate's request with vote binding on delegates.
a. Yes or no	b. Is vote binding on delegates, viz., are delegates pledged?	c. Is consent of presidential candidate required?	
No			Yes
No			
No			
No			
No			
No			
No			Yes
Yes	No	Consent not required but must be filed if delegate's statement of preference for him is to appear on ballot.	
No			
No			
No			
No			
No			

STATE	1. *Delegates selected at State or district conventions or by State executive committee*	2. *Delegates elected at primary with no presidential candidate involved*
Nebraska		
Nevada. (A Presidential primary law enacted in 1953 was repealed in 1955.)	State convention	
New Hampshire		
New Jersey		
New Mexico	State convention	
New York	Delegates-at-large chosen at State conventions; other delegates elected at primary. See col. 2	District delegates elected at primary.
North Carolina	Republicans at district and State Conventions; Democrats at State convention.	
North Dakota	State convention (delegates sign a pledge of loyalty to their party).	
Ohio		
Oklahoma	State convention	
Oregon		

3. *Delegates elected at preferential presidential primary where choice for President is expressed by voters*			4. *Delegates elected at State convention but separate preferential presidential primary where choice for President is expressed by voters at Presidential candidate's request with vote binding on delegates.*
a. Yes or no	b. Is vote binding on delegates, viz., are delegates pledged?	c. Is consent of presidential candidate required?	
Yes Yes	No	Yes	
Yes	Only if he signs a pledge.	No; candidate's name goes on ballot by petition and will be withdrawn at his request.	
Yes	No	No; candidate's name goes on ballot by petition and will be withdrawn if he declines.	
No No			
No			
No			
Yes	Only if he signs a pledge.	Yes	
No			
Yes	Yes, unless nominated by petition.	No; the candidate's name is printed on the ballot at the discretion of the secretary of state.	

STATE	1. *Delegates selected at State or district conventions or by State executive committee*	2. *Delegates elected at primary with no presidential candidate involved*
Pennsylvania	Delegates at large chosen at State conventions; other delegates elected at primary. See col. 3.	
Rhode Island		Both Democrats and Republicans (optional).
South Carolina	State convention	
South Dakota		
Tennessee	State convention	
Texas	State convention	
Utah	Republicans at State convention and district conventions; Democrats at State convention.	
Vermont	State convention	
Virginia	State convention	
Washington	State convention	
West Virginia		
Wisconsin		
Wyoming	State convention	

3. Delegates elected at preferential presidential primary where choice for President is expressed by voters			4. Delegates elected at State convention but separate preferential presidential primary where choice for President is expressed by voters at Presidential candidate's request with vote binding on delegates.
a. Yes or no	b. Is vote binding on delegates, viz., are delegates pledged?	c. Is consent of presidential candidate required?	
Yes	Only if he signs a pledge.	No; the candidate's name is printed on the ballot upon petition of voters.	
No			
No			
Yes	No, unless nominating petition states a preference.	No	
No			
No			
No			
No			
No			
No			
Yes	No	Yes; and must pay filing fee.	
Yes	Yes, unless running as uninstructed delegates.	Yes	
No			

THE NATIONAL PARTY PLATFORMS

DOCUMENT 4 THE 1960 DEMOCRATIC PLATFORM

The function of the party platform is a bit obscure—most American voters have probably never seen the documents prepared by the respective platform committees. A Presidential candidate is in a broad sense committed to the platform, but Al Smith in 1928 expressly repudiated the Democratic pieties on the subject of Prohibition, and no candidate has ever been seriously chafed by the bonds of his platform.

The preparation of the Democratic platform has, at least since 1948, become a task for the liberal wing of the coalition. The 1960 Democratic platform was written by a liberal task force under the direction of Chester Bowles. Although a floor fight was anticipated, the convention adopted this platform without debate on a "unanimous" voice vote. A loud chorus of "Nays" could be heard, but the Southern Democrats did not demand a roll-call vote. They had not undergone a miraculous conversion to the principles expounded in this platform: rather, they were promoting the candidacy of Senator Lyndon B. Johnson and refused to be drawn into a fight at this stage. The Southern Democrats assumed (correctly) that the platform was a "Kennedy trap"—if they took up the gauge of battle on ideological issues, they would destroy Johnson's chances of success among the urban state delegations. At a later stage in the campaign, however, a few Southern state party organizations, notably in Texas and Mississippi, went to the trouble of explicitly repudiating the national Democratic platform and substituting their own versions.

The excerpts of the party platform presented here illuminate the causes of Southern Democratic wrath; this document is clearly tailored to the ideals of the urban, minority-conscious segment of the Democratic party.

In 1796, in America's first contested national election, our Party, under the leadership of Thomas Jefferson, campaigned on the principles of "The Rights of Man."

Ever since, these four words have underscored our identity with the plain people of America and the world.

In periods of national crisis, we Democrats have returned to these words for renewed strength. We return to them today.

In 1960, "The Rights of Man" are still the issue.

It is our continuing responsibility to provide an effective instrument of political action for every American who seeks to strengthen these rights—everywhere here in America, and everywhere in our 20th Century world.

The common danger of mankind is war and the threat of war. Today, three billion human beings live in fear that some rash act or blunder may plunge us all into a nuclear holocaust which will leave only ruined cities, blasted homes, and a poisoned earth and sky.

Our objective, however, is not the right to co-exist in armed camps on the same planet with totalitarian ideologies; it is the creation of an enduring peace in which the universal values of human dignity, truth, and justice under law are finally secured for all men everywhere on earth.

If America is to work effectively for such a peace, we must first restore our national strength—military, political, economic, and moral.

NATIONAL DEFENSE

The new Democratic Administration will recast our military capacity in order to provide forces and weapons of a diversity, balance, and mobility sufficient in quantity and quality to deter both limited and general aggressions.

When the Democratic Administration left office in 1953, the United States was the pre-eminent power in the world. Most free nations had confidence in our will and our ability to carry out our commitments to the common defense.

Even those who wished us ill respected our power and influence.

The Republican Administration has lost that position of pre-eminence. Over the past 7½ years, our military power has steadily declined relative to that of the Russians and the Chinese and their satellites.

FROM: Kirk H. Porter and Donald B. Johnson, eds., *National Party Platforms, 1840–1960,* 2nd ed. (Urbana, Illinois, University of Illinois Press, 1961), pp. 574–600.

ARMS CONTROL

A fragile power balance sustained by mutual nuclear terror does not, however, constitute peace. We must regain the initiative on the entire international front with effective new policies to create the conditions for peace.

There are no simple solutions to the infinitely complex challenges which face us. Mankind's eternal dream, a world of peace, can only be built slowly and patiently.

A primary task is to develop responsible proposals that will help break the deadlock on arms control.

Such proposals should include means for ending nuclear tests under workable safeguards, cutting back nuclear weapons, reducing conventional forces, preserving outer space for peaceful purposes, preventing surprise attack, and limiting the risk of accidental war.

IMMIGRATION

We shall adjust our immigration, nationality and refugee policies to eliminate discrimination and to enable members of scattered families abroad to be united with relatives already in our midst.

The national-origins quota system of limiting immigration contradicts the founding principles of this nation. It is inconsistent with our belief in the rights of man. This system was instituted after World War I as a policy of deliberate discrimination by a Republican Administration and Congress.

To the peoples and governments beyond our shores we offer the following pledges:

THE UNDERDEVELOPED WORLD

To the non-Communist nations of Asia, Africa, and Latin America: We shall create with you working partnerships, based on mutual respect and understanding.

In the Jeffersonian tradition, we recognize and welcome the irresistible momentum of the world revolution of rising expectations for a better life. We shall identify American policy with the values and objectives of this revolution.

To this end the new Democratic Administration will revamp and refocus the objectives, emphasis and allocation of our foreign assistance programs.

The proper purpose of these programs is not to buy gratitude or to recruit mercenaries, but to enable the peoples of these awakening, developing nations to make their own free choices.

As they achieve a sense of belonging, of dignity, and of justice, freedom will become meaningful for them, and therefore worth defending.

Where military assistance remains essential for the common defense, we shall see that the requirements are fully met. But as rapidly as security considerations permit, we will replace tanks with tractors, bombers with bulldozers, and tacticians with technicians.

We shall place our programs of international cooperation on a long-term basis to permit more effective planning. We shall seek to associate other capital-exporting countries with us in promoting the orderly economic growth of the underdeveloped world.

++++

A billion and a half people in Asia, Africa and Latin America are engaged in an unprecedented attempt to propel themselves into the 20th Century. They are striving to create or reaffirm their national identity.

But they want much more than independence. They want an end to grinding poverty. They want more food, health for themselves and their children, and other benefits that a modern industrial civilization can provide.

Communist strategy has sought to divert these aspirations into narrowly nationalistic channels, or external troublemaking, or authoritarianism. The Republican Administration has played into the hands of this strategy by concerning itself almost exclusively with the military problem of Communist invasion.

The Democratic programs of economic cooperation will be aimed at making it as easy as possible for the political leadership in these countries to turn the energy, talent and resources of their peoples to orderly economic growth.

++++

THE ATLANTIC COMMUNITY

To our friends and associates in the Atlantic Community: We propose a broader partnership that goes beyond our common fears to recognize the depth and sweep of our common political, economic, and cultural interests.

We welcome the recent heartening advances toward European unity. In every appropriate way, we shall encourage their further growth within the broader framework of the Atlantic Community.

++++

The new Democratic Administration will restore the former high levels of cooperation within the Atlantic Community envisaged from the beginning by the NATO treaty in political and economic spheres as well as military affairs.

We welcome the progress towards European unity expressed in the Coal and Steel Community, Euratom, the European Economic Community, the European Free Trade Association, and the European Assembly.

We shall conduct our relations with the nations of the Common Market so as to encourage the opportunities for freer and more expanded trade, and to avert the possibilities of discrimination that are inherent in it.

We shall encourage adjustment with the so-called "Outer Seven" nations so as to enlarge further the area of freer trade.

THE COMMUNIST WORLD

To the rulers of the Communist World: We confidently accept your challenge to competition in every field of human effort.

We recognize this contest as one between two radically different approaches to the meaning of life—our open society which places its highest value upon individual dignity, and your closed society in which the rights of men are sacrificed to the state.

We believe your Communist ideology to be sterile, unsound, and doomed to failure. We believe that your children will reject the intellectual prison in which you seek to confine them, and that ultimately they will choose the eternal principles of freedom.

In the meantime, we are prepared to negotiate with you whenever and wherever there is a realistic possibility of progress without sacrifice of principle.

++++

But we will use all the power, resources, and energy at our command to resist the further encroachment of Communism on freedom— whether at Berlin, Formosa, or new points of pressure as yet undisclosed.

We will keep open the lines of communication with our opponents. Despite difficulties in the way of peaceful agreement, every useful avenue will be energetically explored and pursued.

However, we will never surrender positions which are essential to the defense of freedom, nor will we abandon peoples who are now behind the Iron Curtain through any formal approval of the status quo.

Everyone proclaims "firmness" in support of Berlin. The issue is not the desire to be firm, but the capability to be firm. This the Democratic Party will provide as it has done before.

The ultimate solution of the situation in Berlin must be approached in the broader context of settlement of the tensions and divisions of Europe.

The good faith of the United States is pledged likewise to defending Formosa. We will carry out that pledge.

The new Democratic Administration will also reaffirm our historic policy of opposition to the establishment anywhere in the Americas of governments dominated by foreign powers, a policy now being undermined by Soviet threats to the freedom and independence of Cuba. The Government of the United States under a Democratic Administration will not be deterred from fulfilling its obligations and solemn responsibilities under its treaties and agreements with the nations of the Western Hemisphere. Nor will the United States, in conformity with its treaty obligations, permit the establishment of a regime dominated by international, atheistic Communism in the Western Hemisphere.

THE UNITED NATIONS

To all our fellow members of the United Nations. We shall strengthen our commitments in this, our great continuing institution for conciliation and the growth of a world community.

Through the machinery of the United Nations, we shall work for disarmament, the establishment of an international police force, the strengthening of the World Court, and the establishment of world law.

We shall propose the bolder and more effective use of the specialized agencies to promote the world's economic and social development.

THE DOMESTIC ECONOMY

The pursuit of peace, our contribution to the stability of the new nations of the world, our hopes for progress and well-being at home, all these depend in large measure on our ability to release the full potential of our American economy for employment, production, and growth.

Our generation of Americans has achieved a historic technological breakthrough. Today we are capable of creating an abundance in goods and services beyond the dreams of our parents. Yet on the threshold of plenty the Republican Administration hesitates, confused and afraid.

As a result, massive human needs now exist side by side with idle workers, idle capital, and idle machines.

The Republican failure in the economic field has been virtually complete.

Their years of power have consisted of two recessions, in 1953–54 and 1957–60, separated by the most severe peacetime inflation in history.

They have shown themselves incapable of checking inflation. In their efforts to do so, they have brought on recessions that have thrown millions of Americans out of work. Yet even in these slumps, the cost of living has continued to climb, and it is now at an all-time high.

They have slowed down the rate of growth of the economy to about one-third the rate of the Soviet Union.

Over the past 7½-year period, the Republicans have failed to balance the budget or reduce the national debt. Responsible fiscal policy requires surpluses in good times to more than offset the deficits which may occur in recessions, in order to reduce the national debt over the long run. The Republican Administration has produced the deficits—in fact, the greatest deficit in any peacetime year in history, in 1958–59—but only occasional and meager surpluses. Their first seven years produced a total deficit of nearly $19 billion.

While reducing outlays for essential public services which directly benefit our people, they have raised the annual interest charge on the national debt to a level $3 billion higher than when they took office. In the eight fiscal years of the Republican Administration, these useless higher interest payments will have cost the taxpayers $9 billion.

They have mismanaged the public debt not only by increasing interest rates, but also by failing to lengthen the average maturity of Government obligations when they had a clear opportunity to do so.

ECONOMIC GROWTH

The new Democratic Administration will confidently proceed to unshackle American enterprise and to free American labor, industrial leadership, and capital, to create an abundance that will outstrip any other system.

THE NATIONAL PARTY PLATFORMS

Free competitive enterprise is the most creative and productive form of economic order that the world has seen. The recent slow pace of American growth is due not to the failure of our free economy but to the failure of our national leadership.

We Democrats believe that our economy can and must grow at an average rate of 5% annually, almost twice as fast as our average annual rate since 1953. We pledge ourselves to policies that will achieve this goal without inflation.

Economic growth is the means whereby we improve the American standard of living and produce added tax resources for national security and essential public services.

Our economy must grow more swiftly in order to absorb two groups of workers: the much larger number of young people who will be reaching working age in the 1960s, and the workers displaced by the rapid pace of technological advances, including automation. Republican policies which have stifled growth could only mean increasingly severe unemployment, particularly of youth and older workers.

AN END TO TIGHT MONEY

As the first step in speeding economic growth, a Democratic President will put an end to the present high-interest, tight-money policy.

This policy has failed in its stated purpose—to keep prices down. It has given us two recessions within five years, bankrupted many of our farmers, produced a record number of business failures, and added billions of dollars in unnecessary higher interest charges to Government budgets and the cost of living.

++++

CONTROL OF INFLATION

The American consumer has a right to fair prices. We are determined to secure that right.

Inflation has its roots in a variety of causes; its cure lies in a variety of remedies. Among those remedies are monetary and credit policies properly applied, budget surpluses in times of full employment, and action to restrain "administered price" increases in industries where economic power rests in the hands of a few.

A fair share of the gains from increasing productivity in many industries should be passed on to the consumer through price reductions.

++++

A new Democratic Administration will undertake to meet those needs.

It will reaffirm the Economic Bill of Rights which Franklin Roosevelt wrote into our national conscience sixteen years ago. It will reaffirm these rights for all Americans of whatever race, place of residence, or station in life:

a. *"The right to a useful and remunerative job in the industries or shops or farms or mines of the nation."*

FULL EMPLOYMENT

The Democratic Party reaffirms its support of full employment as a paramount objective of national policy.

For nearly 30 months the rate of unemployment has been between 5 and 7.5% of the labor force. A pool of three to four million citizens, able and willing to work but unable to find jobs, has been written off by the Republican Administration as a "normal" readjustment of the economic system.

The policies of a Democratic Administration to restore economic growth will reduce current unemployment to a minimum.

Thereafter, if recessionary trends appear, we will act promptly with counter-measures, such as public works or temporary tax cuts. We will not stand idly by and permit recessions to run their course as the Republican Administration has done.

AID TO DEPRESSED AREAS

Areas of heavy and persistent unemployment result from depletion of natural resources, technological change, shifting defense requirements, or trade imbalances which have caused the decline of major industries. Whole communities, urban and rural, have been left stranded in distress and despair, through no fault of their own.

These communities have undertaken valiant efforts of self-help. But mutual aid, as well as self-help, is part of the American tradition. Stricken communities deserve the help of the whole nation.

The Democratic Congress twice passed bills to provide this help. The Republican President twice vetoed them.

These bills proposed low-interest loans to private enterprise to create new industry and new jobs in depressed communities, assistance to the communities to provide public facilities necessary to encourage the new industry, and retraining of workers for the new jobs.

DISCRIMINATION IN EMPLOYMENT

The right to a job requires action to break down artificial and arbitrary barriers to employment based on age, race, sex, religion, or national origin.

Unemployment strikes hardest at workers over 40, minority groups, young people, and women. We will not achieve full employment until prejudice against these workers is wiped out.

COLLECTIVE BARGAINING

The right to a job requires the restoration of full support for collective bargaining and the repeal of the anti-labor excesses which have been written into our labor laws.

Under Democratic leadership a sound national policy was developed, expressed particularly by the Wagner National Labor Relations Act, which guaranteed the rights of workers to organize and to bargain collectively. But the Republican Administration has replaced this sound policy with a national anti-labor policy.

The Republican Taft-Hartley Act seriously weakened unions in their efforts to bring economic justice to the millions of American workers who remain unorganized.

By administrative action, anti-labor personnel appointed by the Republicans to the National Labor Relations Board have made the Taft-Hartley Act even more restrictive in its application than in its language.

✦✦✦✦

We pledge the enactment of an affirmative labor policy which will encourage free collective bargaining through the growth and development of free and responsible unions.

Millions of workers just now seeking to organize are blocked by Federally authorized "right-to-work" laws, unreasonable limitations on the right to picket, and other hampering legislative and administrative provisions.

Again, in the new Labor-Management Reporting and Disclosure Act, the Republican Administration perverted the constructive effort of the Democratic Congress to deal with improper activities of a few in labor and management by turning that Act into a means of restricting the legitimate rights of the vast majority of working men and women in honest labor unions. This law likewise strikes hardest at the weak or poorly organized, and it fails to deal with abuses of management as vigorously as with those of labor.

We will repeal the authorization for "right-to-work" laws, limitations on the right to strike, to picket peacefully and to tell the public the facts of a labor dispute, and other anti-labor features of the Taft-Hartley Act and the 1959 [Reporting and Disclosure] Act. This unequivocal pledge for the repeal of the anti-labor and restrictive provisions of those laws will encourage collective bargaining and strengthen and support the free and honest labor movement.

PLANNING FOR AUTOMATION

The right to a job requires planning for automation, so that men and women will be trained and available to meet shifting employment needs.

We will conduct a continuing analysis of the nation's manpower resources and of measures which may be required to assure their fullest development and use.

We will provide the Government leadership necessary to insure that the blessings of automation do not become burdens of widespread unemployment. For the young and the technologically displaced workers, we will provide the opportunity for training and retraining that equips them for jobs to be filled.

MINIMUM WAGES

b. *"The right to earn enough to provide adequate food and clothing and recreation."*

At the bottom of the income scale are some eight million families whose earnings are too low to provide even basic necessities of food, shelter, and clothing.

We pledge to raise the minimum wage to $1.25 an hour and to extend coverage to several million workers not now protected.

We pledge further improvements in the wage, hour and coverage standards of the Fair Labor Standards Act so as to extend its benefits to all workers employed in industries engaged in or affecting interstate commerce and to raise its standards to keep up with our general economic progress and needs.

We shall seek to bring the two million men, women and children who work for wages on the farms of the United States under the protection of existing labor and social legislation; and to assure migrant labor, perhaps the most underprivileged of all, of a comprehensive program to bring them not only decent wages but also adequate standards of health, housing, Social Security protection, education and welfare services.

c. *"The right of every farmer to raise and sell his products at a return which will give him and his family a decent living."*

++++

Using our abundance

The Democratic Administration will inaugurate a national food and fiber policy for expanded use of our agricultural abundance. We will no longer view food stockpiles with alarm but will use them as powerful instruments for peace and plenty. . . .

We will use the food stamp programs authorized to feed needy children, the aged and the unemployed. We will expand and improve the school lunch and milk programs.

++++

We will increase consumption abroad. The Democratic Party believes our nation's capacity to produce food and fiber is one of the great weapons for waging war against hunger and want throughout the world. With wise management of our food abundance we will expand trade between nations, support economic and human development programs, and combat famine.

++++

Achieving income parity

While farmers have raised their productive efficiency to record levels, Republican farm policies have forced their income to drop by 30%.

Tens of thousands of farm families have been bankrupted and forced off the land. This has happened despite the fact that the Secretary of Agriculture has spent more on farm programs than all previous Secretaries in history combined.

Farmers acting individually or in small groups are helpless to protect their incomes from sharp declines. Their only recourse is to produce more, throwing production still further out of balance with demand and driving prices down further.

This disastrous downward cycle can be stopped only by effective farm programs sympathetically administered with the assistance of democratically elected farmer committees.

The Democratic Administration will work to bring about full parity income for farmers in all segments of agriculture by helping them to balance farm production with the expanding needs of the nation and the world.

Measures to this end include production and marketing quotas measured in terms of barrels, bushels and bales, loans on basic commodities at not less than 90% of parity, production payments, commodity purchases, and marketing orders and agreements.

We repudiate the Republican administration of the Soil Bank Program, which has emphasized the retirement of whole farm units, and we pledge an orderly land retirement and conservation program.

✦✦✦✦

We will encourage agricultural cooperatives by expanding and liberalizing existing credit facilities and developing new facilities if necessary to assist them in extending their marketing and purchasing activities, and we will protect cooperatives from punitive taxation.

✦✦✦✦

Improving working and living on farms

✦✦✦✦

The new Democratic Administration will begin at once to eradicate long-neglected rural blight. We will help people help themselves with extended and supervised credit for farm improvement, local industrial development, improved vocational training and other assistance to those wishing to change to non-farm employment, and with the fullest development of commercial and recreational possibilities. This is one of the major objectives of the area redevelopment program, twice vetoed by the Republican President.

The rural electric cooperatives celebrate this year the twenty-fifth anniversary of the creation of the Rural Electrification Administration under President Franklin D. Roosevelt.

The Democratic Congress has successfully fought the efforts of the Republican Administration to cut off REA loans and force high-interest-rate policies on this great rural enterprise.

We will maintain interest rates for REA co-ops and public power districts at the levels provided in present law.

✦✦✦✦

In every way we will seek to help the men, women, and children whose livelihood comes from the soil to achieve better housing, education, health, and decent earnings and working conditions.

SMALL BUSINESS

d. *"The right of every businessman, large and small, to trade in an atmosphere of freedom from unfair competition and domination by monopolies at home and abroad."*

The new Democratic Administration will act to make our free economy really free—free from the oppression of monopolistic power, and free from the suffocating impact of high interest rates. We will help create an economy in which small business can take root, grow, and flourish.

We Democrats pledge:

1. Action to aid small business in obtaining credit and equity capital at reasonable rates. Small business which must borrow to stay alive has been a particular victim of the high-interest policies of the Republican administration.

++++

2. Protection of the public against the growth of monopoly.

The last 7½ years of Republican government has been the greatest period of merger and amalgamation in industry and banking in American history. Democratic Congresses have enacted numerous important measures to strengthen our anti-trust laws. Since 1950 the four Democratic Congresses have enacted laws like the Celler-Kefauver Anti-Merger Act, and improved the laws against price discriminations and tie-in sales.

When the Republicans were in control of the 80th and 83rd Congresses they failed to enact a single measure to strengthen or improve the anti-trust laws.

The Democratic Party opposes this trend to monopoly.

We pledge vigorous enforcement of the anti-trust laws.

++++

3. A more equitable share of Government contracts to small and independent business.

++++

HOUSING

e. "The right of every family to a decent home."

Today our rate of home building is less than that of ten years ago. A healthy, expanding economy will enable us to build two million homes a year, in wholesome neighborhoods, for people of all incomes.

At this rate, within a single decade we can clear away our slums and assure every American family a decent place to live.

Republican policies have led to a decline of the home building industry and the production of fewer homes. Republican high-interest policies have forced the cost of decent housing beyond the range of many families. Republican indifference has perpetuated slums.

We record the unpleasant fact that in 1960 at least 40 million Americans live in substandard housing.

One million new families are formed each year and need housing, and 300,000 existing homes are lost through demolition or other causes and need to be replaced. At present, construction does not even meet these requirements, much less permit reduction of the backlog of slum units.

We support a housing construction goal of more than two million homes a year. Most of the increased construction will be priced to meet the housing needs of middle- and low-income families who now live in substandard housing and are priced out of the market for decent homes.

Our housing programs will provide for rental as well as sales housing. They will permit expanded cooperative housing programs and sharply stepped-up rehabilitation of existing homes.

To make possible the building of two million homes a year in wholesome neighborhoods, the home building industry should be aided by special mortgage assistance, with low interest rates, long-term mortgage periods and reduced down payments. Where necessary, direct Government loans should be provided.

Even with this new and flexible approach, there will still be need for a substantial low-rent public housing program authorizing as many units as local communities require and are prepared to build.

HEALTH

f. *"The right to adequate medical care and the opportunity to achieve and enjoy good health."*

Illness is expensive. Many Americans have neither incomes nor insurance protection to enable them to pay for modern health care. The problem is particularly acute with our older citizens, among whom serious illness strikes most often.

We shall provide medical care benefits for the aged as part of the time-tested Social Security insurance system. We reject any proposal which would require such citizens to submit to the indignity of a means test—a "pauper's oath."

For young and old alike, we need more medical schools, more hospitals, more research laboratories to speed the final conquest of major killers.

Medical care for older persons

Fifty million Americans—more than a fourth of our people—have no insurance protection against the high cost of illness. For the rest, private health insurance pays, on the average, only about one-third of the cost of medical care.

The problem is particularly acute among the 16 million Americans over 65 years old, and among disabled workers, widows and orphans.

Most of these have low incomes and the elderly among them suffer two or three times as much illness as the rest of the population.

The Republican Administration refused to acknowledge any national responsibility for health care for elder citizens until forced to do so by an increasingly outraged demand. Then, its belated proposal was a cynical sham built around a degrading test based on means or income —a "pauper's oath."

The most practicable way to provide health protection for older people is to use the contributory machinery of the Social Security system for insurance covering hospital bills and other high-cost medical services. For those relatively few of our older people who have never been eligible for Social Security coverage, we shall provide corresponding benefits by appropriations from the general revenue.

++++

g. *"The right to adequate protection from the economic fears of old age, sickness, accidents, and unemployment."*

A PROGRAM FOR THE AGING

The Democratic Administration will end the neglect of our older citizens. They deserve lives of usefulness, dignity, independence, and participation. We shall assure them not only health care but employment for those who want work, decent housing, and recreation.

Already 16 million Americans—about one in ten—are over 65, with the prospect of 26 million by 1980.

Health

As stated, we will provide an effective system for paid-up medical insurance upon retirement, financed during working years through the Social Security mechanism and available to all retired persons without a means test. This has first priority.

Income

++++

We will amend the Social Security Act to increase the retirement benefit for each additional year of work after 65, thus encouraging workers to continue on the job full time.

THE 1960 DEMOCRATIC PLATFORM   47

To encourage part-time work by others, we favor raising the $1200-a-year ceiling on what a worker may earn while still drawing Social Security benefits.

Retirement benefits must be increased generally, and minimum benefits raised from $33 a month to $50.

Housing

We shall provide decent and suitable housing which older persons can afford. Specifically we shall move ahead with the program of direct Government loans for housing for older people initiated in the Housing Act of 1959, a program which the Republican Administration has sought to kill.

++++

EDUCATION

h. *"The right to a good education."*

America's young people are our greatest resource for the future. Each of them deserves the education which will best develop his potentialities.

We shall act at once to help in building the classrooms and employing the teachers that are essential if the right to a good education is to have genuine meaning for all the youth of America in the decade ahead.

As a national investment in our future we propose a program of loans and scholarship grants to assure that qualified young Americans will have full opportunity for higher education, at the institutions of their choice, regardless of the income of their parents.

The new Democratic Administration will end eight years of official neglect of our educational system.

America's education faces a financial crisis. The tremendous increase in the number of children of school and college age has far outrun the available supply of educational facilities and qualified teachers. The classroom shortage alone is interfering with the education of 10 million students.

America's teachers, parents and school administrators have striven courageously to keep up with the increased challenge of education.

So have states and local communities. Education absorbs two-fifths of all their revenue. With limited resources, private educational institutions have shouldered their share of the burden.

Only the Federal Government is not doing its part. For eight years, measures for the relief of the educational crisis have been held up by the cynical maneuvers of the Republican Party in Congress and the White House.

We believe that America can meet its educational obligations only with generous Federal financial support, within the traditional framework of local control. The assistance will take the form of Federal grants to states for educational purposes they deem most pressing, including classroom construction and teachers' salaries. It will include aid for the construction of academic facilities as well as dormitories at colleges and universities.

✚✚✚✚

The pledges contained in this Economic Bill of Rights point the way to a better life for every family in America.

They are the means to a goal that is now within our reach—the final eradication in America of the age-old evil of poverty.

✚✚✚✚

Energy

The Republican Administration would turn the clock back to the days before the New Deal, in an effort to divert the benefits of the great natural energy resources from all the people to a favored few. It has followed for many years a "no new starts" policy.

It has stalled atomic energy development; it has sought to cripple rural electrification.

It has closed the pilot plant on getting oil from shale.

It has harassed and hampered the TVA.

We reject this philosophy and these policies. The people are entitled to use profitably what they already own.

The Democratic Administration instead will foster the development of efficient regional giant power systems from all sources, including water, tidal, and nuclear power, to supply low-cost electricity to all retail electric systems, public, private, and cooperative.

The Democratic Administration will continue to develop "yard-sticks" for measuring the rates of private utility systems. This means meeting the needs of rural electric cooperatives for low-interest loans for distribution, transmission and generation facilities; Federal transmission facilities, where appropriate, to provide [an] efficient low-cost power supply; and strict enforcement of the public-preference clause in power marketing.

✚✚✚✚

A new Democratic Administration will expand Federal programs to help urban communities clear their slums, dispose of their sewage, educate their children, transport suburban commuters to and from their jobs, and combat juvenile delinquency.

We will give the city dweller a voice at the Cabinet table by bringing together within a single department programs concerned with urban and metropolitan problems.

The United States is now predominantly an urban nation.

The efficiency, comfort, and beauty of our cities and suburbs influence the lives of all Americans.

Local governments have found increasing difficulty in coping with such fundamental public problems as urban renewal, slum clearance, water supply, mass transportation, recreation, health, welfare, education and metropolitan planning. These problems are, in many cases, interstate and regional in scope.

Yet the Republican Administration has turned its back on urban and suburban America. The list of Republican vetoes includes housing, urban renewal and slum clearance, area redevelopment, public works, airports and stream pollution control. It has proposed severe cutbacks in aid for hospital construction, public assistance, vocational education, community facilities and sewage disposal.

We propose a ten-year action program to restore our cities and provide for balanced suburban development, including the following:

1. The elimination of slums and blight and the restoration of cities and depressed areas within the next ten years.

2. Federal aid for metropolitan area planning and community facility programs.

3. Federal aid for comprehensive metropolitan transportation programs, including bus and rail mass transit, commuter railroads as well as highway programs, and construction of civil airports.

4. Federal aid in combating air and water pollution.

5. Expansion of park systems to meet the recreation needs of our growing population.

Regulatory agencies

The Democratic Party promises to clean up the Federal regulatory agencies. The acceptance by Republican appointees to these agencies of gifts, hospitality, and bribes from interests under their jurisdiction has been a particularly flagrant abuse of public trust.

We shall bring all contacts with commissioners into the open, and will protect them from any form of improper pressure.

We shall appoint to these agencies men of ability and independent judgment who understand that their function is to regulate these industries in the public interest.

We promise a thorough review of existing agency practices, with an eye toward speedier decisions, and a clearer definition of what constitutes the public interest.

++++

CONGRESSIONAL PROCEDURES

In order that the will of the American people may be expressed upon all legislative proposals, we urge that action be taken at the beginning of the 87th Congress to improve Congressional procedures so that majority rule prevails and decisions can be made after reasonable debate without being blocked by a minority in either House.

The rules of the House of Representatives should be so amended as to make sure that bills reported by legislative committees reach the floor for consideration without undue delay.

++++

CIVIL LIBERTIES

With democratic values threatened today by Communist tyranny, we reaffirm our dedication to the Bill of Rights. Freedom and civil liberties, far from being incompatible with security, are vital to our national strength. Unfortunately, those high in the Republican Administration have all too often sullied the name and honor of loyal and faithful American citizens in and out of Government.

The Democratic Party will strive to improve Congressional investigating and hearing procedures. We shall abolish useless disclaimer affidavits such as those for student educational loans. We shall provide a full and fair hearing, including confrontation of the accuser, to any person whose public or private employment or reputation is jeopardized by a loyalty or security proceeding.

Protection of rights of American citizens to travel, to pursue lawful trade and to engage in other lawful activities abroad without distinction as to race or religion is a cardinal function of the national sovereignty.

We will oppose any international agreement or treaty which by its terms or practices differentiates among American citizens on grounds of race or religion.

++++

FISCAL RESPONSIBILITY

We vigorously reject the notion that America, with a half-trillion-dollar gross national product, and nearly half of the world's industrial resources, cannot afford to meet our needs at home and in our world relationships.

We believe, moreover, that except in periods of recession or national emergency, these needs can be met with a balanced budget, with no increase in present tax rates, and with some surplus for the gradual reduction of our national debt.

To assure such a balance we shall pursue a four-point program of fiscal responsibility.

First, we shall end the gross waste in Federal expenditures which needlessly raises the budgets of many Government agencies.

The most conspicuous unnecessary item is, of course, the excessive cost of interest on the national debt. Courageous action to end duplication and competition among the armed services will achieve large savings. The cost of the agricultural program can be reduced while at the same time prosperity is being restored to the nation's farmers.

Second, we shall collect the billions in taxes which are owed to the Federal Government but not now collected.

++++

We will add enforcement personnel, and develop new techniques of enforcement, to collect tax revenue which is now being lost through evasion.

Third, we shall close the loopholes in the tax laws by which certain privileged groups legally escape their fair share of taxation.

Among the more conspicuous loopholes are depletion allowances which are inequitable, special consideration for recipients of dividend income, and deductions for extravagant "business expenses" which have reached scandalous proportions.

Tax reform can raise additional revenue and at the same time increase legitimate incentives for growth, and make it possible to ease the burden on the general taxpayer who now pays an unfair share of taxes because of special favors to the few.

Fourth, we shall bring in added Federal tax revenues by expanding the economy itself. Each dollar of additional production puts an additional 18 cents in tax revenue in the national treasury. A 5% growth rate, therefore, will mean that at the end of four years the Federal Government will have had a total of nearly $50 billion in additional tax revenues above those presently received.

By these four methods we can sharply increase the Government funds available for needed services, for correction of tax inequities, and for debt or tax reduction.

++++

CIVIL RIGHTS

We shall also seek to create an affirmative new atmosphere in which to deal with racial divisions and inequalities which threaten both the integrity of our democratic faith and the proposition on which our nation was founded—that all men are created equal. It is our faith in human dignity that distinguishes our open free society from the closed totalitarian society of the Communists.

The Constitution of the United States rejects the notion that the Rights of Man means the rights of some men only. We reject it too.

The right to vote is the first principle of self-government. The Constitution also guarantees to all Americans the equal protection of the laws.

It is the duty of the Congress to enact the laws necessary and proper to protect and promote these constitutional rights. The Supreme Court has the power to interpret these rights and the laws thus enacted.

It is the duty of the President to see that these rights are respected and that the Constitution and laws as interpreted by the Supreme Court are faithfully executed.

What is now required is effective moral and political leadership by the whole Executive branch of our Government to make equal opportunity a living reality for all Americans.

As the party of Jefferson, we shall provide that leadership.

In every city and state in greater or lesser degree there is discrimination based on color, race, religion, or national origin.

If discrimination in voting, education, the administration of justice or segregated lunch counters are the issues in one area, discrimination in housing and employment may be pressing questions elsewhere.

The peaceful demonstrations for first-class citizenship which have recently taken place in many parts of this country are a signal to all of us to make good at long last the guarantees of our Constitution.

The time has come to assure equal access for all Americans to all areas of community life, including voting booths, schoolrooms, jobs, housing, and public facilities.

The Democratic Administration which takes office next January will therefore use the full powers provided in the Civil Rights Acts of 1957 and 1960 to secure for all Americans the right to vote.

If these powers, vigorously invoked by a new Attorney General and backed by a strong and imaginative Democratic President, prove inadequate, further powers will be sought.

We will support whatever action is necessary to eliminate literacy tests and the payment of poll taxes as requirements for voting.

A new Democratic Administration will also use its full powers—legal and moral—to ensure the beginning of good-faith compliance with the Constitutional requirement that racial discrimination be ended in public education.

We believe that every school district affected by the Supreme Court's school desegregation decision should submit a plan providing for at least first-step compliance by 1963, the 100th anniversary of the Emancipation Proclamation.

To facilitate compliance, technical and financial assistance should be given to school districts facing special problems of transition.

For this and for the protection of all other Constitutional rights of Americans, the Attorney General should be empowered and directed to file civil injunction suits in Federal courts to prevent the denial of any civil right on grounds of race, creed, or color.

The new Democratic Administration will support Federal legislation establishing a Fair Employment Practices Commission to secure effectively for everyone the right to equal opportunity for employment.

In 1949 the President's Committee on Civil Rights recommended a permanent Commission on Civil Rights. The new Democratic Administration will broaden the scope and strengthen the powers of the present commission and make it permanent.

Its functions will be to provide assistance to communities, industries, or individuals in the implementation of Constitutional rights in education, housing, employment, transportation, and the administration of justice.

In addition, the Democratic Administration will use its full executive powers to assure equal employment opportunities and to terminate racial segregation throughout Federal services and institutions, and on all Government contracts. The successful desegregation of the armed services took place through such decisive executive action under President Truman.

Similarly the new Democratic Administration will take action to end discrimination in Federal housing programs, including Federally assisted housing.

To accomplish these goals will require executive orders, legal actions brought by the Attorney General, legislation, and improved Congressional procedures to safeguard majority rule.

Above all, it will require the strong, active, persuasive, and inventive leadership of the President of the United States.

✦✦✦✦

As the Party of Hope it is our responsibility and opportunity to call forth the greatness of the American people.

In this spirit, we hereby rededicate ourselves to the continuing service of the Rights of Man—everywhere in America and everywhere else on God's earth.

DOCUMENT 5 **THE 1960 REPUBLICAN PLATFORM**

The Republicans in 1960 were confronted by a novel problem: for the first time, the Twenty-Second Amendment ("No person shall be elected to the office of the President more than twice . . . .") came into operation and deprived them of the services of a sure winner. With the politically impregnable Dwight Eisenhower out of the picture, the Democrats were moving in for the kill, though candidate Kennedy carefully distinguished between savage attacks on the Republican Administration and more benign references to President Eisenhower (who of course had no connection with the Eisenhower Administration).

The Republican strategists were in a bad predicament: if they emphasized the character and standing of President Eisenhower, Vice-President Richard M. Nixon could be accused of running on Ike's accomplishments, of "hiding behind Daddy." On the other hand, if the Nixon planners took off on an independent tack, demanding vigor and enthusiasm, they were implicitly forced to criticize the Eisenhower record. As it turned out, Nixon (to President Eisenhower's annoyance, it seems) decided to go it alone, and the Democrats shortly began circulating a parody in which the Vice-President pro-

claimed, "Everything is in magnificent shape—and you can count on me to get the nation out of the mess." Any successor to a popular President, of course, has the same problem.

This Republican platform reveals the ambivalence of the planners on this crucial point; it is also interesting to compare the views of the GOP "intellectuals" who drafted it with those of their Democratic counterparts of the previous document.

PREAMBLE

The United States is living in an age of profoundest revolution. The lives of men and of nations are undergoing such transformations as history has rarely recorded. The birth of new nations, the impact of new machines, the threat of new weapons, the stirring of new ideas, the ascent into a new dimension of the universe—everywhere the accent falls on the new.

In this Republican Platform we offer to the United States our program—our call to service, our pledge of leadership, our proposal of measures in the public interest. We call upon God, in whose hand is every blessing, to favor our deliberations with wisdom, our nation with endurance, and troubled mankind everywhere with a righteous peace.

FOREIGN POLICY

The Republican Party asserts that the sovereign purpose of our foreign policy is to secure the free institutions of our nation against every peril, to hearten and fortify the love of freedom everywhere in the world, and to achieve a just peace for all of anxious humanity.

The Government of the United States, under the administration of President Eisenhower and Vice President Nixon, has demonstrated that firmness in the face of threatened aggression is the most dependable safeguard of peace. We now reaffirm our determination to defend the security and the freedom of our country, to honor our commitments to our allies at whatever cost or sacrifice, and never to submit to force or threats. Our determination to stand fast has forestalled aggression before [in] Berlin, in the Formosa Straits, and in Lebanon. Since 1954 no

FROM: Kirk H. Porter and Donald B. Johnson, eds., *National Party Platforms,* 1840–1960, 2nd ed. (Urbana, Illinois, University of Illinois Press, 1961), pp. 604–20.

free nation has fallen victim behind the Iron Curtain. We mean to adhere to the policy of firmness that has served us so well.

We are unalterably committed to maintaining the security, freedom and solidarity of the Western Hemisphere. We support President Eisenhower's reaffirmation of the Monroe Doctrine in all its vitality. Faithful to our treaty commitments, we shall join the Republics of the Americas against any intervention in our hemisphere, and in refusing to tolerate the establishment in this hemisphere of any government dominated by the foreign rule of communism.

In the Middle East, we shall continue to support the integrity and independence of all the states of that area including Israel and the Arab States.

✦✦✦✦

Recognition of Communist China and its admission to the United Nations have been firmly opposed by the Republican Administration. We will continue in this opposition because of compelling evidence that to do otherwise would weaken the cause of freedom and endanger the future of the free peoples of Asia and the world. The brutal suppression of the human rights and the religious traditions of the Tibetan people is an unhappy evidence of the need to persist in our policy.

The countries of the free world have been benefited, reinforced and drawn closer together by the vigor of American support of the United Nations, and by our participation in such regional organizations as NATO, SEATO, CENTO, the Organization of American States and other collective security alliances. We assert our intention steadfastly to uphold the action and principles of these bodies.

We believe military assistance to our allies under the mutual security program should be continued with all the vigor and funds needed to maintain the strength of our alliances at levels essential to our common safety.

The firm diplomacy of the Eisenhower-Nixon Administration has been supported by a military power superior to any in the history of our nation or [of] the world. As long as world tensions menace us with war, we are resolved to maintain an armed power exceeded by no other.

Under Republican administration, the Government has developed original and constructive programs in many fields—open skies, atoms for peace, cultural and technical exchanges, the peaceful uses of outer space and Antarctica—to make known to men everywhere our desire to advance the cause of peace. We mean, as a Party, to continue in the same course. . . . To nullify the Soviet conspiracy is our greatest task. The United States faces this challenge and resolves to meet it with courage and confidence.

To this end we will continue to support and strengthen the United Nations as an instrument for peace, for international cooperation, and for the advancement of the fundamental freedoms and humane interests of mankind.

Under the United Nations we will work for the peaceful settlement of international disputes and the extension of the rule of law in the world.

And, in furtherance of President Eisenhower's proposals for the peaceful use of space, we suggest that the United Nations take the initiative to develop a body of law applicable thereto.

Through all the calculated shifts of Soviet tactics and mood, the Eisenhower-Nixon Administration has demonstrated its willingness to negotiate in earnest with the Soviet Union to arrive at just settlements for the reduction of world tensions. We pledge the new Administration to continue in the same course.

We are similarly ready to negotiate and to institute realistic methods and safeguards for disarmament, and for the suspension of nuclear tests.

✛✛✛✛

We recognize that firm political and military policies, while imperative for our security, cannot in themselves build peace in the world.

In Latin America, Asia, Africa and the Middle East, peoples of ancient and recent independence have shown their determination to improve their standards of living, and to enjoy an equality with the rest of mankind in the enjoyment of the fruits of civilization. This determination has become a primary fact of their political life. We declare ourselves to be in sympathy with their aspirations.

We have already created unprecedented dimensions of diplomacy for these purposes. We recognize that upon our support of well-conceived programs of economic cooperation among nations rests the best hopes of hundreds of millions of friendly people for a decent future for themselves and their children. Our mutual security program of economic help and technical assistance; the Development Loan Fund, the Inter-American Bank, the International Development Association and the Food for Peace Program, which create the conditions for progress in less-developed countries; our leadership in international efforts to help children, eliminate pestilence and disease and aid refugees—these are programs wise in concept and generous in purpose. We mean to continue in support of them.

Now we propose to further evolution of our programs for assistance to and cooperation with other nations, suitable to the emerging needs of the future.

++++

NATIONAL DEFENSE

The Republican Party is pledged to making certain that our arms, and our will to use them, remain superior to all threats. We have, and will continue to have, the defenses we need to protect our freedom.

The strategic imperatives of our national defense policy are these:

A second-strike capability, that is, a nuclear retaliatory power that can survive surprise attack, strike back, and destroy any possible enemy.

Highly mobile and versatile forces, including forces deployed, to deter or check local aggressions and "brush fire wars" which might bring on all-out nuclear war.

National determination to employ all necessary military capabilities so as to render any level of aggression unprofitable. Deterrence of war since Korea, specifically, has been the result of our firm statement that we will never again permit a potential aggressor to set the ground rules for his aggression; that we will respond to aggression with the full means and weapons best suited to the situation.

++++

ECONOMIC GROWTH AND BUSINESS

To provide the means to a better life for individual Americans and to strengthen the forces of freedom in the world, we count on the proved productivity of our free economy.

Despite the lamentations of the opposition in viewing the economic scene today, the plain fact is that our 500 billion dollar economy finds more Americans at work, earning more, spending more, saving more, investing more, building more than ever before in history. The well-being of our people, by virtually every yardstick, has greatly advanced under this Republican Administration.

But we can and must do better. We must raise employment to even higher levels and utilize even more fully our expanding, overall capacity to produce. We must quicken the pace of our economic growth to prove the power of American free enterprise to meet growing and urgent demands: to sustain our military posture, to provide jobs for a growing labor force in a time of rapid technological change, to improve living standards, to serve all the needs of an expanding population.

We therefore accord high priority to vigorous economic growth and recognize that its mainspring lies in the private sector of the economy. We must continue to foster a healthy climate in that sector. We reject the concept of artificial growth forced by massive new federal spending and loose money policies. The only effective way to accelerate economic growth is to increase the traditional strengths of our free economy—initiative and investment, productivity and efficiency. To that end we favor:

Broadly-based tax reform to foster job-making and growth-making investment for modernization and expansion, including realistic incentive depreciation schedules.

Use of the full powers of government to prevent the scourges of depression and inflation.

Elimination of featherbedding practices by labor and business.

Maintenance of a stable dollar as an indispensable means to progress.

Relating wage and other payments in production to productivity—except when necessary to correct inequities—in order to help us stay competitive at home and abroad.

Spurring the economy by advancing the successful Eisenhower-Nixon program fostering new and small business, by continued active enforcement of the anti-trust laws, by protecting consumers and investors against the hazard and economic waste of fraudulent and criminal practices in the market place, and by keeping the federal government from unjustly competing with private enterprise upon which Americans mainly depend for their livelihood.

++++

LABOR

America's growth cannot be compartmentalized. Labor and management cannot prosper without each other. They cannot ignore their mutual public obligation.

Industrial harmony, expressing these mutual interests, can best be achieved in a climate of free collective bargaining, with minimal government intervention except by mediation and conciliation.

Even in dealing with emergency situations imperiling the national safety, ways of solution must be found to enhance and not impede the processes of free collective bargaining—carefully considered ways that are in keeping with the policies of national labor relations legislation and with the need to strengthen the hand of the President in dealing with such emergencies.

In the same spirit, Republican leadership will continue to encourage discussions, away from the bargaining table, between labor and management to consider the mutual interest of all Americans in maintaining industrial peace.

Republican policy firmly supports the right of employers and unions freely to enter into agreements providing for the union shop and other forms of union security as authorized by the Labor-Management Relations Act of 1947 (the Taft-Hartley Act).

Republican-sponsored legislation has supported the right of union members to full participation in the affairs of their union and their right to freedom from racketeering and gangster interference whether by labor or management in labor-management relations.

Republican action has given to millions of American working men and women new or expanded protection and benefits, such as:

Increased federal minimum wage;

Extended coverage of unemployment insurance and the payment of additional temporary benefits provided in 1958–59;

Improvement of veterans' re-employment rights;

Extension of federal workman's compensation coverage and increase of benefits;

Legislative assurance of safety standards for longshore and harbor workers and for the transportation of migratory workers;

An increase of railroad workers' retirement and disability benefits.

AGRICULTURE

Americans are the best-fed and the best-clothed people in the world.

Yet, far too many of our farm families, the source of this strength, have not received a fair return for their labors. For too long, Democratic-controlled Congresses have stalemated progress by clinging to obsolete programs conceived for different times and different problems.

Promises of specific levels of price support or a single type of program for all agriculture are cruel deceptions based upon the pessimistic pretense that only with rigid controls can farm families be aided. The Republican Party will provide within the framework of individual freedom a greater bargaining power to assure an equitable return for the work and capital supplied by farmers.

The Republican Party pledges itself to develop new programs to improve and stabilize farm family income. It recognizes two main challenges: the immediate one of utilizing income-depressing surpluses, and the long-range one of steady balanced growth and development with a minimum of federal interference and control.

To utilize immediately surpluses in an orderly manner, with a minimum impact on domestic and foreign markets, we pledge:

Intensification of the Food for Peace program, including new cooperative efforts among food-surplus nations to assist the hungry peoples in less favored areas of the world.

Payment-in-kind, out of existing surpluses, as part of our land retirement program.

Creation of a Strategic Food Reserve properly dispersed in forms which can be preserved for long periods against the contingency of grave national emergency.

Strengthened efforts to distribute surpluses to schools and low-income and needy citizens of our own country.

A reorganization of Commodity Credit Corporation's inventory management operations to reduce competition with the marketings of farmers.

To assure steady balanced growth and agricultural progress, we pledge:

A crash research program to develop industrial and other uses of farm products.

Use of price supports at levels best fitted to specific commodities, in order to widen markets, ease production controls, and help achieve increased farm family income.

Acceleration of production adjustments, including a large scale land conservation reserve program on a voluntary and equitable rental basis, with full consideration of the impact on local communities.

Continued progress in the wise use and conservation of water and soil resources.

Use of marketing agreements and orders, and other marketing devices, when approved by producers, to assist in the orderly marketing of crops, thus enabling farmers to strengthen their bargaining power.

Stepped-up research to reduce production costs and to cut distribution costs.

Strengthening of the educational programs of the U.S. Department of Agriculture and the Land-Grant institutions.

Improvement of credit facilities for financing the capital needs of modern farming.

Encouragement of farmer owned and operated cooperatives including rural electric and telephone facilities.

Expansion of the Rural Development Program to help low-income farm families not only through better farming methods, but also through opportunities for vocational training, more effective employment services, and creation of job opportunities through encouragement of local industrialization.

++++

GOVERNMENT FINANCE

To build a better America with broad national purposes such as high employment, vigorous and steady economic growth, and a dependable currency, responsible management of our federal finances is essential. Even more important, a sound economy is vital to national security. While leading Democrats charge us with a "budget balancing" mentality, their taunts really reflect their frustration over the people's recognition that as a nation we must live within our means. Government that is careless with the money of its citizens is careless with their future.

Because we are concerned about the well-being of people, we are concerned about protecting the value of their money. To this end, we Republicans believe that:

Every government expenditure must be tested by its contribution to the general welfare, not to any narrow interest group.

Except in times of war or economic adversity, expenditures should be covered by revenues.

We must work persistently to reduce, not to increase, the national debt, which imposes a heavy economic burden on every citizen.

Our tax structure should be improved to provide greater incentives to economic progress, to make it fair and equitable, and to maintain and deserve public acceptance.

We must resist assaults upon the independence of the Federal Reserve System; we must strengthen, not weaken, the ability of the Federal Reserve System and the Treasury Department to exercise effective control over money and credit in order better to combat both deflation and inflation that retard economic growth and shrink people's savings and earnings.

++++

GOVERNMENT ADMINISTRATION

Vigorous state and local governments are a vital part of our federal union. The federal government should leave to state and local governments those programs and problems which they can best handle and tax sources adequate to finance them. We must continue to improve liaison between federal, state and local governments. We believe that the federal government, when appropriate, should render significant assistance in dealing with our urgent problems of urban growth and change. No vast new bureaucracy is needed to achieve this objective.

We favor a change in the Electoral College system to give every voter a fair voice in presidential elections.

✦✦✦✦

EDUCATION

. . . Toward the goal of fullest possible educational opportunity for every American, we pledge these actions.

Federal support to the primary and secondary schools by a program of federal aid for school construction—pacing it to the real needs of individual school districts in states and territories, and requiring state approval and participation.

Stimulation of actions designed to update and strengthen vocational education for both youth and adults.

Support of efforts to make adequate library facilities available to all our citizens.

Continued support of programs to strengthen basic research in education; to discover the best methods for helping handicapped, retarded, and gifted children to realize their highest potential.

The federal government can also play a part in stimulating higher education. Constructive action would include:

The federal program to assist in construction of college housing.

Extension of the federal student loan program and graduate fellowship program.

Consideration of means through tax laws to help offset tuition costs.

✦✦✦✦

We are aware of the fact that there is a temporary shortage of classrooms for our elementary and secondary schools in a limited number of states. But this shortage, due to the vigilant action of state legislatures and local school boards, is not increasing, but is decreasing.

We shall use our full efforts in all the states of the Union to have these legislatures and school boards augment their present efforts to the end that this temporary shortage may be eliminated and that every child in this country shall have the opportunity to obtain a good education. The respective states as a permanent program can shoulder this long-standing and cherished responsibility easier than can the federal government with its heavy indebtedness.

We believe moreover that any large plan of federal aid to education, such as direct contributions to or grants for teachers' salaries can only lead ultimately to [the] federal domination and control of our schools to which we are unalterably opposed.

++++

HUMAN NEEDS

The ultimate objective of our free society and of an ever-growing economy is to enable the individual to pursue a life of dignity and to develop his own capacities to his maximum potential.

Government's primary role is to help provide the environment within which the individual can seek his own goals. In some areas this requires federal action to supplement individual, local and state initiative. The Republican Party has acted and will act decisively, compassionately, and with deep human understanding in approaching such problems as those of the aged, the infirm, the mentally ill, and the needy.

This is demonstrated by the significant increase in social security coverage and benefits as a result of recommendations made by the Eisenhower-Nixon Administration.

++++

New needs, however, are constantly arising in our highly complex, interdependent, and urbanized society.

Older citizens

To meet the needs of the aging, we pledge:

Expansion of coverage, and liberalization of selected social security benefits on a basis which would maintain the fiscal integrity of the system.

Support of federal-state grant programs to improve health, welfare and rehabilitation services for handicapped older persons and to improve standards of nursing home care and care and treatment facilities for the chronically and mentally ill.

Federal leadership to encourage policies that will make retirement at a fixed age voluntary and not compulsory.

++++

Health aid

Development of a health program that will provide the aged needing it, on a sound fiscal basis and through a contributory system, protection against burdensome costs of health care. Such a program should:

Provide the beneficiaries with the option of purchasing private health insurance—a vital distinction between our approach and Democratic proposals in that it would encourage commercial carriers and voluntary insurance organizations to continue their efforts to develop sound coverage plans for the senior population.

Protect the personal relationship of patient and physician.

Include state participation.

For the needs which individuals of all age groups cannot meet by themselves, we propose:

Removing the arbitrary 50-year age requirement under the disability insurance program while amending the law also to provide incentives for rehabilitated persons to return to useful work.

A single, federal assistance grant to each state for aid to needy persons rather than dividing such grants into specific categories.

++++

Housing

Despite noteworthy accomplishments, stubborn and deep-seated problems stand in the way of achieving the national objective of a decent home in a suitable environment for every American. Recognizing that the federal government must help provide the economic climate and incentives which make this objective obtainable, the Republican Party will vigorously support the following steps, all designed to supplement and not supplant private initiative.

Continued effort to clear slums, and promote rebuilding, rehabilitation, and conservation of our cities.

New programs to stimulate development of specialized types of housing, such as those for the elderly and for nursing homes.

A program of research and demonstration aimed at finding ways to reduce housing costs, including support of efforts to modernize and improve local building codes.

Adequate authority for the federal housing agencies to assist the flow of mortgage credit into private housing, with emphasis on homes for middle- and lower-income families and including assistance in urban residential areas.

++++

Health

There has been a five-fold increase in government-assisted medical research during the last six years. We pledge:

Continued federal support for a sound research program aimed at both the prevention and cure of diseases, and intensified efforts to secure prompt and effective application of the results of research. This will include emphasis on mental illness.

Support of international health research programs.

We face serious personnel shortages in the health and medical fields. We pledge:

Federal help in new programs to build schools of medicine, dentistry, and public health and nursing, and financial aid to students in those fields.

We are confronted with major problems in the field of environmental health. We pledge:

Strengthened federal enforcement powers in combatting water pollution and additional resources for research and demonstration projects. Federal grants for the construction of waste disposal plants should be made only when they make an identifiable contribution to clearing up polluted streams.

Federal authority to identify, after appropriate hearings, air pollution problems and to recommend proposed solutions.

++++

CIVIL RIGHTS

This nation was created to give expression, validity and purpose to our spiritual heritage—the supreme worth of the individual. In such a nation—a nation dedicated to the proposition that all men are created equal—racial discrimination has no place. It can hardly be reconciled with a Constitution that guarantees equal protection under law to all persons. In a deeper sense, too, it is immoral and unjust. As to those matters within reach of political action and leadership, we pledge ourselves unreservedly to its eradication.

Equality under law promises more than the equal right to vote and transcends mere relief from discrimination by government. It becomes a reality only when all persons have equal opportunity, without distinction of race, religion, color or national origin, to acquire the essentials of life—housing, education and employment. The Republican Party—the party of Abraham Lincoln—from its very beginning has striven to make this promise a reality. It is today, as it was then, unequivocally dedicated to making the greatest amount of progress toward [this] objective.

We recognize that discrimination is not a problem localized in one area of the country, but rather a problem that must be faced by North and South alike. Nor is discrimination confined to the discrimination against Negroes. Discrimination in many, if not all, areas of the country on the basis of creed or national origin is equally insidious. Further we recognize that in many communities in which a century of custom and tradition must be overcome heartening and commendable progress has been made.

The Republican Party is proud of the civil rights record of the Eisenhower Administration. More progress has been made during the past eight years than in the preceding 80 years. We acted promptly to end discrimination in our nation's capital. Vigorous executive action was taken to complete swiftly the desegregation of the armed forces, veterans' hospitals, navy yards, and other federal establishments.

We supported the position of the Negro school children before the Supreme Court. We believe the Supreme Court school decision should be carried out in accordance with the mandate of the Court.

Although the Democratic-controlled Congress watered them down, the Republican Administration's recommendations resulted in significant and effective civil rights legislation in both 1957 and 1960—the first civil rights statutes to be passed in more than 80 years.

Hundreds of Negroes have already been registered to vote as a result of Department of Justice action, some in counties where Negroes did not vote before. The new law will soon make it possible for thousands and thousands of Negroes previously disenfranchised to vote.

By executive order, a committee for the elimination of discrimination in government employment has been reestablished with broadened authority. Today, nearly one-fourth of all federal employees are Negroes.

The President's Committee on Government Contracts, under the chairmanship of Vice President Nixon, has become an impressive force for the elimination of discriminatory employment practices of private companies that do business with the government.

Other important achievements include initial steps toward the elimination of segregation in federally-aided housing; the establishment of the Civil Rights Division of the Department of Justice, which enforces federal civil rights laws; and the appointment of the bi-partisan Civil Rights Commission, which has prepared a significant report that lays the groundwork for further legislative action and progress.

The Republican record is a record of progress—not merely promises. Nevertheless, we recognize that much remains to be done.

Each of the following pledges is practical and within realistic reach of accomplishment. They are serious—not cynical—pledges made to result in maximum progress.

1. *Voting*

We pledge:

Continued vigorous enforcement of the civil rights laws to guarantee the right to vote to all citizens in all areas of the country.

Legislation to provide that the completion of six primary grades in a state accredited school is conclusive evidence of literacy for voting purposes.

2. *Public schools*

We pledge:

The Department of Justice will continue its vigorous support of court orders for school desegregation. Desegregation suits now pending involve at least 39 school districts. Those suits and others already concluded will affect most major cities in which school segregation is being practiced.

It will use the new authority provided by the Civil Rights Act of 1960 to prevent obstruction of court orders.

We will propose legislation to authorize the Attorney General to bring actions for school desegregation in the name of the United States in appropriate cases, as when economic coercion or threat of physical harm is used to deter persons from going to court to establish their rights.

Our continuing support of the President's proposal to extend federal aid and technical assistance to schools which in good faith attempted to desegregate.

We oppose the pretense of fixing a target date 3 years from now for the mere submission of plans for school desegregation. Slow-moving school districts would construe it as a three-year moratorium during which progress would cease, postponing until 1963 the legal process to enforce compliance. We believe that each of the pending court actions should proceed as the Supreme Court has directed and that in no district should there be any such delay.

3. *Employment*

We pledge:

Continued support for legislation to establish a Commission on Equal Job Opportunity to make permanent and to expand with legislative backing the excellent work being performed by the President's Committee on Government Contracts.

Appropriate legislation to end the discriminatory membership practices of some labor union locals, unless such practices are eradicated promptly by the labor unions themselves.

Use of the full-scale review of existing state laws, and of prior proposals for federal legislation, to eliminate discrimination in employment now being conducted by the Civil Rights Commission, for guidance in our objective of developing a Federal-State program in the employment area.

Special consideration of training programs aimed at developing the skills of those now working in marginal agricultural employment so that they can obtain employment in industry, notably in the new industries moving into the South.

4. *Housing*

We pledge:

Action to prohibit discrimination in housing constructed with the aid of federal subsidies.

5. *Public facilities and services*

We pledge:

Removal of any vestige of discrimination in the operation of federal facilities or procedures which may at any time be found.

Opposition to the use of federal funds for the construction of segregated community facilities.

Action to ensure that public transportation and other government authorized services shall be free from segregation.

6. *Legislative procedure*

We pledge:

Our best efforts to change present Rule 22 of the Senate and other appropriate Congressional procedures that often make unattainable proper legislative implementation of constitutional guarantees.

We reaffirm the constitutional right to peaceable assembly to protest discrimination in private business establishments. We applaud the action of the businessmen who have abandoned discriminatory practices in retail establishments, and we urge others to follow their example.

Finally we recognize that civil rights is a responsibility not only of states and localities; it is a national problem and a national responsibility. The federal government should take the initiative in promoting inter-group conferences among those who, in their communities, are earnestly seeking solutions [to] the complex problems of desegregation— to the end that closed channels of communication may be opened, tensions eased, and a cooperative solution of local problems may be sought.

In summary, we pledge the full use of the power, resources and leadership of the federal government to eliminate discrimination based on race, color, religion or national origin and to encourage understanding and good will among all races and creeds.

✦✦✦✦

CONCLUSION

We have set forth the program of the Republican Party for the government of the United States. We have written a Party document, as is our duty, but we have tried to refrain from writing a merely partisan document. We have no wish to exaggerate differences between ourselves and the Democratic Party; nor can we, in conscience, obscure the differences that do exist. We believe that the Republican program is based upon sounder understanding of the action and scope of government. There are many things a free government cannot do for its people as well as they can do them for themselves. There are some things no government should promise or attempt to do. The functions of government are so great as to bear no needless enlargement. We limit our proposals and our pledges to those areas for which the government of a great republic can reasonably be made responsible. To the best of our ability we have avoided advocating measures that would go against the grain of a free people.

✦✦✦✦

ELECTING
A PRESIDENT

DOCUMENT 6 THE ELECTORAL COLLEGE

The framers of the Constitution, aware that George Washington would be the first President but unable to agree on a system of election, eventually improvised a compromise "solution" and left the rest to posterity. As political experimenters of demonstrated talent, they would probably be startled to learn that the Electoral College has remained in operation since the founding of the Republic.

The consequence of this conservatism, inertia, or lack of imagination—whichever may be appropriate—is that we still elect the President indirectly. On election day the American voter casts his ballot not for a Presidential nominee, but for his state's Republican or Democratic slate of electors. The number of electors on each of these slates—the state's electoral votes—is computed by totaling its number of Congressmen plus its two Senators. Technically, a state may divide its electoral votes in any fashion it chooses, but in recent years the tradition has been "winner take all"—the candidate winning the state's popular majority also carries his state's entire slate of electors to victory. (This method contributes enormously to the power of the big urban states, with sizable blocs of votes, in the councils of both parties.) Each voter assumes that the slate of electors he votes for will carry out the mandate of the state's popular majority, and normally this electoral vote is pure routine: the winning party's electors, worthy local politicians all, assemble at the state capitol and cast their independent votes for their party's Presidential candidate. In 1960, however, a Republican elector in Oklahoma achieved brief notoriety by abandoning Nixon and Lodge for Byrd and Goldwater on the ground that the Founding Fathers wanted him to "think for himself."

In recent years, the eccentricities of the Electoral College have been exploited more systematically by Southern political figures in an effort to blackmail the Democratic Presidential candidates. In Mississippi in 1960, for example, the state Democratic party ran a slate of "unpledged electors" (Kennedy's name was nowhere on the ballot!), and several electors in Alabama were chosen on the same basis. The

72

hope is that in a close election such a body of unaffiliated electors could hold the balance of power between the national candidates and possibly, if unappeased, throw the election into the House of Representatives.

The following document provides a more detailed summary of procedures for the operation of the Electoral College system.

The various political parties nominate their candidates for office of President and Vice President at national conventions usually held in June, July, or August prior to the general November election in presidential election years. The national conventions are not regulated by State or Federal law. National conventions have no legal standing but are simply representative of the political sentiments of the particular political party holding the convention.

However, the persons nominated at the respective conventions for the offices of President and Vice President are usually under State law entitled to have their names placed on the general election ballot. This is a mere formality since the President and Vice President are actually under the United States Constitution elected by electors. These electors are State officers, being nominated and elected according to State law and paid some form of compensation, usually only necessary traveling expenses, by the individual States.

The practice of States differs as to printing of names of presidential electors on the general election ballot. Some States print the names of only the electors on the ballot, others print the names of both the electors and the presidential and vice presidential candidates on the ballot, and still others print only the names of the presidential and vice presidential candidates on the ballot. This latter method is termed the "short ballot." In most States where the names of the presidential and vice presidential candidates are printed on the ballot, the names are taken from the certificates of nomination required to be filed in nominating the electors. A voter in marking his ballot is actually voting for the electors and not for the presidential and vice presidential candidates.

The result in the electoral college vote is the same provided electors cast their ballots for their party's choice. A specific pledge is required of electors in Oregon that they will vote for the nominees on their

FROM: *Nomination and Election of the President and Vice President of the United States, Including the Manner of Selecting Delegates to National Political Conventions,* House Document Number 332, Eighty-Sixth Congress, Second Session (Washington, D.C., Government Printing Office, 1960), pp. 22–23.

party's ticket. In California electors must pledge themselves to vote for a member of the party that nominated them. Regardless of any pledge exacted by a State government, or punishment which a State might inflict for failure to observe such a pledge, the vote of a duly accredited elector cast by him as a member of the electoral college must be counted as valid under Federal law.

In accordance with a law enacted by Congress in 1934, the electors chosen by the voters meet at their State capitols on the first Monday after the second Wednesday in December . . . and cast their ballots. The results of their balloting, accompanied by the necessary certificates signed by their State governors, are sent by registered mail to the President of the Senate. The ballots are opened before a joint meeting of the Senate and House, held by law on the following January 6, with the Vice President (President of the Senate) presiding. Two tellers are appointed from each House; the presiding officer opens the returns and hands them to the tellers who record the votes. The candidates for President and Vice President receiving the largest number of votes, providing that number is at least a majority (now 269 out of the total of 537), are declared elected, and are given the oath of office 2 weeks later. . . .

In the event that no candidate for President has received a majority of the electoral votes, the choice of a Chief Executive becomes the responsibility of the House of Representatives and the choice of a Vice President devolves upon the Senate. In balloting for President, the House votes by State delegations, each delegation having one vote. The vote of States whose delegations are evenly divided [is] not counted.

In the election of a Vice President by the Senate each Senator has one vote. In the case of an evenly divided House failing to elect a President, the Vice President elected by the Senate takes the office until such time as the House can break its deadlock and pick a President to serve for the remainder of the term.

Due to the reapportionment of the House of Representatives according to the 1950 census . . . there was a change in the number of electors which each State was entitled to elect beginning with the November general election in 1952. The United States Constitution, article II, section 1, provides that each State is entitled to one elector for each of its Senators and Representatives in Congress.

DOCUMENT 7 ELECTORAL COLLEGE REFORM

Although in the twentieth century no President has been elected with a smaller popular vote than his opponent (in 1912 the Republican majority split between two candidates), the existence of the Electoral College has created a good deal of concern. (In fact, in the 1960 election Richard Nixon came within roughly 55,000 votes of becoming a popular-minority President.) A number of alternative techniques of election have been proposed. These range from simple, direct election by national totals to various proposals for rearranging the present system. Some proposals would require a constitutional amendment; others, such as the division of a state's electoral vote in proportion to the vote cast for the candidates, could be instituted by state legislation.

As a careful reading of this selection will indicate, there are tremendous political stakes involved in any change. Direct popular election, for example, would give the great urban states a completely dominant role. On the other hand, the establishment of Congressional districts as electoral units—with one elector from each district in the state and two at large—would reflect in the Electoral College whatever gerrymanders (rigging of election districts) ingenious state legislatures had devised. (Perhaps with the Supreme Court's decision in Baker v. Carr [1962] that obvious gerrymandering violates the constitutional requirement of equal protection of the laws, this objection may disappear in time.)

However, the fact that no state has taken action to alter its mode of choosing electors (for example, by employing a district system or dividing the electoral vote proportionally, giving 55 per cent of the electors to the man with 55 per cent of the vote) suggests that reform is not imminent. And the proponents of reform are so divided in their motivation that it seems unlikely that the supporters of direct election will support the district system, and even more unlikely that the advocates of the other proposals will "mortgage the Presidency to the cities."

SUMMARIES AND BACKGROUNDS
OF PENDING PROPOSALS

Sixteen pending Senate joint resolutions would change in some way the constitutional method of electing the President. Generally, they follow four basic approaches:

1. Eliminating electors and changing contingent elections.
2. The district system.
3. The proportional system.
4. Direct national election.

1. Eliminating electors and changing contingent elections

This is regarded as proposing only minimal changes. It would incorporate in the Constitution the present practice of awarding all of a State's electoral votes to the candidate receiving the largest number of popular votes. The electoral votes of the States would be retained but electors would be eliminated. The resolution of elections in the House of Representatives when no candidate has a majority would also be changed. This type of proposal has been called direct election by States because it provides that the people vote directly for candidates for President and cast their votes by State units of electoral votes.

✦✦✦✦

2. The district system

This plan . . . retains both the office of elector and the electoral votes of the States. The two electors which each State is entitled to by virtue of its Senators are to be elected by a plurality of the popular votes cast in the State at large. The electors corresponding to its Representatives are to be elected in single-elector districts to be established by the legislatures. The districts are to be compact, contiguous in territory and containing as nearly as practicable the number of persons entitling the State to one Representative in the Congress. A majority of electoral votes is necessary for election in the electoral college, in the absence of which election is by the House and Senate in joint assembly with each Member having one vote and a majority of the votes of the combined authorized membership being necessary for election.

The district system of electing presidential electors was employed by a number of States in the early history of the Nation. . . .

FROM: *The Electoral College: Operation and Effect of Proposed Amendments to the Constitution of the United States,* Staff Memorandum, Subcommittee on Constitutional Amendments of the Committee on the Judiciary, Eighty-Seventh Congress, First Session (Washington, D.C., Government Printing Office, 1961), pp. 1–51.

Until the 87th Congress, proposals of the district system provided that electors would be chosen by congressional districts. This form of the district system became known as the Mundt-Coudert plan. The present Senate Joint Resolution 12 differs from the Mundt-Coudert proposal in that it requires separate and independent presidential elector districts, instead of using congressional districts. A proposed amendment filed by the sponsors of Senate Joint Resolution 12 since the hearings provides for binding electors by pledges. This provision will be discussed in a later section.

3. The proportional system

Eight of the pending resolutions propose that electors be abolished but that electoral votes be retained and that each State's electoral votes be divided among the candidates in proportion to their shares of the total popular vote within the State. This is commonly called the Lodge-Gossett plan, which was the name it bore when approved by the Senate in 1950. Three of the pending resolutions are identical with this 1950 legislation, Senate Joint Resolution 4 (by Senator Dodd), Senate Joint Resolution 17 (by Senator Kefauver), and Senate Joint Resolution 28 (by Senator Saltonstall). Voting qualifications are the same in each State as those for electing the most numerous branch of the State legislature. Each State's electoral votes are divided in the same proportion as the total popular vote of the State with the computation carried to the nearest one-thousandth. Forty percent of the total number of electoral votes is necessary for election. In the event no candidate receives 40 percent, election is by the House and Senate in joint assembly with each Member having one vote and a majority of the votes being necessary for election. The other five proposals of the proportional system vary in some respects.

The proportional system has been before the Congress at various times since it was first introduced by Representative Lawrence of New York in 1848. The Senate approved the "Lodge-Gossett" plan by a vote of 65 to 27 in 1950, but it failed in the House when a motion to suspend the rules for its consideration was defeated by a vote of 210 to 134.

4. Direct national election

Senate Joint Resolution 1 (by Senators Smith of Maine, Beall, Chavez, Morse, and Aiken), and Senate Joint Resolution 23 (by

Senator Mansfield and Senator Keating) propose amendments by which election of the President and Vice President would be by national direct vote of the people. The electoral college system would be totally abolished. Both the electoral votes of the States and the office of presidential elector would be eliminated.

Senate Joint Resolution 1 also contains detailed provisions for nomination of candidates for President and Vice President by national primary elections. Nominating primaries are to be held on the first Tuesday after the first Monday in August. If no candidate receives a majority of the total number of votes cast in a primary, a runoff primary election is to be held 28 days later. Only the candidates officially nominated in the primaries as candidates of a political party may appear on the ballot in the general election. However, voters are permitted to write in votes for other persons. The votes cast in each State are to be certified to the Secretary of State of the United States, who counts the votes. A majority of the total number of popular votes is necessary for election. If no person receives a majority, a runoff election is conducted 28 days after the general election between the two persons receiving the highest number of votes.

++++

Direct national election was considered in the original Constitutional Convention and defeated by a vote of nine States to two, Delaware and Pennsylvania being the States to vote in favor of it. The first proposed constitutional amendment for direct national election was introduced by Representative William McManus of New York in 1826. In 1934, such a proposal, sponsored by Senator Norris of Nebraska, was brought to a vote on the floor of the Senate. It was defeated 59 to 29. In 1950, when the Senate approved the proportional system, Senator Langer of North Dakota offered as a substitute direct popular election along with national nominating primaries. The Langer substitute was rejected by a vote of 60 to 31. Senator Humphrey of Minnesota then offered as a substitute an amendment which provided only for election by direct national vote and it was defeated by a vote of 63 to 28. In 1956, when the Senate considered the proportional-district system compromise, Senator Langer again offered an amendment for nomination and election by national popular vote. This was defeated by a vote of 69 to 13. Senator Lehman of New York then offered an amendment providing only for election by national popular vote, which was rejected by a vote of 66 to 17.

OPERATION AND EFFECTS
OF VARIOUS PROPOSALS

The hearings held by the Subcommittee on Constitutional Amendments disclosed widespread support for changing our method of electing the President. According to a poll of 254 heads of political science departments, almost 91 percent of them favor some constitutional amendment on this subject. The complaints against the present system are summarized by the following statement of Prof. James M. Burns:

Most Americans, regardless of party, are agreed on the failings of the electoral college. It is unfair, inaccurate, uncertain, and undemocratic. Unfair, because the presidential candidate losing a State by even a close margin forfeits all of that State's electoral votes. Inaccurate, because in most elections the winner's electoral votes are inflated grotesquely out of proportion to his popular vote. Uncertain, because Presidential electors are not legally bound to vote for the candidate who carries the State. And undemocratic, because if no candidate wins a majority of the electoral college the verdict is rendered in the House of Representatives, where each State delegation, no matter how large, casts but a single vote in choosing among the three top candidates.

Three aspects of the system are objects of this criticism and would be affected by proposed constitutional amendments:

1. The office of presidential elector;
2. The method of selecting a President when no candidate commands a majority of electoral votes; and
3. The so-called unit-rule method which credits a State's entire electoral vote to the candidate receiving the most popular votes.

Since the first two are subject to the least disagreement and difference of treatment, they will be analyzed first.

THE OFFICE OF PRESIDENTIAL ELECTOR

The present constitutional provision is simply that each State shall appoint electors in such manner as its legislature may direct, and that these electors shall then meet in their respective States and cast ballots for President and Vice President. The people vote only indirectly for President by choosing electors who in turn vote directly for the President. Two features of the present constitutional office of elector will be altered by all proposed amendments. They are (1) the constitutional independence of the elector to exercise his discretion in voting, and (2) the plenary power of State legislatures over appointment of electors.

The proposals differ as to a third point, whether the elector should be retained in any capacity.

Independence of electors

Alexander Hamilton wrote in the 68th Federalist that the electoral college system provided that the election of the Chief Executive—

should be made by men most capable of analyzing the qualities adapted to the station, and acting under circumstances favorable to deliberation, and to a judicious combination of all the reasons and inducements which were proper to govern their choice. A small number of persons selected by their fellow citizens from the general mass will be most likely to possess the information and discernment requisite to such complicated investigation.

Historian James Bryce stated that the electoral college was—

expected to secure the choice by the best citizens of each State, in a tranquil and deliberate way, of the man whom they, in their unfettered discretion, should deem fittest to be the Chief Magistrate of the Union.

✦✦✦✦

There was little discussion of this point in the Constitutional Convention. . . . It was assumed by all that George Washington would be the first President and few looked beyond that. George Mason thought that electors would seldom choose the President in practice; he predicted that 19 of every 20 presidential elections would be decided in the House of Representatives.

In any event, the Constitution provided no bar against electors exercising their discretion and voting independently of their constituents' desires. Does the State legislatures' power to regulate the "appointment" of electors enable them to compel electors to vote in a particular way? The force of popular opinion upon electors along with such devices as nomination by party machinery, instructions and pledges have operated with great success in controlling their votes in the electoral college. However, most authorities agree that if an elector chooses to violate a pledge or ignore popular mandates and statutory instructions, he is free to do so. In 1951, the Supreme Court of the United States held that a pledge could constitutionally be required of a candidate for elector, as a condition of his being placed on the ballot in a primary election, but the Court expressly left unanswered an argument that such pledges would be unenforceable if violated because of "an assumed constitutional freedom of the elector . . . to vote as he may choose in the electoral college" (*Ray* v. *Blair* 343 U.S. 213).

After the rise of the two-party system caused electors to become mere "dummies," proposed amendments in the Congress began to include provisions for abolition of the office of elector.

++++

Concern with the constitutional independence of electors is dismissed by some as "trivia." From 1789 to 1960, in no more than eight instances of a possible 14,000 can it be said that individual electors have departed from their mandates and none of these has ever affected the result of an election. However, three of these eight instances have occurred since 1948 and there is current evidence of substantial efforts to exploit the elector's constitutional independence.

In 1948, a Tennessee elector who was on both the Democratic and States Rights' tickets was elected as a result of popular votes cast for the Democratic ticket. Nevertheless, he voted in the electoral college for the States Rights' candidate. Although he had indicated his intentions before he was elected, his presence on the Democratic ticket of electors made it impossible for the voters of Tennessee to record all of the State's electoral votes for the Democratic nominee. In 1956, an Alabama Democratic elector voted for a person other than the Democratic nominee. In 1960, Mr. Henry D. Irwin, a Republican elector from the State of Oklahoma, cast his vote for Senator Harry F. Byrd instead of Mr. Richard Nixon.

++++

Effects of proposals upon independence of electors. All pending proposals would eliminate any possibility for success of such a movement as Mr. Irwin's. All proposals of direct election, proportional division, and the unit-rule system abolish the office of presidential elector.

++++

Power of State legislatures over appointment of electors

The functioning of the national two-party system has been so successful in producing virtually uniform presidential election methods that many Americans are said to have the misconception that they have a right to vote for the President. Of those who understand that they only vote for electors, many mistakenly believe that presidential electors must be chosen by popular election. Many apparently think that it is a constitutional requirement which causes all the electoral votes of a State to be cast for the candidate receiving the most popular votes. None of these beliefs are true. These customary practices are subject to alteration by any State legislature at any time.

The Constitution grants to each State legislature a plenary power over the appointment of electors. This is evidenced by the variety of methods employed during the early years of the Republic. In some States, the legislature itself chose the electors. In others, they were elected by the people by statewide election upon a general ticket or by the people voting in districts fixed by the legislature. In some, a combination of electors chosen by districts and electors chosen at large was employed.

✦✦✦✦

. . . The States may expressly require or permit that electors be given a free hand to vote for whomever they choose in the electoral college. This plenary power of legislatures enabled the election of unpledged electors in the States of Mississippi and Alabama in 1960 and the casting of electoral votes for persons who were not candidates. Of course, unpledged electors are actually a return to the operation of the system as contemplated by Alexander Hamilton. Voters delegate the choice to such electors and do not know for whom they are voting for President. If unpledged electors were to hold the balance of power in a close election, they could personally control the outcome by voting for either major candidate or they could throw the election into the House of Representatives by voting for a third person. . . .

Most States' present laws either expressly, or by implication, contain provisions which for practical purposes amount to a pledge that the elector will vote in a certain way. . . . The present laws of at least three, and possibly six, States permit the election of unpledged electors. . . . Of course, all State legislation on the subject may be changed by the legislatures at any time.

Since . . . 1892, no State legislature has varied from the general ticket method of choosing electors, although any State is free to adopt a district or proportional system if it chooses. Generally, a State has no reason to adopt for itself alone a system which splits its unit vote. This would only diminish its weight in the election and the dominant party in a State generally wishes to preserve its potential power to deliver all its electoral votes with a plurality of the popular vote. However, where a State legislature is dominated by a party which fears its candidate may not be able to capture a plurality, it is free to change the rules for temporary partisan advantage. . . .

. . . Although the power is seldom used, the present system is subject to State-by-State manipulation between elections for the purposes of the party in power.

Effects of proposals upon legislatures' plenary power over appointment of electors. All pending proposals would remedy the above-mentioned difficulties and uncertainties. Direct popular election, the proportional system and direct election by State units all abolish the elector and provide for direct voting for candidates for President. The district proposal guarantees that electors will be elected by the people. All impose a uniform system which cannot be varied by State legislatures.

++++

Voting qualifications. Like all aspects of appointment of electors, voting qualifications are now left to the States. Any amendment abolishing electors and requiring direct voting for presidential candidates should also deal with the qualifications of voters. Since the district system requires popular election of electors, it raises the same problem. All pending proposals provide that voting qualifications shall be those requisite for voting for members of the most numerous branch of the State legislature, which is the same as the present constitutional provisions for elections of Representatives and Senators.

++++

State laws. All proposals will require some modification of State laws. The amendments abolishing electors would require new laws providing for direct voting by the people for persons for the office of President. Laws now providing for certifications of the duly appointed electors and their votes would be amended to provide for certification of popular vote totals. Senate Joint Resolution 12 would require that States establish single-elector districts, provide for direct voting for electors and set up procedures for electors to pledge their votes in advance.

Nominations. Constitutionally, the elector both nominates and elects the President when there is a majority of electoral votes for one candidate, or merely nominates, when there is no majority, for election in the House of Representatives. The operation of the two-party system and its national nominating conventions, which generally insures that opposing sets of party electors are nominated in the States, is now exclusively regulated by the States. If electors are abolished and States are empowered to regulate the manner of elections, State law will determine if and how candidates for President get on the ballot just as State law now determines how electors get on the ballot. The proposals which would give Congress a reserve regulatory power over the manner of elections would enable it to legislate upon the nominating process and even regulate the national party conventions or require national primary elections.

Thus, it appears that the proposals which eliminate electors contain provisions which purport to fill the gaps created by the elector's disappearance. They differ only on whether to leave the electors' present functions exclusively to the States, or whether to give Congress the same reserve regulatory authority which it now has over congressional elections.

✦✦✦✦

CONTINGENT ELECTIONS IN THE HOUSE OF REPRESENTATIVES

The method of electing the President when the electoral college fails to produce a majority is called the contingent election. The Constitution presently places in the House of Representatives the choice of the President in this situation. In the House, the vote is by States with the delegations of each State having one vote and a majority of all the States' votes necessary for election. Each State's vote is determined by the majority of its delegation. In the event a State delegation is evenly split, the State will have no vote.

In the case of the election of a Vice President, if no candidate receives a majority of the electoral votes, the Senate proceeds to choose from those receiving the two highest totals of electoral votes. A majority of the Senators is required to elect.

Twice in our history, the House of Representatives has elected the President in this manner, in 1801 and again in 1824. The most notable instance was the 1824 election when Andrew Jackson led his nearest opponent, John Quincy Adams, by approximately 50,000 popular votes in a four-man race. Allegedly as a result of manipulations and trading between Clay and Adams supporters, Adams was elected over Jackson.

The pending proposals and the record of the hearings show general agreement that this should be changed, with relatively slight disagreement on the form which the change should take. The chief criticism is the inequity which results from giving all States equal power in electing the President. The Representative from each of the five States having but one Member in the House would have the same voice as the entire 41-member delegation from the State of New York.

Of equal concern is the danger that the House might itself become deadlocked and Inauguration Day might arrive without a duly elected President. This is particularly likely if some third party movement controls enough State delegations to hold the balance of power. Throwing elections into the House and causing deadlocks there has been the announced purpose of third party movements in recent years. In 1948, a change of less than six-tenths of 1 percent of the votes [for] Mr. Truman in two States would have thrown the election into the House where the delegations of four States which had been carried by the States Rights' candidate could have deadlocked the election.

✦✦✦✦

There is little basic disagreement among the proposed amendments concerning the correction of this provision. Of course, direct popular election proposals completely eliminate the need for resolution of elections in the Congress. . . .

Under one of the proportional plan resolutions, Senate Joint Resolution 2, a simple plurality of electoral votes is sufficient to elect, and in the event of a tie, the candidate with the most popular votes is elected. . . . All other proportional plans require 40 percent of the electoral votes for election in the first instance and if no candidate receives 40 percent, election is by the House and Senate assembled jointly with each Member having one vote, except for Senate Joint Resolution 96, which retains the present method. . . .

Of the resolutions which abolish electors but retain the unit rule method of casting electoral votes, Senate Joint Resolution 113 would change the present method and substitute election by the Senate and House of Representatives in joint session where no candidate has a majority of the electoral votes.

THE UNIT-RULE METHOD
OF COUNTING ELECTORAL VOTES

The chief cause of complaints against the electoral college system and also the subject of greatest disagreement is the so-called unit-rule method of counting electoral votes. It is called the unit rule because all the electoral votes of a State are cast as a unit for the candidate who wins a plurality of its popular votes. It is also called the general ticket method because the State's electors are elected upon a general ticket by which each voter votes for the entire number of electors to which his State is entitled.

The unit-rule method is not required by the Constitution. The States are free to adopt other methods of selecting presidential electors but considerations of political power have established it as a general practice for more than a century. Madison and Jefferson favored the district system if it were uniformly adopted, but they influenced Virginia to switch to the general ticket system in 1800 so that their party might secure all its electors. Madison wrote later that the use of the general ticket spread because "it was the only expedient for baffling the policy of the particular States which have set the example." It is generally assumed, therefore, that a constitutional amendment is necessary if the unit-rule system is to be changed.

How far would each proposal go in preventing States from casting their electoral votes in a unit? This question will first be considered, followed by discussion of the effects of each proposal upon particular consequences which are now attributed to the unit rule.

Effect of district system on unit rule. This proposal would split the unit votes of States by requiring that people choose electors by districts. Each State's presidential electors corresponding to its two Senators will be elected from the State at large. Electors corresponding to Representatives will be elected in single-elector districts within each State. Every voter in the Nation will thus vote for only three electors, one from his district and two from his State.

✦✦✦✦

Historically, use of the district system has had mixed results in breaking up State unit votes. From 1789 to 1892, there were 52 instances of States using some form of district system. In 36 instances, the State's votes were still cast as a unit. . . . Analysis of how the district system would have operated in 1960 indicates that a considerably higher proportion of State unit votes would have been split but that many States' votes would have still been cast in [a] bloc.

If congressional districts had been used for a district plan in 1960, electoral votes would still have been cast in a bloc by 21 States— Alaska, Arizona, Delaware, Georgia, Hawaii, Iowa, Kansas, Louisiana, Maine, Massachusetts, Nebraska, Nevada, New Hampshire, New Mexico, North Dakota, Oregon, Rhode Island, South Dakota, Utah, Vermont, and Wyoming. These States had a total of 119 electoral votes. In an additional 7 States with a total of 51 electoral votes, only 1 vote in each would have been split from the State unit. They are Arkansas (1 of 8), Colorado (1 of 6), Connecticut (1 of 8), Idaho (1 of 4), Indiana (1 of 13), Montana (1 of 4), and Oklahoma (1 of 8). In 6 more States having a total of 75 electoral votes, the minority party would have captured less than 25 percent of the total electoral vote of each. They are Kentucky (2 of 10), Ohio (5 of 25), South Carolina (2 of 8), Virginia (3 of 12), West Virginia (2 of 8), and Wisconsin (3 of 12). . . .

Two qualifications should be made. The district system does not use congressional districts and avoidance of their malapportionment and gerrymandering might vary the district patterns. Also a district system might cause larger voter turnout in districts in otherwise safe States where local party strength varies from statewide strength. These figures, along with the historical record of the district system, merely suggest that in some States, the division of political sentiment is sufficiently uniform throughout the State that voting by districts would produce the same result as voting by States.

In many States, especially the most populous ones which have large distinctively rural and urban areas, the district system would very effectively split State unit votes. For instance, using the same analysis, in 1960 New York's vote would have split 25–20, California 19–13, Illinois 15–12, Pennsylvania 17–15, and Michigan 10–10.

Effect of proportional system on unit rule. The proportional system continues the State as the only electoral district or unit and divides its votes according to the popular votes received on a statewide basis. It would, therefore, split the unit vote of all States with the share of each candidate depending only upon the percentage of the popular vote received. The modified version sponsored by Senate Case of South Dakota would split State unit votes only where the minority party receives one-third of the popular vote. In 1960, this would have split the unit votes of all States but Louisiana. . . .

Effect of direct national election upon unit rule. The States would cease to be of any significance as voting units. The Nation becomes the only electoral unit. Since electoral votes of States would be abolished, there would be no State units to split.

PARTICULAR CONSEQUENCES OF UNIT-RULE SYSTEM AND EFFECTS OF PENDING PROPOSALS

Objections voiced to the unit rule or general ticket system are not taken as abstract propositions. Certain inequities or undesirable results are attributed to the operation of the unit rule and urged as reasons for its correction by constitutional amendment. Proposed changes are justified as remedying one or more of these undesirable consequences. In general, they are: (1) disfranchisement of voters, (2) the possibility of minority presidents, (3) pivotal States, (4) sure States, (5) the effects of accident and fraud, and (6) the influence of pressure and minority groups or "swing votes." These alleged defects or evils will be discussed in order along with the effect on each of the proposed changes.

1. The disfranchisement of voters

Above the minimum of three, additional electoral votes to which a State is entitled are based upon population. Nevertheless, as much as 49 percent of a State's voters may see the portion of its electoral votes attributable to them cast for a candidate whom they oppose. It is not merely that their votes are wasted in the sense that they were cast for a loser. The unit rule not only extinguishes the voice of State minorities, but it allows State majorities to speak for them.

Effect of district system upon "disfranchisement of voters." In States where the district system does not split the State unit vote, this effect of the present system obviously will be unchanged. Voters who are in the minority in both their State and district will not be reflected in the counting of their State's electoral votes.

Where the State unit vote is split, it will be because voting strengths vary from district to district throughout the State. Minority voters who are presently disfranchised by their votes being counted out at the State level by the unit rule will become effective in the State's electoral vote where they are combined in local pockets large enough to deliver a plurality in their district. For instance, the voters in an urban or rural district who might otherwise be in the minority on a statewide basis will be able to deliver an electoral vote to the candidate of their choice.

Some charge that the district system merely transfers the alleged inequity of the unit rule from the State to the district level. This ignores the fact that the minority which loses in the district still may capture the State's two at-large electors if they are in the majority on a state-wide basis. If they lose in both the district and the State, their votes would have been ineffective under either the present system or the district system.

Effect of proportional plan upon disfranchisement of voters. The votes cast by the minority would be reflected in the electoral vote of their State whenever they are sufficient to be reflected in a proportional division of the State's electoral vote to the nearest one one-thousandth. The location of the minority votes within the State would be immaterial. Suppose a State has 10 electoral votes and a total of 1 million popular votes are cast. (The national average in 1960 was 128,776 popular votes per electoral vote.) A candidate receiving 400,000 votes would be awarded 4 electoral votes, where under the present system he would receive none. Or a candidate receiving 100,000 votes would capture 1 electoral vote. A candidate receiving only 100 votes would receive .001 electoral vote.

Senator Case's modified proportional plan would give effect to minority votes only if they amounted to one-third of the State total.

Effect of direct national election upon disfranchisement of voters. Since State electoral votes would be abolished, every popular vote, wherever cast, would be of equal effect in the election. No person's vote would be counted out at the State level and all would count equally in the nationwide tabulation.

2. Minority Presidents

This is an alleged defect which is closely related to the disfranchisement of voters criticism. The term "minority President" is frequently used with two different meanings. It may refer to a President who is elected without a majority of the popular vote, but nevertheless with more popular votes than any of his opponents. This has happened in 14 elections.

The term is here used to refer to a President who is elected despite the fact that he has fewer popular votes than his leading opponent. Considering the public's emphasis on national popular vote totals in measuring a President's victory, this danger is the feature of the present system to which many raise the greatest objection.

In 1824, although Andrew Jackson received more popular and electoral votes than did John Quincy Adams, the latter was elected by the House of Representatives. In 1876, although Samuel J. Tilden polled 247,448 votes more than Rutherford B. Hayes, the resolution of contested slates of electors by an Electoral Commission created by Congress resulted in Hayes being elected by 1 electoral vote. In 1888, although Benjamin Harrison received 90,728 fewer popular votes than did Grover Cleveland, Harrison was elected by 233 electoral votes to Cleveland's 168.

Several "near-misses" may be added in which slight shifts of votes in a few States would have caused the popular vote loser to capture the election. In 1916, Woodrow Wilson won reelection with a nation-wide popular plurality of more than 590,000 votes over Charles Evans Hughes. Yet, Hughes would have been elected if he had carried California, a State which he lost by only 3,806 votes. In the election of 1884, Grover Cleveland had a 23,000-vote plurality over James G. Blaine. The election turned on the outcome in the State of New York, which Cleveland won by only 1,149 votes. In 1844, Polk defeated Clay by 170 electoral votes to 105 and by a popular vote margin of 38,000 votes. A switch of 3,000 votes in the State of New York would have changed the result and elected Clay. In 1948, a shift of 17,000 votes in Illinois, 3,500 votes in Ohio, and 9,000 votes in California would have transferred 78 electoral votes from Mr. Truman to Mr. Dewey, and the latter would have been elected despite the fact that his opponent had polled 2 million more popular votes.

Former President Dwight D. Eisenhower, while declining to endorse a particular proposed reform, has urged modernization and improvement of the electoral college system, which he describes as "outdated, particularly in that it tends to be unrepresentative of the votes actually cast for a presidential candidate."

Although the unit rule often works to widen the electoral vote margin, the same factors can cause it to produce the opposite result because it causes great blocs of electoral votes to be shifted from one candidate to another by the tipping of relatively few popular votes. So long as it is possible for a handful of popular votes in one State to cause a candidate to receive a large bloc of electoral votes while millions of votes are "counted out" by the operation of the unit-rule system, the danger of a minority President is aggravated.

✦✦✦✦

However, it must be pointed out that the danger of a minority President is not due solely to the unit-rule system. Two other features of the present system contribute to it: (1) The minimum of three electoral votes for each State, and (2) the allocation of additional electors on the basis of population.

The first of these is based upon the underlying Federal principle of equality of States which allots to each State two electors corresponding to its Senators along with the minimum allowance of one Representative to each State which guarantees one additional elector. Based upon the 1960 census, it causes 36 States to have greater weight in the presidential election than they would have had if electoral votes were awarded solely on population. This is shown by the following table [see facing page]:

The 13 least populous States have a combined electoral vote of 47 and a population of about 7,300,000. Each electoral vote therefore represents 155,000 people. The 11 most populous States have a combined electoral vote of 268 and a combined population of almost 102 million, so that each electoral vote represents approximately 380,000 people, more than twice the average of the 13 least populous States. Obviously, any system which preserves the Federal principle and its

RATIO OF ELECTORAL VOTES TO POPULATION IN EACH STATE FOR 1964 AND 1968 PRESIDENTIAL ELECTIONS (BASED ON 1960 CENSUS)

RANK AND STATE	RATIO	RANK AND STATE	RATIO
1. Alaska	75,389	28. Kansas	311,230
2. Nevada	95,093	29. Connecticut	316,904
3. Wyoming	110,022	30. Washington	317,024
4. Vermont	129,960	31. Tennessee	324,281
5. Delaware	148,764	32. Louisiana	325,702
6. New Hampshire	151,730	33. Alabama	326,674
7. North Dakota	158,112	34. Georgia	328,593
8. Hawaii	158,193	35. Wisconsin	329,315
9. Idaho	166,798	36. Virginia	330,579
10. Montana	168,692		
11. South Dakota	170,129	National average	333,314
12. Rhode Island	214,872		
13. Utah	222,657	37. Kentucky	337,573
14. New Mexico	237,756	38. Minnesota	341,386
15. Maine	242,316	39. North Carolina	350,473
16. District of Columbia	254,652	40. Florida	353,682
17. Arizona	260,452	41. New Jersey	356,870
18. West Virginia	265,774	42. Indiana	358,654
19. Nebraska	282,266	43. Missouri	359,984
20. Oklahoma	291,036	44. Massachusetts	359,984
21. Colorado	292,325	45. Michigan	372,533
22. Oregon	294,781	46. Ohio	373,325
23. Arkansas	297,712	47. Texas	383,187
24. South Carolina	297,824	48. Illinois	387,736
25. Iowa	306,369	49. New York	390,286
26. Maryland	310,069	50. Pennsylvania	390,323
27. Mississippi	311,163	51. California	392,930

three-vote minimum allows for the possibility that a majority of the electoral vote may go to a candidate who receives fewer popular votes. Indeed, this was the original purpose of the electoral vote "bonus" for smaller States, so that the greater populations of the larger States could not dictate the selection of the President. It was part of the compromise which made the Constitution possible.

The allotment of additional electors on the basis of population also contributes to the possibility of a "minority President." The total popular vote in a State has no relevancy to its electoral votes. A State's electoral votes will be counted just as effectively in the electoral college if only one person goes to the polls. The following table shows the ratio of popular votes to electoral votes in the 1960 election:

NUMBER OF POPULAR VOTES PER ELECTORAL VOTE
IN EACH STATE IN 1960 PRESIDENTIAL ELECTION

RANK AND STATE	RATIO OF POPULAR VOTES TO ELECTORAL VOTES	RANK AND STATE	RATIO OF POPULAR VOTES TO ELECTORAL VOTES
1. Alaska	20,254	27. Nebraska	102,183
2. Nevada	35,756	28. West Virginia	104,723
3. Mississippi	37,271	29. Kentucky	112,446
4. Wyoming	46,961	30. Oklahoma	112,894
5. South Carolina	48,336	31. Kansas	116,103
6. Alabama	51,294	32. Maryland	117,261
7. Arkansas	53,564	33. Colorado	122,708
8. Vermont	55,772	34. Iowa	127,381
9. Georgia	61,112		
10. Hawaii	61,568	National average	128,776
11. Virginia	64,287	35. Oregon	129,404
12. Delaware	65,321	36. Washington	137,952
13. Montana	69,395	37. Minnesota	140,172
14. North Dakota	69,608	38. Wisconsin	144,090
15. New Hampshire	73,940	39. Missouri	148,802
16. Idaho	75,113	40. Connecticut	152,809
17. South Dakota	76,669	41. Massachusetts	154,343
18. New Mexico	77,777	42. Florida	154,418
19. Louisiana	80,789	43. Pennsylvania	156,441
20. Maine	84,353	44. New York	162,018
21. Utah	93,677	45. Indiana	164,258
22. Tennessee	95,617	46. Michigan	165,905
23. Texas	96,327	47. Ohio	166,474
24. North Carolina	97,754	48. New Jersey	173,319
25. Arizona	99,623	49. Illinois	176,200
26. Rhode Island	101,384	50. California	203,331

The percentage of civilians of voting age who voted in the 1960 presidential elections varied from 25.6 percent in Mississippi to 80.7 percent in Idaho. Nine States were below 50 percent and 14 States were above 75 percent. With electoral votes based upon population without regard to voter participation, there is necessarily a built-in and deliberate risk that the weight of popular votes will not correspond to the weight of electoral votes. Voter participation varies according to voting qualifications within the States and interest among those who are qualified. However, the unit-rule system is charged with causing low voter participation in so-called safe States.

Effect of district system upon possibility of minority President. As shown above, a President may be elected with a minority of the popular vote under any system which retains the electoral voting strengths of the States. Since the district system would not alter the present electoral vote allocations, it retains one feature which contributes to the possibility of a minority President.

Where it splits State unit votes, the district system will affect one feature which makes minority Presidents possible. Just how far it will go in splitting State unit votes so that they more nearly reflect the popular vote in these States is difficult to analyze. The makeup of the districts would have a bearing. Districts which meet the standards of compactness, contiguity, and equality of population can nevertheless be drawn to political advantage. Congressional districting has shown, for instance, how an urban center may be divided among one or more adjoining rural areas with the result that its citizens are outvoted in all districts.

++++

Where State unit votes are split by the district system, it could result in a situation which is not possible under the present system—a candidate could receive a majority of a State's electoral votes with a minority of its popular votes.

This is illustrated by the following hypothetical illustration stated by Mr. Gus Tyler:

Assume that a State having a population of 4 million is divided into 10 districts, each with a population of exactly 400,000. Assume that of the 400,000 persons in each district, 150,000 turn out to vote on Election Day. Then assume that candidate A receives a 10,000-vote margin in 7 of the 10 districts, and that candidate B receives a 50,000-vote margin in the remaining 3 districts. . . . This would mean that candidate A had gotten 710,000 votes—46 percent of the statewide total—and that candidate B had gotten 790,000 votes—54 percent of the total, yet candidate A would get 7 electoral votes (1 for each of the 7 districts he won) and candidate B would get only 5 electoral votes (1 for each of the 3 districts he won, plus 2 for his statewide edge). Thus, with only 46 percent of the popular vote in the State, candidate A would receive 58.3 percent of the State's electoral votes.

The above illustration assumes districts of equal population and equal voter turnout. Variations in either of these factors could cause a wider disparity between the electoral vote and the popular vote.

++++

The number of persons represented by each district elector will, of course, be the population of the district. The present ratio of population to electors in the districts will also increase but to a much lesser extent. The districts will each contain "as nearly as practicable the number of persons which entitled the State to one Representative in the Congress." This figure will be the same (or as nearly the same as practicable) for different districts within each State but it will vary from State to State. Because each State is entitled to one Representative regardless of population and because of the operation of the complex mathematical formula for the decennial apportionment of Representatives, the average population of congressional districts varies substantially among the States. The optimum population of elector districts in each State is determined by dividing its total population by its number of Representatives.

✦✦✦✦

It is seen that in States which will be districted (those having 2 or more Representatives), the average population represented by each district elector will vary from 303,461 in New Hampshire to 484,633 in Maine. Limiting the comparison to those States having 3 or more districts, the range is from 372,084 in West Virginia to 470,443 in Nebraska. Looking only at the States which have 10 or more districts, the disparity becomes very narrow, going from 394,312 in Georgia to 431,981 in Missouri.

The exact effect of these changes upon the already existing possibility of a minority President is difficult to analyze. The greatest number of persons now represented by any one electoral vote is 392,930 for each of California's electors. The smallest is 75,389 in Alaska, which will continue to be so under the district system. The greatest number of persons per vote under the district system will become the 8,390,000 persons represented by each of New York's at-large electors. But such extremes involve only the at-large electors. The majority of electors, those chosen by districts, will become more nearly uniform throughout the country in the number of persons represented by each. Perhaps this will tend to make a minority President less likely. Voting patterns will determine whether the leveling effect in the ratio of district electors to population compensates for the great increase in the present ratios for the at-large electors.

Effect of proportional system upon minority President possibility. Like the district system, the proportional plan is aimed at only one of the three factors which contribute to this alleged danger of the present system. It continues the allocation of electoral votes to States. However, it will split the State unit vote of every State by dividing the electoral votes in proportion to each candidate's share of the popular vote. By insuring that every citizen's vote, even though in the minority within his State, is reflected in the electoral votes, it would seem to reduce the danger of a minority President. Critics of the proportional plan, however, contend that the realities of the sectional strengths of the two major parties must be considered in this respect and argue that adoption of the proportional plan might make a minority President more likely.

In closely contested two-party States, either party now has a chance with a slight plurality to gain all the electoral votes of those States. Under the proportional system, the electoral vote of such States might be almost evenly divided. However, in "safe" or "one-party" States, the minority party could expect to receive only a small portion of its electoral votes. If each party had the same number of safe States so that comparative gains and losses would even out, this obviously would not be a valid consideration, and this argument invariably turns to Democratic strength in the South for illustrations. An oft cited example is the election of 1900, when William McKinley had a total popular vote of 7,219,000 or 52.8 percent. William Jennings Bryan had a popular vote of 6,358,000 or 47.2 percent. McKinley won with 292 electoral votes to Bryan's 155. If the proportional system had been used, with the same popular vote figures, Bryan would have had 218 electoral votes and McKinley 214. Yet Bryan had carried only 17 States, 11 of them in the South, 2 border States, and 4 Western States, while McKinley had carried 28 States, including all the Eastern, Middle Western, and Pacific Coast States, 3 border States, and 2 Western States. In other words, under the proportional system, McKinley would have lost many more electoral votes outside the South because of Democratic minority votes than he would have gained by virtue of Republican minority votes in solid Democratic States.

In the 1956 debates, Senator Paul H. Douglas of Illinois used the 1952 election to illustrate the same point. He concluded that although President Eisenhower would still have been elected under the Lodge-Gossett plan by 288.457 electoral votes to 240.241 for Stevenson, the proportional plan would have defeated him if the South had stayed solidly Democratic . . . even though Eisenhower would have polled almost 3 million more popular votes. . . .

It is said along the same lines that the effect of unequal voter participation would be magnified by the proportional system. Professor Norman Johnson illustrates this by comparing the Northern States of

Indiana and Iowa with the Southern States of Alabama and Georgia in the 1960 election. Mr. Nixon carried Indiana and Iowa by a combined plurality of 394,578 votes out of a total of 3,409,180. This popular vote margin would have provided an electoral vote margin of 2.705 in these two States. Yet, a combined Democratic plurality of 264,448 votes out of 1,297,591 votes cast in Alabama and Georgia would have given Mr. Kennedy a net margin there of 4.579 electoral votes, more than enough to offset his losses in the two Northern States. The combined effect of the four States' votes would have given Mr. Kennedy a margin of 1.874 electoral votes despite a popular vote margin for Mr. Nixon of some 130,000 votes. Under the present system, the two candidates broke even in the electoral votes of the four States.

Effect of direct national election. By definition, election of the President by national direct popular vote would totally eliminate the possibility of a minority President. In fact, it is the only proposal which would do so.

3. The "pivotal State"

A further charge against the unit-rule system is that it strongly tends to overemphasize the political importance of the large populous States. This has meant that presidential candidates have come almost exclusively from such States. Except for Mr. Landon of Kansas in 1936 and the incumbent President Truman of Missouri in 1948, both major parties have limited their presidential nominations in the last half century to men from the eight largest States. Able men from small States are given little chance to secure nominations from either major party, and are generally not even regarded as "presidential timber." Both major parties are accused of greater concern with the capacity of their candidate to carry certain pivotal States than to command the support of voters throughout the Nation as a whole.

The pivotal State also tends to monopolize the attention of the candidates and their campaign efforts with the result that presidential campaigns are not carried to the Nation as a whole. States which are not regarded as doubtful, or which are considered of less importance, are relatively ignored. Citizens in the smaller States are less apt to see or hear the candidates in person and may be inclined to think that their interests are of less importance to the candidates. For the same reason, it is charged that issues, party platforms, and campaign promises are formulated with a view to these pivotal States.

At this point, the argument becomes a pragmatic one—addressed to the substantive programs of presidential candidates. These States for the most part have large metropolitan areas and heavy concentrations of urban voters who may be able to determine the winner of the State's electoral vote. Former President Truman, supporting a district system, stated:

> The electoral college was first devised to protect the small States from dominance by the larger States, as for example, Delaware and Rhode Island from being dominated by Virginia and New York.
>
> The problem we face today is that of the emergence of the big cities into political overbalance, with the threat of imposing their choices on the rest of the country.

Former President Hoover sounded a similar note in writing to Senator Kefauver concerning the subcommittee's hearings:

> Your subject is important. It confronts the same difficulties as were met by the Founding Fathers—that is, to prevent domination by a few large States.

In other words, despite the imbalance in the electoral college favoring small States, the large urban States have come into dominance because of the operation of the unit rule. Most defenders of the present system do not dispute this point. They concede that the present electoral system has an urban bias but justify it as compensating for other claimed inequities in our State and Federal Governments which are said to favor rural interests at the expense of urban areas. The following are representative of several statements to this effect submitted to the subcommittee by political scientists.

Dean Stephen K. Bailey, Maxwell Graduate School of Citizenship and Public Affairs, Syracuse University:

> I am presently opposed to any change in the electoral college system. I believe the electoral college system presently overrepresents big urban States and minorities within those urban States. I am prepared to admit the injustice of this. At such a time when the House of Representatives ceases to overrepresent egregiously, nonurban and rural areas, I would be willing to advocate some modification in the electoral college system.

++++

Effect of district system upon "pivotal States." The special emphasis given to pivotal States would be diminished to the extent that the district system splits the unit votes of such States.

++++

Effect of proportional system. By splitting the electoral vote of all States in proportion to the popular vote, the proportional system would also diminish the emphasis now placed upon the key pivotal States. A closely divided popular vote would be a closely divided electoral vote. However, the States which have large numbers of electoral votes by virtue of large populations, would continue to be prime sources of substantial electoral votes. For instance, one-half of the electoral votes of the State of New York would still be worth more than the combined electoral votes of the 7 smallest States. Candidates could be expected to still be greatly concerned with the voting results in such States. Urban areas would command the same proportion of each State's electoral vote as they command of its popular vote.

Effect of direct national election. Under this system, the candidates would be looking to popular votes wherever they are located. Any combination of votes sufficient to produce a plurality would be sufficient to elect. The boundaries within which voters were located would be immaterial. Candidates could be expected, however, to give greater attention to areas with the largest popular votes. . . .

4. The "sure State"

Another complaint against the unit-rule system is that it perpetuates so-called solid or one-party States. Voting figures show a high correlation between the closeness of statewide popular vote totals and the amount of voter participation. In the doubtful State there is a strong incentive for the voter to vote. In States where the outcome is a foregone conclusion, there is much less incentive for the voter, regardless of his political inclinations, to take the trouble to register his preference. . . .

Effect of district system. Whether the district system will cause increased campaign efforts and voter participation in so-called sure States depends upon patterns of minority party strength. Where the strength of parties in the minority on a statewide basis is spread uniformly throughout the State, they may find themselves in a collection of sure districts. If a minority party cannot capture a plurality within a district, it still will not reflect its popular votes in the electoral vote totals of the State. Conversely, where minority party voters are sufficiently sectionalized that they win a district's popular vote, they will gain an electoral vote even though they remain a minority on a statewide basis.

✦✦✦✦

Effect of proportional system on sure States. The incentive of minority voters to turn out in previously sure States would not depend upon geographical location or concentration in sections. Even though minority voters are spread uniformly throughout the State, its proportion of the State's popular vote total would be reflected accordingly in its electoral vote. No party could be assured of receiving any State's entire electoral vote.

Effect of direct national election on sure States. Again, State lines would cease to be of importance. Popular votes cast by minority party supporters in sure States would be reflected in the national vote totals, vote by vote, in the same manner as the votes of the majority party in the State.

5. The "swing vote" of minority groups

The pivotal States are generally the highly populated States where both parties are relatively strong and each has a chance to carry the State. This encourages and invites great emphasis upon small organized minority or pressure groups within these States, which are usually united by racial, ethnic, or economic interests. It is generally admitted that within many of the pivotal States, there are small blocs of voters which may hold the balance of power, causing both major parties to give special attention to the demands of these groups.

++++

The result is that as a practical political matter, the vote of a member of such a swing group may be many times more important to a candidate than thousands of other votes throughout the country. The unit-rule system gives such minority blocs a strategic position which some charge causes both parties to make unduly large concessions and strong bids for their support. . . .

Many defenders of the unit-rule system concede that it operates in this fashion but point to other inequities for which it is said to compensate. Others state that the result of the unit rule is not to give minority groups an undue influence, but in the words of Senator Case of New Jersey to "make it necessary for both major parties to recognize the legitimate interests of such groups."

Effect of district system upon swing votes. The district system would have a pronounced effect here. The votes of minority blocs become of importance under the unit rule because of their balance-of-power position. The swing vote concept assumes that the State is otherwise relatively evenly divided so that the vote of the small pressure group or minority group can tip the State's electoral vote either way. This complaint against the present system is usually directed at the pivotal States where unit votes are likely to be split. If the minority bloc voters are isolated in a few districts, their vote will become important only for their districts and the extent to which they may influence the two at-large electors.

Effect of proportional system upon swing votes. The undue importance of such votes in every State would also be greatly diminished by the proportional system. The votes of minority blocs would have no more influence in the division of the electoral vote than the same number of votes cast by any other group of persons.

Effect of direct national election. Here, too, the emphasis upon the swing vote would be almost totally eliminated. The votes of a 200,000 minority group in a particular State would be only 200,000 votes toward a necessary national total of 30 to 40 million votes. These 200,000 votes would take on the same appearance to a candidate as any other 200,000 in the same State or anywhere else in the Nation. Of course, if the two parties were otherwise closely divided on a national basis, a national minority bloc vote might hold the balance of power in the national election in the same manner as it may now hold it at the State level.

On January 1, 1961, Mr. Roy Wilkins, executive secretary of the NAACP, warned against any scheme to change the electoral college, saying that past reform efforts had been designed to cut down the voting strength of Negro citizens in large northern cities.

✦✦✦✦

OTHER POSSIBLE EFFECTS AND CRITICISMS OF DISTRICT SYSTEM

Possible gerrymandering and malapportionment of districts

Prior to the 87th Congress, recent proposals of the district plan (known popularly as the Mundt-Coudert plan) provided that presidential electors should be elected in the same manner as Senators and Representatives. Electors corresponding to Senators would have been elected from the State at large and those corresponding to Representatives would be elected in the same districts from which Representatives were chosen. The principal sponsor of Senate Joint Resolution 12, Senator Mundt, states that past hearings demonstrated that the Mundt-Coudert proposal was subject to a valid criticism that congressional districts were actually and potentially subject to unfair gerrymandering and malapportionment by Senate legislatures. Therefore, the current proposal provides for independent single-elector districts to be composed of compact and contiguous territory, containing as nearly as practicable the number of persons which entitled the State to one Representative in Congress. Such districts, once established, are not to be changed until after the next census.

Senator Mundt envisions that presidential elector districts established under these standards will sharply curtail unfair congressional districting because it would be extremely difficult for a State legislature to jutsify one set of districts for electors and another for Representatives. Senator Morton, a cosponsor of Senate Joint Resolution 12 also believes that the requirement of nongerrymandered electoral districts will influence State legislatures to set up fair congressional districts.

Senator Kefauver holds a different opinion:

Instead of re-forming congressional districts, I fear that State legislatures are more likely to merely adopt these districts—in their present forms—as presidential elector districts, thus carrying over into presidential elections the harmful effects of gerrymandering. The same political pressures and opportunity for partisan advantage would operate on the legislatures in this presidential electoral districting as now influence congressional redistricting. If political considerations cause disproportionate or unfair districting, it is doubtful if the anti-gerrymandering provision will be enforced as a practical matter.

The standards set forth in Senate Joint Resolution 12 are those which have come to be accepted as fair standards for districting of congressional seats. However, as provisions of the U.S. Constitution, they would be on a higher footing than similar standards for congressional districts have ever been.

The United States Constitution does not require that Representatives be elected in districts. Congress has a reserve power to regulate the manner of congressional elections but there is no current Federal statute requiring elections of Representatives by districts. Two States still elect some Representatives at Large and several may elect their entire delegations at large in 1962 because of legislative stalemates resulting from the recent reapportionment of seats. Congress never exercised its power to regulate congressional elections until 1842 when legislation required that Representatives be elected by districts. The 1842 legislation also required that districts be composed of contiguous territory. In 1872, the requirement was added that districts be of substantially equal population. In 1901, the feature of compactness was added. From 1901 until 1929, the legislative standard for districts was the same as the constitutional standard would be under Senate Joint Resolution 12. Since 1929, there has been no Federal law of any sort on congressional districts.

It is agreed that neither party has a monopoly on unfair apportionment and gerrymandering of congressional districts. In the hearings, this was approached as a bipartisan problem and it was recognized by all that the dominant political party in any State is equally apt to be guilty of the practice.

✦✦✦✦

OTHER POSSIBLE EFFECTS
AND CRITICISMS OF PROPORTIONAL SYSTEM

Encouragement of splinter parties

The criticism most often made of the proportional system is that it would encourage splinter parties and endanger our two-party system. A splinter party could reflect its popular votes in the electoral college by polling small percentages of the popular vote within a State and could obtain roughly the same proportion of the national electoral votes as it obtains of the total popular vote throughout the Nation.

Supporters of the proportional plan deny that this would be its effect. They claim that most American voters want a chance of voting with the winner; that whether his vote is counted out at the State level by a State unit rule, or at the national level where it is insufficient by virtue of its total, he is no more apt to cast his vote for a third party candidate who has no chance of winning the national election. The requirement of only a 40 percent plurality of the electoral votes for election is also cited as a deterrent to third party movements since it insures that a third party could not throw the election into Congress with less than 20 percent of the total electoral vote.

Both arguments are difficult of exact proof or critical analysis. The proportional system is often equated by its critics to proportional representation, or "P. R.," a system of representation in European countries which allows minority parties to elect delegates to parliamentary bodies. This term would certainly apply to the proportional plan if the electoral college were a deliberative body and electors were divided proportionally among all parties which polled popular votes. Supporters of the proportional system maintain that the "P. R." concept is irrelevant because the college of electors is eliminated and electoral votes are retained only for the Federal purpose of weighting voting strengths among the various States. The object is to choose one Chief Executive for the Nation, which led Senator Henry Cabot Lodge to state in 1950: "Even the cleverest surgeon cannot divide one man up—proportionally or otherwise—and expect him to live."

Indeed, it is stated that dividing electoral votes so as to more accurately reflect popular votes would minimize, rather than encourage, the influence of multiple parties and pressure factions. Small groups in large pivotal States now hold positions of great importance because they may add or withhold enough votes from either party to swing the State's entire bloc of electoral votes. As examples are cited the Liberal Party in New York and the candidacy of Henry Wallace in 1948, which is considered to have thrown two States to Mr. Dewey.

✦✦✦✦

Advantages of one-party States

Critics of the proportional system argue that elimination of the unit rule and substitution of proportional division would penalize two-party States and make the votes of the so-called one-party States more attractive and sought after by presidential candidates.

As an example, it is cited that under the unit-rule system, Mr. Kennedy won the States of Connecticut, New York, New Jersey, and Pennsylvania by a combined margin of 613,000 votes. He won Georgia and Louisiana by a combined margin of 360,000 votes. If the proportional plan had been in effect, he would have gained a margin of 3.835 electoral votes in the larger group of States and a margin of 5.196 in the latter two States. In other words, a popular margin of 613,000 in closely contested States would have netted less than three-quarters as much of an electoral vote advantage as a popular margin of only 360,000 in one-party States.

This analysis is directed only to the net "advantage" in each group of States. Under the proportional system, Mr. Kennedy would have captured a total of 52.267 electoral votes from the first four States, as against only 12.546 electoral votes from the latter two States . . . . Under any system, a candidate must obtain a majority (or at least 40 percent) of the entire electoral vote of the Nation and, therefore, seek an aggregate of electoral votes as well as an aggregate of "advantages." Mr. Kennedy's votes in the first four States would still have contributed four times as much to his election as the votes of the latter two States.

Under the proportional plan, Mr. Kennedy would have received 23.638 of New York's 45 electoral votes. This would have been more than his combined proportional shares of the electoral votes of Arkansas, Georgia, North Carolina, and South Carolina, from which he would have obtained 22.911 of a total of 42 electoral votes. Under the proportional plan, 50 percent of the electoral votes of New York continues to be more than the combined electoral votes of the seven smallest States and would be 11 percent of the total necessary for election.

Effect upon restrictions on voting

An argument is made along the same lines that the proportional plan will magnify the effect of unequal voter participation. In the example stated above, it shows how a smaller margin in the popular votes of one State may be worth more than a larger margin in another because of differences in voter participation. It is argued that the proportional plan would place a premium on keeping the voter turnout low in so-called one-party States and provide little incentive for those with low voting participation to broaden suffrage or relax restrictions on voting.

Effect upon weight of individual votes

Mr. Gus Tyler's statement in the hearings . . . analyzes the present system as one of "balancing inequities." He states that there are three inequities inherent in the present system: (1) The "block-vote" inequity or the operation of the unit-rule system, (2) the "three-vote minimum" inequity which gives each State a minimum of three electoral votes regardless of its population, and (3) the "population basis" inequity which awards electoral votes above the minimum of three on the basis of population without regard to the number of popular votes cast in the State. The third inequity is said by [Mr.] Tyler to mean that those who vote on election day are voting not only for themselves, but also for those who do not turn out to vote. This creates an advantage for those who do vote in States where relatively few votes are cast because the fewer the votes, the more important are those of persons who do vote. Each of these three inequities is said to work to the advantages of different kinds of States, the first to the advantage of the larger States, the second to the advantage of the least populous States, and the third to the advantage of States with low-voter participation. The effect of all three is said to strike a kind of political balance among the States.

Mr. Tyler maintains that introduction of the proportional system would throw off this political balance by eliminating the populous States' advantage from the block vote while having no effect upon the other two inequities which give advantages to the least populous and low-vote States. He goes on to state that under the proportional system, the populous States tend to be the most closely contested and would often give each of the candidates of the two major parties virtually the same number of electoral votes. The one-party States, by contrast, even though their total number of electoral votes [was] smaller, would give their highest candidate a larger electoral vote margin, thus making the voters in these States more effective in determining the outcome of the election.

This argument is closely related to that concerning the relative advantage of one-party States. The opposing viewpoint is the same in both instances. Also, there is considerable evidence from the past three presidential elections that one-party States in this respect are fast disappearing.

OTHER EFFECTS AND CRITICISMS OF DIRECT NATIONAL ELECTION

Weight of individual votes

In the words of Senator Keating, direct national election means "one voter, one vote." An obvious and certain effect of direct national election will be to equalize the weight of every individual vote.

Elimination of Federal principle in presidential elections

It is equally obvious that States as such, or the people voting by States, would have no significance. The Federal principle would be totally abrogated in the choice of the President. . . .

In introducing Senate Joint Resolution 23, Senator Mansfield argued that the electoral college system is contrary to our Federal system as it is now generally expected to function and that direct national election would reinforce its contemporary practice. He stated:

To the only significant argument which still serves to underwrite the electoral college system; that is, that it is a part of the Federal system, and as such must be preserved, I can only reply that, in my opinion, the Federal system is not strengthened through an antiquated device which has not worked as it was intended to work when it was included in the Constitution and which, [if] anything, has become a divisive force in the Federal system by pitting groups of States against groups of States. As I see the Federal system in contemporary practice, the House of Representatives is the key to the protection of district interests as district interests, just as the Senate is the key to the protection of State interests as State interests. These instrumentalities, and particularly the Senate, are the principal constitutional safeguards of the Federal system, but the Presidency has evolved, out of necessity, into the principal political office, as the courts have become the principal legal bulwark beyond districts, beyond States, for safeguarding the interests of all the people in all the States. And since such is the case, in my opinion, the Presidency should be subject to the direct and equal control of all the people.

Nationalization of voting qualifications

Under direct national election, the vote of every person in the country would compete directly against that of every other voter, regardless of where they live. The degree of voting participation would determine the extent to which the people of each State influence the outcome.

Critics of direct election argue that it would result in a race among the States to lower voting qualifications, in order that each State might have the greatest possible voice in selecting the President. It is suggested, for instance, that ridiculous voting ages might be the result in some States and that all States would be driven to the lowest common denominator of voting qualifications.

Both pending proposals for direct national election provide that voting qualifications in each State shall be those requisite for voting for the most numerous branch of the State legislature. In order to generate a larger popular vote in presidential elections, a State would have to adopt the same broadened suffrage requirement for election of their State legislatures. Since the same provision controls voting qualifications in electing Senators and Representatives, these elections would also follow the same course. A State would have the same electorate for State legislators, Senators, Representatives, and the President and could not adopt unreasonably low requirements solely for presidential elections. Some argue that nationalization of the presidential election would necessarily produce demands for national voting qualifications. Voters of a given political persuasion in one State would have an interest in seeing that persons of like persuasion in other States are permitted to vote and fairness would require uniform voting laws throughout the Nation. This sort of demand is frequently made under the present system, however, and in either instance a further constitutional amendment would be necessary, requiring ratification by three-fourths of the States after submission by two-thirds of the Congress.

Nationalization of election laws

With direct national election, a voter in any State would have an interest in the fairness and accuracy of the election machinery in every other State. Voters in Maine, for instance, could see their votes nullified by opposing votes counted in Alaska, just as readily as by votes cast in Maine. It is said that this would produce demands for national election laws and Federal administration of election machinery. This is not denied by advocates of direct national election. Senator Margaret Chase Smith states that "fostering of national uniform laws on elections" is an "objective to be sought rather than opposed."

Chances of ratification

The most frequent argument made against direct national election in the Congress is that it would be futile for Congress to submit such an amendment to the States; that it would have no chance of ratification by three-fourths of the States because 36 of the States have added weight in the election of the President because of the electoral college system. Many witnesses in the hearings never reached the merits of this proposal and dismissed it on this assumption.

++++

HYPOTHETICAL RESULTS OF PAST ELECTIONS

It is common and expected in any analysis of proposed reforms of the electoral college to show how they would have altered the results of past elections. This is used as a two-edged sword. Where it is shown that a proposed system would not have altered past results, it is argued that such an amendment would be useless. On the other hand, if it can be shown that a system would have caused a different result and elected the "wrong man", this too is argued against a proposed change.

Election analysts and political scientists agree that it is not realistic to apply a proposed change to a past election except with strong qualification and caution that it is done solely to illustrate hypothetically the operation of a particular plan. It should not be done to show that different results would have occurred. Any different system would have produced different party platforms, campaign strategy, and techniques of voter appeal. Voting patterns and participation would vary. Indeed, the nominees might not have been the same in any given election if a different system had been in use.

For the 1960 elections, it is therefore utterly impossible to compute realistic hypothetical results under different systems, even though such efforts are worthwhile to illustrate as far as possible how various systems would operate. The following testimony of Mr. Neal R. Peirce, of Congressional Quarterly, is believed to be a worthwhile summary of the qualifications which should be made in applying proposed changes to past elections:

Surely, the campaign would have been waged differently by both parties if another electoral vote system or a direct popular system had been in effect. The emphasis would have switched away from the big key States, at least to some extent. If the proportional method or a direct vote had been in effect, each vote from every State would have been of approximately equal impact, and the campaign efforts would have been spread more evenly throughout the country.

Or let us assume that the district system had been in effect in 1960. The emphasis would then have switched to the close districts all around the country. The downtown districts generally assumed safe for the Democrats, or areas in which the Republicans always win, would have received less attention by the presidential candidates.

The truth of the matter is that we have no way of knowing just how the results of the 1960 election might have varied if another electoral system had been in effect with correspondingly altered national campaigns and patterns of voter behavior. Either candidate might have gained or lost votes as a result of different voting patterns. As we review the hypothetical results under other systems, showing that Mr. Nixon would have been a likely winner under many of them, it is important to remember that even under the current system a shift of a few thousand votes in three or four States could have made Mr. Nixon President today. The basic fact of 1960 was that it was an exceedingly close election, and the fact that some other systems of counting the vote show a slight Kennedy margin and others a slight Nixon margin is primarily an illustration of the element of pure chance in any system under which 2 candidates receive virtually the same number of votes out of almost 69 million cast.

CAMPAIGN COSTS

DOCUMENT 8 FINANCING PRESIDENTIAL CAMPAIGNS

The fantastic amounts expended in the elections of 1960—the authors of the following document suggest that a total of $165 to $175 million was spent on the elections of that year, with at least $20 million expended on the Presidential contest—have led to demands for reform. Just about everybody seems to agree with Alexander Heard and his commission that something has to be done, but the problem is what? No significant body of opinion favors the rigorous British system, which sets a specific limit on the amount a candidate can spend (so much per voter in his constituency, with variations to allow for sparsely settled districts) and enforces these limitations with severe sanctions.

It is one thing to express concern and another thing to develop specific remedies. Past efforts to limit expenditures have proved farcical; while an individual candidate could honestly list his expenditures in running for office as, say, $750, there could be three or four "independent" committees working on his behalf and spending $10,000 each.

Of course, underlying the commission's concern is a fundamental issue in democratic politics: can a viewpoint literally be priced out of the electoral market? Or, conversely, can a well-financed candidate dominate a contest by virtue of his money—not by "buying voters," but by preempting radio, television, and newspaper advertisements, and flooding his constituency with workers and literature? Moreover, to what degree does the need for money lead political parties to seek wealthy nominees who will be willing to pay the bill? (The British limit the amount a candidate can put into his own cause.) In short, to what extent has American politics become a "rich man's game"? Perhaps more pertinent, to what extent have political candidates become dependent on (or committed to) big donors?

The Heard report, representing the predominant American view, makes several recommendations to curb these trends. It seems to abandon hope of effective regulation of campaign expenditures; in-

stead it suggests encouraging bipartisan political donations, offering tax credits to stimulate a larger number of small donations, and most important, providing "full exposure" by bringing before the public honest statements of political outlays.

The faith of the American people in constitutional government has been regularly renewed by an uninterrupted series of presidential elections. This testing of the popular will every 4 years has survived many periods of crisis and change. Presidential campaigns and elections over the decades have served as shining emblems of effective democracy, opening new doors of hope to people seeking freedom all around the world.

In 1960, approximately 150 foreign correspondents covered each of the 2 presidential nominating conventions. Some 75 of them accompanied each of the presidential and vice presidential candidates during some portion of the campaign. On Election Day itself, 56 of 86 accredited embassies responded positively to President Eisenhower's suggestion that teams of observers be sent to view, at first hand, the manner of holding presidential elections in different parts of the United States. In addition, from at least 20 nations came groups composed primarily of scholars who studied the campaign in minute detail.

These observers saw a presidential campaign molded by the long heritage of American political life, a heritage consistently embracing two important elements: (1) a profound belief in widespread citizen participation; and (2) an equally deep belief in voluntary action—a belief that politics should be animated by the voluntary efforts of individuals, groups, and organizations rather than by government.

Many problems have been encountered in the long story of presidential campaigns, campaigns varying from that of 1860 when Abraham Lincoln never left Springfield nor made a single speech, to that of 1960 when John F. Kennedy made 360 speeches while traveling 44,000 miles in 43 States, and Richard M. Nixon gave 212 speeches and journeyed 65,000 miles through 50 States.

No problem, however, has become more troublesome than that of providing adequate financial support for campaigns.

A chronic difficulty in maintaining adequate support has long been the lurking suspicion that contributing to political parties is somehow a shoddy business. This is unfortunate. Improvement of public under-

FROM: *Financing Presidential Campaigns,* President's Commission on Campaign Costs (Washington, D.C., Government Printing Office, 1962), pp. 1–12.

standing of campaign finance is essential. This Commission hopes the American people will come to regard contributions to parties with the same sense of obligation they display toward contributions to educational and charitable institutions.

Active, widespread political participation is the key to successful democracy in the United States and voluntary effort is the great sustaining force of our political parties.

The rocketing costs of presidential campaigns, and the recurring difficulties parties encounter in meeting these costs, require us to seek new methods and incentives for financing our political parties.

We agree with President Kennedy, former President Eisenhower, and other leaders of both parties that the existing system of presidential campaign finance poses serious problems. It is not desirable to have candidates for high office, especially for President and Vice President, dependent on individuals or organizations with special interests who are willing to make large contributions in the form of cash or campaign services. As President Kennedy has stated, "it is not healthy for the democratic process—or for the ethical standards in our government —to keep our national candidates in [the present] condition of dependence."

Many of the existing legal regulations of campaign finance have become a mockery. They are not realistic in light of today's campaign requirements. As a consequence, many provisions of the law are evaded or avoided, a condition contributing to the unfavorable climate that has surrounded fund-raising efforts.

In this climate, the political parties have found it increasingly difficult to meet satisfactorily the "great financial burdens" of presidential campaigns noted by the President. Further, the parties have lacked the continuity of leadership and the staff necessary for efficient fund raising and campaigning.

Mindful of these problems, we have sought to find ways that

a. Presidential candidates and the political parties supporting them can be helped in raising funds;

b. Public confidence in the ways these campaigns are financed can be increased;

c. Public respect for the system of legal regulation can be instilled; and

d. Presidential campaign costs can be reduced.

There is a wide range and diversity of opinion as to how the problems of financing presidential campaigns can best be solved. We have had the benefit of hundreds of suggestions from experienced individuals and organizations who are knowledgeable about financing political activities. We have considered these suggestions in the light of three basic beliefs shared by all members of the Commission:

a. In a strongly organized and effectively functioning two-party system;

b. In widespread participation by citizens in the political system through the political party of their choice; and

c. In the desirability of voluntary, private action wherever such effort will suffice to meet the common needs of the society.

While our recommendations are directed toward problems of presidential and vice presidential campaign finance, in accordance with our charge, [they also] carry implications for campaigning for other offices. We are aware of the possibility of overemphasis [on] a presidential campaign to the detriment of congressional, State, and local races, but it is our view that the measures we propose would have a desirable effect on all political fund raising.

We recommend—

1. That individuals and private organizations—including corporations, labor unions, farm organizations, civic societies, and other appropriate groups—be encouraged to take part in and to make expenditures for voluntary *bipartisan* political activities, and where an individual or organization is subject to taxation, that the reasonable costs of such activities be declared a deductible expense for tax purposes.

2. That for an experimental period extending over two presidential campaigns:

Political contributors be given a credit against their Federal income tax of 50 percent of contributions, up to a maximum of $10 in credits per year;

Contributors be permitted, alternatively, to claim the full amount of their contributions as a deduction from taxable income up to a maximum of $1,000 per tax return per year;

The only contributions eligible for these benefits be ones made to the national committee of a party, and to a State political committee designated by such a national committee (provided that no more than one committee per State be designated by a national committee).

3. That an effective system of public disclosure be adopted which requires that the principal sources and uses of money in presidential campaigns be reported to a Registry of Election Finance;

That toward this end periodic reports be submitted by all political parties, committees, and other campaign groups receiving or disbursing as much as $2,500 per year, any part of which aided a presidential or vice presidential candidate for nomination or election;

That such reports show total income and outgo, and itemize contributions that aggregate $250 or more from one source (including purchase of tickets to dinners or other fund-raising events), expenditures of $100 or over and transfers of funds and debts;

That candidates for nomination or election to those offices be required to submit similar reports;

That any individual or family (husband, wife, and dependent children) contributing to the above committees as much as $5,000 in the aggregate in a single year, or spending and contributing a combined total of that much on behalf of such a candidate or candidates, shall also submit reports of such disbursements;

That similar reports of both direct or indirect expenditures be required of individuals and groups taking part or spending money in bipartisan political activities as urged in our first recommendation, if such expenditures total $5,000 or more in a year; and

That the present meaningless ceilings on individual contributions and on total expenditures by political committees be abolished.

4. That the present equal treatment of corporations and labor unions by Section 610, Title 18, *United States Code,* that prohibits direct, partisan campaign contributions and expenditures, be maintained and strictly enforced.

5. That all other statutes regulating the financing of political parties and candidates be vigorously enforced.

6. That the political parties take full advantage of opportunities to modernize and increase the effectiveness of their fund-raising practices.

7. That research to increase campaign efficiency and help reduce campaign waste be encouraged among individuals and organizations, public and private.

8. That the Congress provide funds to pay the reasonable and necessary costs of preparing and installing in office new administrations during the "transition" period between the election and inauguration of a new President.

9. That a further temporary suspension of section 315 of the Federal Communications Act be enacted to permit broadcasters to make their facilities available on an equal basis to the nominees of the major political parties for President and Vice President without the legal compulsion of doing likewise for minor party candidates for those offices.

10. That a nonpartisan White House Conference on Campaign Finance be called by the President of the United States to launch broad solicitation programs by all parties following the adoption of measures to stimulate such giving, such a conference to include representatives designated by the important political parties, as well as representatives from various sectors of political life and the communications media, and to lay the groundwork for further continuing efforts to encourage voluntary, private action in meeting campaign costs.

11. That the several States consider measures similar to those recommended in this report along with others that would help to reduce

the costs of campaigning and make it easier for the parties and candidates to meet them, and that the Post Office Department make its change-of-address files available to the parties as well as to election boards as a way of assisting in local registration drives.

12. That, after a trial period with the measures here proposed, the President should provide for another nonpartisan evaluation of presidential campaign finance, and that, if the objectives sought by our proposals have not been realized, study be given to additional measures to achieve them, especially a "matching incentive" system to stimulate party solicitation.

We have been asked to recommend ways to improve the financing of campaigns of presidential and vice presidential candidates. This should be achieved through the political parties the candidates are chosen to represent. Our political parties are indispensable instruments of democratic government. Through their leadership, we strive to achieve our national aspirations; by their workings, we seek to keep government responsible to the people.

The work of all political parties, minor as well as major, can be stimulated by new measures that will encourage their broad financial support and by removing certain statutory restraints that at present tend to inhibit their activities. Our recommendations are directed to measures that would facilitate the work of the parties. We have tried to avoid recommendations that would introduce rigidities into the party system or that would adversely affect the internal operation of the political parties.

The magnitude of the problem with which we are concerned is obvious. Expenditures on behalf of all candidates for all public offices in the United States probably reached $165 to $175 million in 1960. While the share of this total spent on behalf of presidential and vice presidential candidates cannot be estimated with precision, the two major parties reported expenditures of almost $20 million in their national campaigns alone; the corresponding totals in 1952 and 1956 were $11.6 million and $12.9 million, respectively. Both parties ended the campaigns of 1956 and 1960 in debt. In 1960, the Democrats spent $3.8 million more than they raised and the Republicans spent $700,000 more than they raised.

In considering methods of financing presidential campaigns, we have recognized the interrelationship between national financial requirements and the financial needs of party activities at other levels. We recognize as well the dependence of national-level committees on State and local fund raising. Also, there is a special need for adequate annual income to finance the continuing tasks that the party committees must perform.

Under present practices, the parties encounter enormous difficulty in raising adequate funds at the proper time. Given the erratic flow of funds and the periodic crises in campaign finance, individuals and organizations providing substantial gifts at critical moments can threaten to place a candidate in moral hock. In consequence, a disturbing and fundamental failure of present practices is the widespread cynicism about the democratic system they produce.

The heavy dependence of political parties in presidential campaigns upon substantial gifts from and expenditures by a relatively small number of individuals and organizations lends itself to widespread misinterpretation. While the great majority of such contributors to presidential campaigns is not motivated by expectation of specific preferment, nonetheless, for the vitality and acceptance of the democratic system, we hope to see a significant increase in the number of contributors, both to spread the cost of campaigns and to diffuse more widely through the population the sense and the reality of participation in the politics of democracy.

PARTY BEHAVIOR IN CONGRESS

DOCUMENT 9 THE REPUBLICAN-
DIXIECRAT
COALITION

In no real institutional sense does the United States have a national two-party system; it was pointed out in the headnotes to Documents 1 and 2 that the basic unit in the American party system is the state organization. Every four years the two coalitions of state parties face each other in a contest for the Presidency, a battle which centers far more on the personal qualities of the candidates than it does on the programs approved by the conventions. Once the Presidential contest has been decided, the coalitions break up into their fifty state components, while the President tries to rally a Congressional coalition to support his legislative program from among these disparate fragments. Lacking a unified party to follow him, the President looks uneasily up Pennsylvania Avenue at the Capitol and wonders what the ancestral enemies of executive authority are concocting for his benefit. For operational purposes, the "separation of powers" may best be defined as the distance between the White House and the Capitol dome.

In recent years, as Congressman Frank Thompson points out in this selection, a clear pattern has emerged under both Democratic and Republican administrations. A President who has been elected by his appeal to the urban voter faces the so-called conservative coalition dominated by Southern Democrats and rurally oriented Republicans. Because Southern Democrats are from non-competitive political regions (as are roughly two-thirds of the House of Representatives), they achieve seniority and thus the chairmanship of key committees. (Between 1930 and 1964, the GOP controlled Congress for only four years, but the senior Republicans who took the chairmanships under these rare circumstances were overwhelmingly from non-urban districts.) The power of Southern Democratic chairmen, backed by the votes of Southern and Republican Representatives, represents a powerful road-block in the path of "liberal" or urban-oriented measures. The

116

formidable power of the House Rules Committee further unbalances the scales: in the Eighty-Seventh Congress, 1960–62, the conservative Democrats in this body, with GOP support, refused to permit two major pieces of social legislation to go before the House and silently disposed of twenty-two more by the expedient of doing nothing! Thus a President who hopes to satisfy his urban supporters must really work against tremendous odds.

The following document traces the pattern of the Republican-Dixiecrat alliance from its roots in 1937 through its influence on the legislation of the 1960's.

++++

[MR. THOMPSON:] The gentleman from Missouri seems to have some doubt in his mind about the existence of a coalition between Republicans and some southern Democrats here in the House.

++++

Based on last year's analysis, the average House Republican voted with the coalition 82 percent of the time on these coalition rollcall votes. Republicans and Southern Democrats hold 264 seats in the House, 45 more than a constitutional majority needed to pass or defeat any bill.

The operation of the coalition is a matter of record and has been most successful on legislation such as education, social welfare, public housing, immigration, taxes, labor, antitrust, civil rights, public works, and resource development.

Mr. Speaker, I include at this point in the *Record* a research paper on this subject which reviews the history of the Republican-southern Democratic coalition in the House from 1937 to 1959:

The Republican-Southern Democratic coalition, or conservative coalition, as it is sometimes called, has exerted vast influence over the outcome of various types of legislation since its loose formation 22 years ago.

The 1st session of the 86th Congress saw a tightening of the coalition's voting alliance under the leadership of Minority Leader Halleck and Judge Smith, chairman of the House Rules Committee.

The scope and effectiveness of the coalition as described in this study is limited to legislation reaching the House floor, where its impact can be measured by analysis of rollcall votes. Of course, much of the important work of the coalition takes place in standing committees, and particularly in the House Rules Committee, where many measures are pigeonholed or watered

FROM: Speech by Representative Frank Thompson, January 27, 1960, *Congressional Record*, Eighty-Sixth Congress, Second Session (Washington, D.C., Government Printing Office, 1960), Vol. 106, pp. 1441–42.

down before a rule is granted. These aspects of coalition activity are not subject to the same type of precise analysis.

The purpose of this study is to analyze the party lineup in the 86th Congress and to briefly review the history of the Republican-Southern Democratic coalition since its beginnings in 1937 so that its operation in the present Congress may be placed in proper perspective.

THE 86TH CONGRESS—BASIC ARITHMETIC

An understanding of the role of the coalition in the 86th Congress must begin with an analysis of the real party alinement in the House. On paper it would appear that the Democratic majority in the House is the largest since New Deal days—280 Democrats, 152 Republicans. The party lineups are:

Southern Democrats	104
Border Democrats	24
Northern and western Democrats	152
Republicans	152
TOTAL	432[a]

[a] *Excludes vacancies (Illinois, Ohio, New York, Pennsylvania).*

But on the basis of three key rollcall votes in the first session on which the conservative coalition achieved its maximum strength (Thomas amendment—housing bill financing; H.R. 3—States rights issue; Landrum-Griffin substitute—labor bill), the approximate real party alinement is:

COALITION

Southern Democrats	80
Border Democrats	9
Northern and western Democrats	6
Republicans	130
TOTAL	225

LIBERALS

Southern Democrats	20
Border Democrats	15
Northern and western Democrats	143
Republicans	18
TOTAL	196

Absentees and vacancies, 16.

THE CONSERVATIVE COALITION, 1959

A congressional quarterly study of Republican-Southern Democrats voting alinements during the first session of the 86th Congress shows that a majority of both groups opposed a majority of northern and western Democrats on 11 of the 87 House rollcall votes. The coalition won on 10 of the 11, or 91 percent. By comparison, the coalition won on 64 percent of the showdown votes in 1958 and 81 percent in the 1957 session.

A separate Congressional Quarterly study also reveals that southerners split with the rest of the House Democrats on 23 percent of all rollcalls during the 1959 session. They included votes on such issues as housing, civil rights, taxes, labor legislation, States rights (H.R. 3), farm price supports, surplus disposal policies, and Hawaiian statehood.

During the 1959 session, southern Democrats cast 82 percent of their votes with the Republicans and against the majority of their own party on these coalition rollcalls. The 12 southern Democratic committee chairmen cast 86.5 percent of their votes with the Republicans on these coalition rollcalls, only 10 percent with the majority of their own party.

On these same votes, 79 percent of the northern and western Democratic votes were cast with the party majority. Republicans cast 88 percent of their votes with southerners on these key rollcalls, only 9 percent with northern and western Democrats.

Coalition voting frequency would have been [even] greater if the House Rules Committee had permitted such measures as the area redevelopment bill, the civil rights bill, and [the] Federal aid school bill to reach the House floor.

THE COALITION GERMINATES: 1937

Beginnings of the Republican-Southern Democratic coalition in Congress can be traced back to 1937, the 1st session of the 75th Congress.

Franklin Roosevelt had just won his landslide reelection victory over Alf Landon and Democrats controlled the House by a 333 to 89 margin. Major New Deal reform measures were already on the statute books and the overwhelming Democratic victory in 1936 had provided a clear mandate for the Roosevelt administration to continue its New Deal reform and economic recovery programs.

But there were rumblings of discontent among powerful conservative forces in the Nation. The Supreme Court had already ruled several New Deal programs unconstitutional. Southerners were smarting over the repeal of the two-thirds nominating rule at the 1936 Democratic Convention, which denied them their traditional veto power over presidential choices. Resentment against the White House efforts to pack the Supreme Court began to grow in Congress.

On the national scene, organized labor was beginning to assert itself as an economic force, aided by enactment of the Wagner and Walsh-Healy Acts. Sitdown strikes became a new economic weapon in the hands of unions. Organizational strikes were being conducted in the basic industries. However, the Liberty League was strongly resisting these inroads and confidently expected the Supreme Court to rule the Wagner Act unconstitutional in a test case.

When the Court upheld the act in April 1937, it became clear to many conservatives in the industrial North and the low-wage farm areas of the

South that only by forging a bipartisan conservative alliance in Congress could they hope to stem the tide of new dealism, with its growing emphasis on the needs of city dwellers, minority groups, workers, small farmers, and other underprivileged segments of the population.

This was the year that conservatives succeeded in seizing control of the House Rules Committee. They were able to change its role from that of a traffic cop in scheduling measures reported by standing committees for floor action, subject to majority leadership decisions, to that of a policy-making body—dictating to all Members which bills it deemed worthy of being considered on the House floor.

During the 1937 session, almost 10 percent of all House rollcalls showed Republicans and a majority of southern Democrats voting against a majority of Democrats from the rest of the country. Democrats divided sharply on such votes as those to authorize an investigation of sitdown strikes, antilynching legislation, alien relief, and immigration measures. The coalition also succeeded in blocking consideration of the fair labor standards bill for the remainder of the session. However, a concerted drive by the administration resulted in passage of the bill in the second session, after it was pried out of the Rules Committee by a discharge petition.

EARLY COALITION VICTORIES

During the 1st session of the 76th Congress, the coalition won two important victories—forcing an investigation of the NLRB because of alleged "prolabor" rulings and in passing the Hatch Act to prohibit political activity by Federal employees. Cleavages between northern and southern Democrats widened on such issues as housing, civil rights, labor legislation, immigration bills, relief measures, and regulation of business.

THE COALITION DURING WORLD WAR II

Although the outbreak of World War II in Europe curtailed the New Deal domestic programs, the influence of the conservative coalition continued to grow. By 1941, coalition voting frequently had increased to more than 13 percent of all House rollcalls.

During the war years, the coalition succeeded in passing the Smith antistrike bill, a States' rights armed services' voting bill, established the Un-American Activities Committee as a permanent House committee, and watered down the price control program and the excess profits tax measures.

By 1945, coalition voting alinements took place on 16 percent of all House rollcalls, as a combination of Rules Committee power, seniority, and attrition among northern Democrats in off-year elections helped conservatives strengthen their grip on the legislative machinery of the House.

THE COALITION IN POSTWAR YEARS

In the immediate postwar period of the 79th Congress the coalition used its power to pass the Case strike-control bill, to exclude farm labor from

120

NLRB jurisdiction, to turn over the U.S. Employment Service to the States, and to take the first steps toward gutting the price control program. This latter action soon resulted in a wave of speculation, profiteering, and inflation, costing the American public billions of dollars in lost purchasing power.

After the election of the Republican 80th Congress in 1946, the coalition achieved its greatest numerical strength. It succeeded in passing the Taft-Hartley Act and in overriding President Truman's veto of the measure. It reduced coverage under the Social Security Act, overrode Truman's veto of the "rich man's" tax reduction bill, and further weakened price and rent controls.

The hand of the coalition was also seen in blocking such measures as an effective public housing program, Federal aid to education, civil rights, an increase in the minimum wage, an adequate farm program, and other legislation which President Truman proposed to the 80th Congress. His 1948 "whistle stop" campaign against the "special interests" which dominated the 80th Congress won for him his upset victory over [Thomas] Dewey and formed the basic plank of his Fair Deal program.

THE COALITION VERSUS THE FAIR DEAL

The Republican-Southern Democratic coalition in the 81st Congress was a major force in blocking enactment of important segments of the Truman legislative program and in watering down others. A majority of Republicans and southern Democrats voted together against administration proposals on about 30 percent of all substantive rollcalls in the House.

The high frequency of coalition voting is at least partially explained by the change in House rules on the opening day of the session. The House Rules Committee was stripped of its power to pigeonhole bills reported by standing committees by adoption of the 21-day rule, which permitted committee chairmen to call up bills reported by [their committees] if they were not acted upon by the Rules Committee within a 21-day period. This meant that many of the controversial administration bills reached the floor for debate and vote which otherwise would have been held up in the Rules Committee.

Among the measures brought to the floor under the new 21-day rule were Hawaiian and Alaskan statehood bills, a rivers and harbors bill, the National Science Foundation bill, an antipoll tax bill, a VA hospital bill, and a joint resolution providing for U.S. participation in international organizations. In addition, the threat of using the new rule forced a reluctant Rules Committee to act on minimum wage, social security, and public housing legislation, all of which were subsequently enacted into law.

The conservative coalition did succeed in defeating an attempt to repeal the Taft-Hartley Act; in rejecting the Brannan farm plan; in permitting "local option" decontrol of rents; in defeating the National Minerals Act; in watering down the minimum wage bill; in passing the natural gas and basing point bills (both vetoed); in reducing foreign aid funds and funds for public housing; in rejecting controls over commodity speculation, and in watering down an FEPC bill.

A coalition attempt to repeal the 21-day rule early in the 2d session of the 81st Congress failed. However, the new rule was repealed by the coalition on the opening day of the 82d Congress. Since that time, the Rules Committee has tightened its hold over the legislative machinery of the House.

THE COALITION DURING THE EISENHOWER YEARS

During the Eisenhower administration, the coalition has continued to play a dominant role. It has won a number of important victories, including those in which it turned over offshore oil resources to a few coastal States, reduced funds for the soil conservation program, blocked liberalization of the unemployment compensation system, watered down several public housing bills, passed the natural gas bill, defeated school construction legislation, watered down a minimum wage bill increasing the extent of coverage, blocked an investigation of administration fiscal and monetary policies, defeated the Kennedy-Ives labor reform bill, blocked consideration of the community facility loan program.

The coalition has also appeared on such issues as antitrust legislation, water pollution control measures, civil rights, natural resource development, public works, foreign aid, H.E.W. appropriation measures, and legislation affecting the District of Columbia.

SUMMARY

Over the years since 1937, the Republican-Southern Democratic voting coalition has operated with varying degrees of effectiveness, being most successful on legislation dealing with education, social welfare, labor, regulation of business, public works and resource development, civil rights, immigration, taxes and other economic issues, and those where States' rights have been involved.

It is in these areas that the major differences between the Republican and Democratic parties are to be found. These are also the types of issues [that were] of such vital concern to Northern and Western Democrats in the 1960 campaign.

Scholars and political writers have attempted to explain the basis for the Republican-Southern Democratic coalition in these broad areas of legislation. Many factors have been mentioned, including the high degree of party discipline among Republicans and the correspondingly low degree of party unity, loyalty, and responsibility to the party platform among congressional Democrats from the South.

Other factors often mentioned are the procedural roadblocks in the House legislative machinery, controlled by coalition leaders; the seniority system which assures conservatives of the chairmanships of a majority of the committees and subcommittees; the one-party system in most Southern States; the lack of communication and unity of purpose among Northern and Western

Democrats; the antiquated apportionment formulas in many States, which give rural areas disproportionate representation in State legislatures and in Congress; and the basic need for a realinement of the American political party system.

✦✦✦✦

DOCUMENT 10 PARTY GOVERNMENT OR PERSONAL INDEPENDENCE?

The "independent" status of a member of the legislature can be evaluated from two viewpoints: first, with respect to his own constituents; and, second, vis-à-vis the President. According to the first criterion, the classic statement of autonomy was probably made by Edmund Burke in 1783 when he informed his Bristol electors that they had sent him to the House of Commons to think for the common good and not to act as their agent. He was promptly defeated. While most American legislators have a considerable range of decision on most issues before them, each is well aware of the peculiar sensitivities of his district. For example, many Southern Democrats, such as Senator Fulbright of Arkansas, have considerable freedom on foreign-policy issues so long as they hold the fort against civil-rights legislation and integration. Agile Representatives have been known to vote on both sides of a matter: a conservative from a marginal urban district, for example, may support emasculating amendments to a public-housing measure in the preliminary stages of debate and later, even if they are defeated, support the final bill. At election time he will emphasize one vote before the Chamber of Commerce, the other to the Friends of Urban Renewal. Or, to cite a variation of this practice, on May 15, 1963, Democratic Senator Edward Kennedy voted with the Republicans in favor of an amendment to the feed grains bill that was strongly supported by the New England farmers. However, he held off voting until he knew the amendment had been defeated, neatly getting the best of both worlds.

The criterion of Congressional independence from "executive dictation" is quite another matter, and one on which there is bipartisan consensus. Since the day when President Washington went personally to the Senate to ask advice on a pending treaty and was told politely but coldly that the Senators would consider the matter among themselves and let him know the outcome, the Congress of the United States has been eternally watchful for signs of Presidential imperialism.

Even President Harry Truman's occasional visits to his old haunts in the Senate were viewed with suspicion as harbingers of "usurpation." As was noted in Document 9, the Congress has its own political system, and it is a matter of honor in the House and Senate not to accept Presidential orders. A considerable amount of factional scheming also enters the picture because the Congressional baronage is uniformly conservative and has a strong vested interest in preventing the President from developing a "royal faction" which might, if properly organized, undercut their prerogatives—for example, by altering the seniority rule.

This document from hearings before the Joint Committee on the Organization of Congress includes a discussion of party responsibilities to constituents, the President, and the national party itself.

++++

MR. MICHENER: What you want is independence on the part of the Congressman.

MR. VOORHIS: Exactly.

MR. MICHENER: You do not want Congressmen here who are elected on the platform that they will uphold the hands of the Executive in everything he asks, regardless.

MR. VOORHIS: No.

MR. COX: Platforms are made to get votes. Do you feel you are bound, as a responsible functioning Member of Congress, by the platform of any party or any organization? Does your sense of responsibility to the country at large permit this?

MR. VOORHIS: I think we certainly do. I think a Member has a certain duty to the position that has been taken before the people, in a responsible manner by a party convention, and I would just amend your statement by saying that I do not believe a Member of Congress should come here committed to do whatever anybody says.

I do not think that it should be limited to the Executive that happens to be in office at a given time. I should say he should come here prepared to do what he believes to be right and just and what he believes to be best for the Nation.

I think it is his primary duty to let the people know, as nearly as he possibly can, what he believes about those things before he gets elected.

FROM: Testimony in Hearings of the Joint Committee on the Organization of Congress, March 13 to June 29, 1945, Seventy-Ninth Congress, First Session (Washington, D.C., Government Printing Office, 1945), pp. 37, 123–24, 364–69, 794–95, 844–48, 851–53, 876–79.

PARTY BEHAVIOR IN CONGRESS

MR. COX: Will you broaden my suggestion to include pressure groups?

MR. VOORHIS: That is right, I would.

++++

MR. COX: Under the Kefauver resolution, the party in power would use the system to further its advantage over the minority; there isn't any question about it. You are talking about under the Kefauver plan, you would have to set up a committee, you understand, to determine as to who shall be called and as to what questions shall be asked, and who should ask them, and all of that. That is something that the party in power would control.

SENATOR FULBRIGHT: What is wrong with that? The party in power is supposed to control.

MR. COX: And it is subject to abuse.

THE VICE CHAIRMAN: They do not abuse the regular committee system, Mr. Cox. Most of the testimony is absolutely freewheeling.

MR. COX: Yes.

THE VICE CHAIRMAN: And more inquisitive questions come from the minority than the majority.

SENATOR FULBRIGHT: I notice in our committee hearings you see much less partisanship than you do when the thing gets on the floor of the House. I have noticed that in the few committees I have been on. I am not nearly so conscious of a party division in committee hearings as on the floor of the House.

Furthermore, this is party government. We have two parties. I think it is proper that the party in power does control it; otherwise you have got absolute chaos. Somebody has got to control both of the Houses. That is why we have parties. I think the trouble we have now is that there is very little party discipline. Both of our parties have developed splits in them; they have developed basic differences with which we are all familiar.

Whether that will work itself out or not I do not know, but I do think that the party in power ought to have control of the situation, and if they do not do it right, then they should be removed. In other words, there should be some responsibility attached to the party. The people would have nothing to vote on if one party or the other did not take the responsibility. I think it is very difficult for the voters now to choose, because both parties have very strong diverse elements. Now neither is strictly conservative or liberal, but each has got strong elements of the other faction.

MR. MICHENER: Don't you think that in the final analysis the decision rests with the people back home? We now have pressure groups.

SENATOR FULBRIGHT: Well, of course, I do not think that is proper for anybody. He is supposed to exercise his own judgment regardless of who is President. I do not think very many do that, but I do think that we do lack certain responsibility. I do think that the party in power ought to have the power and responsibility for doing the thing right, and if they do not do it right, they should be removed and the power and responsibility given the other party. The fact that this would enable the party in power to have greater influence to me seems a good thing. They ought to be able to run it. However, that does not mean the Executive would be running it. I think it would not weaken the party in the Congress at all.

✦✦✦✦

[MR. SMITH:] I want to discuss [for] just a moment the question of party responsibility, because there have been several suggestions made about that in the committee hearings thus far and in all the reports that we have.

In the Heller report there is a considerable statement concerning party responsibility, so I want to say, if I may, a few words about that.

I think party responsibility, which I have studied very carefully in connection with my present work, is a very complex subject and very difficult to bring about, because it can only be done by a series of things and not by any one thing. For instance, in order to have party responsibility, it becomes necessary to have party leadership, and that is very difficult to determine. We have, over in our minority, a form of leadership. We have outstanding Senators who have proposed programs and policies in a position where they exercise what might be called leadership but their leadership is disregarded by other members of our own party, and I have heard severe criticism among members of our party of the domineering leadership that is being exercised. I do not know the answer unless there is some way of achieving a recognition of leaders so that the members of the party will say "Yes; we do recognize these men as our leaders, and we will take the program that they give us and follow it through." If that cannot be done, then I do not see how you can get much party leadership except the scattered or sporadic leadership of individuals.

SENATOR WHITE: Off the record.

(Discussion was [carried on off] the record.)

MR. SMITH: Then, it seems to me that before we can get party responsibility in the legislature, even through a legislative council or

126

through anything else, it becomes necessary to have the formation of some party principles and some party program.

SENATOR PEPPER: You have in mind that the minority party should have the rigorous discipline and the perpetual harmony which prevails in the majority party?

THE CHAIRMAN: For the record, please record the laughter which the able Senator's (from Florida) remarks occasioned, both among members of the committee and those who are in attendance.

SENATOR WHITE: And if you will, it was a horse laugh.

MR. SMITH: Please record that the laugh takes the place of any reaction on the part of the witness, because I am in the same position.

I have tried and most of my work over the last year has been an attempt to obtain some positive party program, some set of principles by which we could say that the minority in the Senate stands for certain definite things as a matter of principle, high principle, and that we shall gage or judge all the legislation on the basis of those principles. I must confess that I have not been able to make much headway on the proposal. We have had program discussions. I have held evening meetings which one newspaper called night school for the Republican Senators. We have tried, for instance, very, very carefully on the question of Bretton Woods to bring about some understanding. . . . I hoped that that would be the means of clarifying the question among the Senators so that we would be able to say, "Now, are we for this thing or are we against this thing? What changes shall we propose? Shall we come to some carefully devised program on it?" I confess the thing is right up in the air where it was. Every Senator is free to do what he pleases. We are for some things and against other things and not the same men are for the same things, and so on. Party agreement on principles is a very difficult thing to secure.

If we had a legislative council, might not these practical things that I have been trying to show, which are in part my own barriers—might they not arise in connection with a legislative council or even an executive council?

THE VICE CHAIRMAN: Will you yield right there?

MR. SMITH: Yes.

THE VICE CHAIRMAN: I have been trying to figure out from the recommendations made in these reports as well, and the best that I can figure out is that perhaps the party's responsibility to the committees —in other words, if it is a part of a party platform—is that a member of that party holding his position on the committee by virtue of that party's position in the House [should] help expedite that legislation to the floor [while] reserving then his own right to oppose or support it as he sees fit. In other words, it seems bad to me that if a thing is in a national party platform or part of a well defined party program, that one member on a committee, holding office by virtue of that party's position, could block the legislation in reaching the floor. But after it reaches the floor, I do not question any man's right to support or to oppose the legislation.

MR. SMITH: That is right, but we have another problem there. Let us say we call a minority conference on some matter involving party policy. Every Member is free to express his views and explain his position. Let us say that after the proposition is fully debated, the overwhelming majority of those present conclude that a certain position should be taken as a matter of party policy. A very small number do not agree. As our party rules now stand no Member can be bound to take a position against his own wishes. At that point, and in order to make party action on principle effective, I should think that the few Members who will not follow party policy should retire from the room while party strategy is determined. In one particular case that was not done and some of these Members who disagreed with the party policy sat in the room and heard the entire discussion of the party strategy, what the party would do on Monday morning to make its policy effective, and the strategy somehow or other got over to the opposition, and they were able to block the strategy. You see, we cannot have party principles and party policies without some mechanism or understanding that the Members will abide by decisions made by the majority of party members.

✦✦✦✦

SENATOR PEPPER: Just before departing, I would like to say the whole thing of general responsibility on organization in the Senate has been very loose. There is even a question as to whether the majority leader has any jurisdiction over the committees. It is more or less a combination of independent autonomous bodies in the Senate. While usually the chairman is disposed to cooperate, it does seem to me that the whole organization, at least in the Senate, should be tightened up so that the leadership has a little more direction.

MR. SMITH: Senator Pepper, may I ask if it would be your belief that it would be desirable to work toward some fairly cohesive party discipline in the Senate?

SENATOR PEPPER: Yes; as a general rule.

MR. SMITH: You would not think it would go to the extreme of a

Hanna or Reed or a Joe Cannon dictatorship over all the members of the party?

SENATOR PEPPER: That all depends on the degree of authority that the discipline might involve. In the Senate, the steering committee of the two parties selects the membership on the various committees. Of course, it is possible that if a committee member put on a committee by the steering committee persisted in being—and too frequently, in their opinion—out of accord with the party policy, they might ask him to resign and ask him if he would not feel it would be better for him to go along generally with party policy, and if not, would he not feel it was proper for him to resign and let them put somebody else on the committee who did go along with party policy. That is the technique by which it could be handled if that result were desired.

We have had some cases where there have been chairmen of committees who were not in accord with the general party policy and who have been chairmen of very important committees. Before some of those appointments were made, there was some discussion between the steering committee and the prospective chairman about what his views generally were, and in one or two instances I have heard it reported that they did not think the chairman carried out his duties in accord, generally, with what the steering committee thought would be his policy. In a case like that, it would have been, I assume, possible for the steering committee to say, "If you find yourself conscientiously out of accord with your party on this matter and especially since you have the chairmanship, would you think it proper that you might relinquish your chairmanship so someone who might fit in with the general party program could be made chairman?" So you get into the question of the resolution of individual conviction in conflict with the general party policy.

++++

[MR. COYLE:] There were one or two other points I noticed in England. Some British members of Parliament, like the young Tories, are restive under party discipline. A good many people are worried about the extent to which the political parties discipline their members. No matter what a man's personal opinion may be when the issue is up, the whip gets after him and he has to vote right. Otherwise the next time he comes up for election the party is likely to say they will not give him a district in which to run. One of the advantages, it appears to me, in the Members of Congress having to be from their own State is that the Democratic and Republican Parties in this country cannot park favored Congressmen around in easy districts somewhere where they do not know the people at all but are just brought in with a lot of ballyhoo and shoved on the voters.

In England the parties stand, in the British mind, for principles. They were rather shocked when I told them although our parties theoretically stand for different principles, actually they are instruments for running the elections and when they make up the party platforms, they come out almost the same. That is shocking to an Englishman.

But modern life in England is getting so complicated that two parties are not enough to represent all the principles there are. If the Tory Party represents, in general, big business, and the Labor Party represents labor unions, all the other principles haven't any party to represent them. When another question comes up like the Beveridge full employment plan, for example, Beveridge joined the Liberal Party, and now the Liberal Party represents that as a principle, and yet many other members, including young Tories and many Labor members, are naturally in favor of the same program, but if their party decides against it they must vote no. The effect is a tendency to get more than two parties and then to have to rely on party coalitions rather than on free voting.

MR. MICHENER: Do these different groups submit to discipline?

MR. COYLE: They apparently do, yes; and if they don't they get badly disciplined, too.

MR. MICHENER: We had a few years ago the purge where that thing was attempted.

MR. COYLE: And it did not succeed.

MR. MICHENER: Where the administration wrote its program of "must legislation," and the Congress was advised, through the whips, or the Executive himself, to vote for it or else, and if they did not vote for it then the "or else" was attempted, and the American people, as a whole, responded very decidedly against it.

MR. COYLE: And they did the same under Woodrow Wilson.

MR. MICHENER: Yes.

MR. COYLE: I was surprised to find a good many Englishmen are envying the relative freedom of our Congressmen from party discipline. A man can get away from his party in this country if he decides to do it. The result is, when a thing comes up that is not included in the main line of orientation of either the Democratic or Republican Party, that the parties often split on that and men vote their own opinions. I find a surprising number of Englishmen who envy us that and feel that any effort to enforce party discipline in this country would not be an advance.

THE VICE CHAIRMAN: That is an interesting observation, because several people have recommended strengthening party discipline almost to the point of absolute control.

MR. COYLE: Party discipline involves just the same thing that you mentioned, Mr. Michener, the ability to purge a man who would not play ball. In England the parties can purge him because if they do not put him up for a seat he has to quit or run as an independent.

THE VICE CHAIRMAN: The difference there, of course, is that we have a popular primary here, and I do not believe they have in England. I believe the choice is always in the party as to who will represent that party.

MR. COYLE: Of course, the primary gives the people one more shot at it, although still the party has an influence on who gets nominated. However, our parties have to nominate somebody they can get away with in the primary, too, and it is more democratic. In England, as I understand it, the party chooses the candidates and puts them up for seats, and so, of course, it can discipline them.

THE VICE CHAIRMAN: In a great many of our States the candidate in the primary is above his party. In other words, he is not the choice of anyone in the party machinery, and oftentimes runs counter to the organized political machine or organization in that area. Very often he wins if the issue is strong enough, and then the party must accept him and he represents that party although he is not the product of its machinery.

MR. COYLE: I have been impressed with the political habits in both countries that either favor or do not favor the maintenance of two major parties.

On the Continent where they have lots of parties Parliaments did not work so very well. I think the strictness of party discipline in England is contributing to the rise of independent MPs. They turn up on their own hook or else start little parties of various kinds. We can more easily avoid getting too large an influx of small parties. I believe there is an advantage in having only two major parties in Congress, that is, a real majority party as well as a powerful minority party. I think many of the healthy aspects of our political life could not be maintained if you had 20 parties in Congress and had to work through party coalitions. I believe it is sound policy when a candidate is chosen by the people through the primary, and the party takes him, instead of driving him into running as an independent. In England, I am not sure how long the two-party system is going to continue. The Liberal Party, it seems to me, is coming up.

[MR. HELLER:] This I consider is very important as concerns my

++++

work: Each House should establish a majority policy committee, composed of the chairman of each major standing committee and chairmanned by the majority leader, and [a] minority policy committee composed of ranking minority members.

This is the capstone of my whole report. It is a one-party planning and management committee in each House which would coordinate and guide all the legislative affairs of Congress. Advantages of the majority policy committee are briefly as follows:

1. They would furnish a locus of responsibility for actions and inactions in each House.

2. A majority policy committee could readily coordinate all work of the several standing committees in each House.

3. A majority policy committee could furnish much of the needed synthesis of divergent interests in each House.

4. When the President belonged to the same party as the members of the majority policy committee, the latter would institutionalize within Congress a group with which the President or executive department heads could have regular communication without exposure to partisan politics.

5. The majority policy committee would be the most effective means for improving congressional performance on fiscal matters.

I know of nothing that would affect the standard of living of all citizens more than an improvement in congressional performance [on] fiscal matters. Government fiscal policy has a pronounced effect on the country's production; if the wrong fiscal policy is adopted at any given time, the inflationary or deflationary forces which may be at work are accentuated rather than offset.

✦✦✦✦

MR. COX: What are you leaving for the rest of the Congress to do, rather than promote the dictates of this supercommittee, as you recommended?

MR. HELLER: You would still have, sir, 15 standing committees in each House.

MR. COX: You are putting the members on those committees in a strait jacket. This supercommittee would have the control.

MR. HELLER: They would not control. I do not think it is possible in our Congress of 531 people for anybody to control much of anything, by its very nature.

MR. COX: Then what is the sense of this supercommittee?

MR. HELLER: In the first place you would have a one-party accountability to the people. In the old days when world conditions were relatively simple and domestic conditions were relatively simple, it was more within the realm of possibility to forecast in the party platform what the party intended to do and could do. Today, with conditions as complex as they are, it is most difficult, if not impossible, to forecast events over a period of time and live up to party promises. The situation is dynamic. Therefore, it is necessary that people have, as a concrete expression of what each party stands for, a correspondingly dynamic mechanism as a substitute for the static party platform. The publicly announced policy decisions of the majority and minority policy committees would give the electorate a basis for formulating their judgment about the party in the light of current situations as they develop.

This does not mean to imply that party platforms can be pushed around unless conditions have changed to the extent necessary to justify such action. Even then, any change in policy from that stated in the platform should be specifically recognized as a part of any policy committee statement.

I have also said in the report that this mechanism would provide an easy means of communication between the President and Congress at all times on a formalized basis without exposure to too much partisan politics.

And last but not least, this policy committee would furnish a mechanism for the appropriate coordination of the fiscal affairs of Congress because you would have an over-all planning committee in whose hands would be the formulating of the policy which would be best for the country at any given time. For example, if an inflationary policy were appropriate, then all of the spending and revenue raising would be directed toward that objective.

++++

SENATOR PEPPER: It impresses me, if I might interrupt, that this is simply an enlarged form of a steering committee. I do not mean that the term "steering" is preferable, but we are accustomed to steering committees and we do not have a policy committee. As it is now it depends, as I understand it, pretty much on the temperament of the individual leader; it does in the Senate, about which alone I have knowledge. Some leaders have broadened their base of inquiry in such and such a way, and some have not. Some talk to a few men about what they are going to recommend and some do not, and some set up an organization that reaches to all parts of their party in the Senate so that they are in constant contact with them, and so they may come to their office from time to time and keep in touch with them. Now if you had a system like this you would pre-suppose a reduction in the number of committees.

++++

So the Senate divides up into a certain small number of com-mittees and you would have little overlapping, I suppose, of the membership on those committees. This total number of committee chairmen would be a very responsible body. They would have seniority, they would have experience, and they would have achieved the chairmanship on responsible committees. They would be set up as the official advisers and policy counselors, and they would formulate the general policy of the party in the Senate, we will say.

Now an individual chairman might say, "This will not come be-fore my committee, this legislation you are talking about," and I do not agree with that at all. They might thresh it out with him and say, "Here is what we said in our platform; this is the major senti-ment of the party. We feel like you ought to go along as far as you can on this thing, and we have got a party responsibility in con-nection with it."

On the other hand, the individual chairman would not be bound in any way. He could still go into his committee and oppose it. But there would be a group of 15 to 20 members that would be around the table with him and threshing this thing out.

I do not think the thing works in the Senate that way at the present time. You know what the Congress is. It seems to me in the final analysis the executive determines what is the party policy. The executive practically makes a recommendation to Congress that we should adopt certain legislation, for example, and without any con-sultation, except maybe he may consult a few of the leaders, the majority leader and maybe two or three others, but there is never any opportunity for representation of the rank and file of the party in the formulation of that policy, as a general rule.

++++

SENATOR WHITE: There is quite a bit I am tempted to say about this whole situation, about the responsibility of the majority, how the majority shall meet that responsibility, and in particular I have some problems that confront me as to the minority, but I think I will take it up at some other time.

I just cannot help saying this: Of course, the majority, I firmly believe, should have not only the powers of the majority but should have the responsibilities of the majority. I definitely am committed to that. They have a very great advantage over the minority in reaching a conclusion as to what their position should be.

In the first place, they have had the sanction recently of the people of the country that their platform carries with it approval of those who hold office and who ran for office and were elected on that platform. They have the very distinct advantage of executive advice, so that the majority ought to be able, within reasonable limits, to determine what the party policy is, and it ought to be able to make that party policy effective in legislation.

Now, the minority is in a very much worse situation. In the first place, you are the minority and mathematics plays a part. If you are agreed as a minority upon what a program shall be, or what the minority attitude toward a particular piece of legislation shall be, you know perfectly well that unless you are pretty persuasive and you are able to chip off some of the majority, that you are riding to disaster anyway. You know you are going to be beaten, because you know, as I have said a good many times, when we had 16 Republican Senators, 16 Republican Senators are not going to run the Senate of the United States with 96 Members, and when we had 23 or 25 we were in the same situation, although relatively, perhaps, a little improved, and even with 40 we are still the minority.

But in addition to that, we find this situation: We are here as a minority, with our platform and our candidates running on the platform repudiated by the people. Take myself: I have had some letters that have been called to my attention recently that the Republican platform is thus and so, and why did I not announce forthwith and forthrightly that I was standing on [that] platform. Well, I don't know what my obligation is to a platform that has been rejected by the people. I do not feel a great sense of obligation to look back and read a platform which the people of the United States have not approved and take that as my guiding star.

Of course, we of the minority have our steering committee, our chairman of our conference.

SENATOR PEPPER: How do you select your steering committee?

SENATOR WHITE: I was about to say. The chairman of our conference, the leader on the floor and with our ex officio members of the steering committee, and the committee on committees on the Republican side nominate the other members, and the full conference elects the other members of our steering committee. But since I have been here, we have never attempted in our conferences to assign anybody. Men come in and talk about things, but when we conclude our conversations every member is just as free to do as he pleases as he was when he came in. You cannot get party cohesiveness under that situation.

There is another thing that militates very greatly against party cohesiveness and makes it difficult not only for the majority but difficult for the minority. I do not suppose any of us would want to say we disapprove of independent voting in the country. I would not want to say that, and yet independent voting in the country exacts its price. Independent voting in the country finds a reflex immediately in voting in the legislative bodies. When you find that your constituents are not going to vote the Republican ticket because of any loyalty, or they are not going to vote the Democratic ticket because of any loyalty, but they are going to pick and choose independently, that is what the Members of Congress are going to do when they get into the Congress. They are not going to yield themselves cheerfully and completely to a party organization and a party program.

That is one of the prices we pay for independent voting. It is one of the contributions that independent voting in the country is making to the ineffectiveness of party organizations. It is pretty difficult even with the majority, which the Democratic Party now has, to formulate a program with any assurance that you have got the votes to put it through. It is difficult to formulate a policy and say, "This is our policy and we are going to the country on it," because you do not know whether you have got the votes even with your seeming majority.

MR. RHAME: Senator, you have been mentioning some of the disadvantages that the minority party has. It has one important advantage. The members of the minority party can vote against some proposal when some of the members of the minority party favor going farther than the proposal and some of the minority members oppose going as far as the proposal. That is one of the reasons that we felt it desirable to have a minority policy committee. The people would know what the position of the minority party was with respect to a given type of legislation, so that they would know when the next election time came around whether they were going to get more or less of what they had been getting if they voted a new party into power.

SENATOR WHITE: I think Senator Pepper of the majority party and I of the minority party recognize how unstable our party allegiance in the legislative body is. You can occasionally rally your followers and unify them, but most of the time you cannot. That goes for the majority as well as the minority.

136   PARTY BEHAVIOR IN CONGRESS

MR. HELLER: Our forefathers were very smart people, the framers of the Constitution. They must have thought about that very fact, that lots of talk and disagreement would delay the enactment of the legislation to a point where it would cool off long enough and the need for the legislation then would not exist.

SENATOR WHITE: I have been in the minority—and I have been in the majority when I was in the other House—I have been in the minority over here in the Senate with a minority so small that it was just hopeless. There are advantages in both situations. You do not have the responsibility, and yet you are constantly being asked, "Why does not your party do this, that, and the other thing." The answer is, you haven't got the votes.

MR. HELLER: It is just that simple.

SENATOR WHITE: Yes.

✦✦✦✦

SENATOR WHITE: You have spoken about the obligation of carrying out party-platform pledges. Do you think that obligation is the same in the case of the party which was defeated in the election? Putting it another way, I have had a good many letters in the last several months asking me about the Republican Party pledges as to this, that, or the other thing and why didn't I see to it that the pledges were carried out? The first answer is I couldn't. The second question in my mind has always been, What obligation I, as a member of the Republican Party, was under with respect to a platform which was rejected by the people and upon which the candidate stood, who was defeated at the polls? I do not have clearly in my mind just what my obligation is with respect to a platform which turns out to have only minority support in the country.

MR. MONRONEY: Isn't it a fact that both major-party platforms are virtually a rewrite of the same thing? There is no real division on basic issues before the country so that the election resolves itself not into a choice of platform but more or less a choice between candidates. The candidate is the thing in issue rather than the platform in our election.

SENATOR WHITE: I think today in our political life the people are very much more interested in the person of the candidate and his character and his point of view as he outlines it in his speeches that he makes around the country rather than in the platform. The platform, it seems to me, in our party scheme is wholly secondary to the person of the candidate.

✦✦✦✦

[MR. SILVEY:] I believe the people who go to political party conventions are interested in this country and are interested in presenting a document to the American people which reflects their thinking. They do not have to say that they give it to the people as a solemn covenant but they do say that and because they do, because it is printed in the papers and people read it, it becomes known as a compact between the political party and the electorate.

Now, Senator White, you have raised the question when one of the parties is rejected in the election by the voters, are the members of that party who do get elected obligated to observe the provisions of the platform which the people did not accept?

My opinion is this, that if there is in both party platforms the same subject treated in the same way then the elected members of the minority party are obliged to observe that part of the compact, for the reason that the voters made their choice after looking at the things which are common to both platforms and after looking in addition at the things that in one platform were more appealing or were emphasized better or were stated differently and they made their choice on those additional things.

There is also the matter of trust and confidence in past performance which has much weight with the voters. I could mention a couple of illustrations of current questions, but I promised not to throw current questions into this subject because we do not want to change the focus of discussion from the organization of Congress to an issue now before the Congress, but I can think of a couple of questions now before Congress which were in both party platforms, and therefore I would say about those subjects that the members of the minority party do have an obligation under their platform to keep the promises they made to the people.

SENATOR WHITE: You mean if what they promised is either identical or substantially the same as that in the winning platform.

MR. SILVEY: That is right.

SENATOR WHITE: But with respect to those matters divergent between the two platforms?

MR. SILVEY: Then I would say the voters have rejected those things and the country wants what was in the majority and not what was in the minority platform.

✦✦✦✦

You see, the platform is sometimes considered to be a sterile document because it is not translated into comic-book style and presented to the people. But even though the newspapers do not continually pick up and emphasize [the] exact language of the platform, the candidates of the parties, both the leading candidate and the lesser candidates, always pick out their speech material from the platform. That is proper and right, they should. And so really all during the 10 weeks of a political campaign the statements and speeches, press interviews, radio talks, and utterances of all the candidates of the party are an extension and elaboration of the platform. In this way, the voters really learn to know pretty well what is in the platform.

The personality of the candidates has something to do with the election, yes, but the subject-matter of their campaign is the subject-matter of the platform.

Now, with respect to the question of responsibility of the two parties to the electorate as they function in the Congress, I want to make a statement concerning the difference between the individual action of the Senator or Representative and the action of the Senator or Representative as an officer of his party in Congress.

Certainly, there should be no gag rule on individual members. They ought to be free in Congress and out of Congress to express themselves and to act upon any idea which they choose to speak or act upon, according to the way they personally want to do it. But when a member of a party accepts a position in his party organization in the Congress, then he has an official position to fulfill and he is required to perform in a way that will carry out the party's obligations and promises to the voters. Such a Congressman is like a person who gets elected—shall I say, to an official position in a labor union? A labor-union officer has an obligation to carry out the point of view of the membership on questions in which they are interested and as such points of view are expressed in convention resolutions.

A labor-union officer has private opinions and he has a perfect right as an individual citizen to express them in an individual capacity as, for instance, if he were one of a company of congenial people engaged in conversation.

But when he is making an address as the official, responsible spokesman of the organization which elects him, he is bound by virtue of his acceptance of the office to the decisions of the organization in convention assembled. If he is morally unable or personally unable to accept those convention decisions he resigns his office and somebody else takes it who can carry out the organization's wishes.

I cite this because there is no attempt in preaching party responsibility to gag members. Progress in a democracy is made by the expression of our ideas, not by the repression of them. We do, however, feel that when a man takes a party position in Congress he is responsible to the electorate in terms of his party's declarations to the voters.

THE VICE CHAIRMAN: Would you yield there? As to that party position, that would be analogous to a committee chairmanship or a committee membership that comes to him by virtue of his party's being in power.

MR. SILVEY: I would feel that to be so.

THE VICE CHAIRMAN: That is a line I draw between individual reaction and party responsibility; that is, that I hold my position on a committee because my party is in power. The chairman does likewise.

MR. SILVEY: Yes.

THE VICE CHAIRMAN: Therefore, my action on that committee must be measured to a large degree by my party's platform. Reaching the House I then become an individual member, expressing my own personal desires because I hold my position there by virtue of being elected.

MR. SILVEY: That is right, that is the way I think of it.

The suggestion for a majority and a minority policy committee contained in this report really impressed the people who studied it and comes out of a very large background of work and research which commends it to us and I hope to you.

Such an organization of Congress would enable the parties to carry the case to the voters more easily because a party must—and remember, I speak of all these things out of the desirability of continuing the two-party system in America—a party must carry its record to the voters not only in terms of what it has done but in terms of what it has failed to do.

The minority party has a peculiar privilege and opportunity with such machinery in Congress to make hay at the expense of the weaknesses and faults of the majority party, which is all to the good of the political structure and the progress of democracy in America. For example, let me pick up again an illustration—an unnamed question where the same subject is touched on in practically identical terms in both party platforms. The majority party has the responsibility to carry it out because it got elected. . . .

THE PARTY SYSTEM
EVALUATED

A CRITIQUE BY THE
AMERICAN POLITICAL
SCIENCE ASSOCIATION

This report, prepared by a committee of distinguished political scientists, summarizes concisely and incisively a great body of complaints about the workings of the American political system. In essence the committee recommends that the United States institute the British party system, arguing that the transformation of American life under the impact of the industrial revolution has established the institutional preconditions for true national parties, parties which would be program-oriented and internally disciplined.

This report is of course Presidentially rather than Congressionally oriented, and its recommendations are designed to satisfy Presidential needs. The existing party system is made to order for Congressional magnates, and they are under no pressure to change it. Indeed, Congress has gone to some lengths to forestall the development of a "Presidential party," as mentioned in the headnote to Document 10. For example, the Hatch Acts, which prevent civil servants from engaging in political activity, were primarily designed to prevent a President from using government employees as cadres in his own political machine.

If reports could change political systems, this one should surely have revolutionized our behavior, but the fact is that more than a decade has passed with little indication of movement in the directions recommended by Professor Schattschneider and his colleagues. Critics of the report have suggested that given the size and diversity of the United States—the ethnic, religious, regional, social, and economic divisions that sunder the populace—the committee's advice is at best premature and at worst dangerous. The looseness of the American party system, these critics have alleged, plays a vital role in muffling and accommodating discontent, in insulating the body politic from the contagion of local infections. Some have mordantly suggested that if the United States had a party system based on the British model,

141

with ideological confrontation at every election at every level, the nation would be in constant and perilous turmoil. (*Just to make the dispute more interesting, several distinguished British political scientists have recently noted that the British system appears to be moving in the direction of the American—with greater emphasis on the personality of the party leader and less and less of a clear programmatic distinction between the organizations!*)

I. *THE ROLE OF THE POLITICAL PARTIES*

THE PARTIES AND PUBLIC POLICY

Throughout this report political parties are treated as indispensable instruments of government. That is to say, we proceed on the proposition that *popular government . . . requires political parties which provide the electorate with a proper range of choice between alternatives of action.* The party system thus serves as the main device for bringing into continuing relationship those ideas about liberty, majority rule and leadership which Americans are largely taking for granted.

For the great majority of Americans, the most valuable opportunity to influence the course of public affairs is the choice they are able to make between the parties in the principal elections. While in an election the party alternative necessarily takes the form of a choice between candidates, putting a particular candidate into office is not an end in itself. The concern of the parties with candidates, elections and appointments is misunderstood if it is assumed that parties can afford to bring forth aspirants for office without regard to the views of those so selected. Actually, the party struggle is concerned with the direction of public affairs. Party nominations are no more than a means to this end. In short, party politics inevitably involves public policy in one way or another. *In order to keep the parties apart, one must consider the relations between each and public policy.*

This is not to ignore that in the past the American two-party system has shown little propensity for evolving original or creative ideas about public policy; that it has even been rather sluggish in responding to such ideas in the public interest; that it reflects in an enlarged way those differences throughout the country which are expressed in the operation of the federal structure of government; and that in all

FROM: E. E. Schattschneider, chairman, Commission on Political Parties of the American Political Science Association, "Toward a More Responsible Two-Party System," *American Political Science Review*, Vol. XLIV, No. 3, Part II, supplement (September 1950), pp. 15–36.

political organizations a considerable measure of irrationality manifests itself.

Giving due weight to each of these factors, we are nevertheless led to conclude that the choices provided by the two-party system are valuable to the American people in proportion to their definition in terms of public policy. *The reasons for the growing emphasis on public policy in party politics are to be found, above all, in the very operations of modern government.* With the extraordinary growth of the responsibilities of government, the discussion of public affairs for the most part makes sense only in terms of public policy.

THE NEW IMPORTANCE OF PROGRAMS

One of the most pressing requirements of contemporary politics is for the party in power to furnish a general kind of direction over the government as a whole. *The crux of public affairs lies in the necessity for more effective formulation of general policies and programs and for better integration of all of the far-flung activities of modern government.*

Only large-scale and representative political organizations possess the qualifications needed for these tasks. The ascendancy of national issues in an industrial society, the impact of the widening concern of government with problems of the general welfare, the entrance into the realm of politics of millions of new voters—all of these factors have tended to broaden the base of the parties as the largest political organizations in the country. *It is in terms of party programs that political leaders can attempt to consolidate public attitudes toward the work plans of government.*

Modern public policy, therefore, accentuates the importance of the parties, not as mere brokers between different groups and interests, but as agencies of the electorate. Because it affects unprecedented numbers of people and because it depends for its execution on extensive and widespread public support, modern public policy requires a broad political base. That base can be provided only by the parties, which reach people touched by no other political organization.

THE POTENTIALITIES OF THE PARTY SYSTEM

The potentialities of the two-party system are suggested, on the one hand, by the fact that for all practical purposes the major parties monopolize elections; and, on the other, by the fact that both parties have in the past managed to adapt themselves to the demands made upon them by external necessities.

Moreover, in contrast with any other political organization today in existence, the major parties even now are forced to consider public policy at least broadly enough to make it likely for them to win elections. If public esteem of the parties is much less high than it might be, the depressed state of their reputation has resulted in the main from their past indifference to broadly conceived public policy. This indifference has fixed in the popular mind the idea of spoils, patronage and plunder. It is hence not astonishing when one hears a chosen representative assert for the public ear that in his state "people put principles above party." Much of the agitation for nonpartisanship—despite the impossibility of nonpartisan organization on a national level—is rooted in the same attitudes.

Bad reputations die hard, but things are no longer what they used to be. Certainly success in presidential campaigns today is based on broad national appeals to the widest possible constituencies. To a much greater extent than in the past, elections are won by influences and trends that are felt throughout the country. *It is therefore good practical politics to reconsider party organization in the light of the changing conditions of politics.*

+++++

II. *WHAT KIND OF PARTY SYSTEM IS NEEDED?*

There is little point to talking about the American party system in terms of its deficiencies and potentialities except against a picture of what the parties ought to be. Our report would be lacking in exactness without an indication of the sort of model we have in mind.

Americans are reasonably well agreed about the purposes served by the two major parties as long as the matter is discussed in generalities. When specific questions are raised, however, agreement is much more limited. We cannot assume, therefore, a commonly shared view about the essential characteristics of the party system. But we can and must state our own view.

In brief, our view is this: *The party system that is needed must be democratic, responsible and effective*—a system that is accountable to the public, respects and expresses differences of opinion, and is able to cope with the great problems of modern government. Some of the implications warrant special statement, which is the purpose of this section.

1. *The Need for an Effective Party System*

In an era beset with problems of unprecedented magnitude at home and abroad, it is dangerous to drift without a party system that helps the nation to set a general course of policy for the government as a whole. In a two-party system, when both parties are weakened or confused by internal divisions or ineffective organization it is the nation that suffers. When the parties are unable to reach and pursue responsible decisions, difficulties accumulate and cynicism about all democratic institutions grows.

An effective party system requires, first, that the parties are able to bring forth programs to which they commit themselves and, second, that the parties possess sufficient internal cohesion to carry out these programs. In such a system, the party program becomes the work program of the party, so recognized by the party leaders in and out of the government, by the party body as a whole, and by the public. This condition is unattainable unless party institutions have been created through which agreement can be reached about the general position of the party.

Clearly *such a degree of unity within the parties cannot be brought about without party procedures that give a large body of people an opportunity to share in the development of the party program.* One great function of the party system is to bring about the widest possible consent in relation to defined political goals, which provides the majority party with the essential means of building public support for the policies of the government. Democratic procedures in the internal affairs of the parties are best suited to the development of agreement within each party.

2. *The Need for an Effective Opposition Party*

The argument for a stronger party system cannot be divorced from measures designed to make the parties more fully accountable to the public. *The fundamental requirement of such accountability is a two-party system in which the opposition party acts as the critic of the party in power, developing, defining and presenting the policy alternatives which are necessary for a true choice in reaching public decisions.*

Beyond that, the case for the American two-party system need not be restated here. The two-party system is so strongly rooted in the political traditions of this country and public preference for it is so well established that consideration of other possibilities seems entirely academic. When we speak of the parties without further qualification, we mean throughout our report the two major parties. The inference is not that we consider third or minor parties undesirable or ineffectual within their limited orbit. Rather, we feel that the minor parties in the long run have failed to leave a lasting imprint upon both the two-party system and the basic processes of American government.

In spite of the fact that the two-party system is part of the American political tradition, it cannot be said that the role of the opposition party is well understood. This is unfortunate because democratic government is greatly influenced by the character of the opposition party. The measures proposed elsewhere in our report to help the party in power to clarify its policies are equally applicable to the opposition.

The opposition most conducive to responsible government is an organized party opposition, produced by the organic operation of the two-party system. When there are two parties identifiable by the kinds of action they propose, the voters have an actual choice. On the other hand, the sort of opposition presented by a coalition that cuts across party lines, as a regular thing, tends to deprive the public of a meaningful alternative. When such coalitions are formed after the elections are over, the public usually finds it difficult to understand the new situation and to reconcile it with the purpose of the ballot. Moreover, on that basis it is next to impossible to hold either party responsible for its political record. This is a serious source of public discontent.

BETTER INTEGRATED PARTIES

1. *The Need for a Party System with Greater Resistance to Pressure*

As a consciously defined and consistently followed line of action keeps individuals from losing themselves in irresponsible ventures, so a program-conscious party develops greater resistance against the inroads of pressure groups.

The value of special-interest groups in a diversified society made up of countless groupings and specializations should be obvious. But organized interest groups cannot do the job of the parties. Indeed, it is only when a working formula of the public interest in its *general* character is made manifest by the parties in terms of coherent programs that the claims of interest groups can be adjusted on the basis of political responsibility. Such adjustment, once again, calls for the party's ability to honor its word.

There is little to suggest that the phenomenal growth of interest organizations in recent decades has come to its end. Organization along such lines is a characteristic feature of our civilization. To some extent these interest groups have replaced or absorbed into themselves older local institutions in that they make it possible for the government and substantial segments of the nation to maintain contact with each other. It must be obvious, however, that *the whole development makes necessary a reinforced party system that can cope with the multiplied organized pressures.* The alternative would be a scheme perhaps best described as government by pressure groups intent upon using the parties to deflect political attention from themselves.

By themselves, the interest groups cannot attempt to define public policy democratically. Coherent public policies do not emerge as the mathematical result of the claims of all of the pressure groups. The integration of the interest groups into the political system is a function of the parties. Any tendency in the direction of a strengthened party system encourages the interest groups to align themselves with one or the other of the major parties. Such a tendency is already at work. One of the noteworthy features of contemporary American politics is the fact that not a few interest groups have found it impossible to remain neutral toward both parties. To illustrate, the entry of organized labor upon the political scene has in turn impelled antagonistic special interests to coalesce in closer political alignments.

In one respect the growth of the modern interest groups is exerting a direct effect upon the internal distribution of power within the parties. They counteract and offset local interests; they are a nationalizing influence. Indeed, the proliferation of interest groups has been one of the factors in the rise of national issues because these groups tend to organize and define their objectives on a national scale.

Parties whose political commitments count are of particular significance to interest organizations with large memberships such as exist among industrial workers and farmers, but to a lesser extent also among businessmen. Unlike the great majority of pressure groups, these organizations through their membership—and in proportion to their voting strength—are able to play a measurable role in elections. Interest groups of this kind are the equivalent of organizations of voters. For reasons of mutual interest, the relationship between them and the parties tends to become explicit and continuing.

A stronger party system is less likely to give cause for the deterioration and confusion of purposes which sometimes passes for compromise but is really an unjustifiable surrender to narrow interests. *Compromise among interests is compatible with the aims of a free society only when the terms of reference reflect an openly acknowledged concept of the public interest.* There is every reason to insist that the parties be held accountable to the public for the compromises they accept.

2. The Need for a Party System with Sufficient Party Loyalty

It is here not suggested, of course, that the parties should disagree about everything. Parties do not, and need not, take a position on all questions that allow for controversy. The proper function of the parties is to develop and define policy alternatives on matters likely to be of interest to the whole country, on issues related to the responsibility of the parties for the conduct of either the government or the opposition.

Needed clarification of party policy in itself *will not cause the parties to differ more fundamentally or more sharply than they have in the past.* The contrary is much more likely to be the case. The clarification of party policy may be expected to produce a more reasonable discussion of public affairs, more closely related to the political performance of the parties in their actions rather than their words. *Nor is it to be assumed that increasing concern with their programs will cause the parties to erect between themselves an ideological wall.* There is no real ideological division in the American electorate, and hence programs of action presented by responsible parties for the voter's support could hardly be expected to reflect or strive toward such division.

It is true at the same time that ultimately any political party must establish some conditions for membership and place some obligations on its representatives in government. Without so defining its identity the party is in danger of ceasing to be a party. To make party policy effective the *parties have the right and the duty to announce the terms to govern participation in the common enterprise.* This basic proposition is rarely denied, nor are precedents lacking. But there are practical difficulties in the way of applying restraints upon those who disregard the stated terms.

It is obvious that an effective party cannot be based merely or primarily on the expulsion of the disloyal. To impose discipline in any voluntary association is possible only as a last resort and only when a wide consensus is present within the association. Discipline and consensus are simply the front and rear sides of the same coin. *The emphasis in all considerations of party discipline must be,* therefore, *on positive measures to create a strong and general agreement on policies.* Thereafter, the problem of discipline is secondary and marginal.

When the membership of the party has become well aware of party policy and stands behind it, assumptions about teamwork within the party are likely to pervade the whole organization. Ultimately it is the electorate itself which will determine how firmly it wants the lines of party allegiance to be drawn. Yet even a small shift of emphasis toward party cohesion is likely to produce changes not only in the structure of the parties but also in the degree to which members identify themselves with their party.

Party unity is always a relative matter. It may be fostered, but the whole weight of tradition in American politics is against very rigid party discipline. As a general rule, the parties have a basis for expecting adherence to the party program when their position is reasonably explicit. Thus it is evident that the disciplinary difficulties of the parties do not result primarily from a reluctance to impose restraints but from the neglect of positive measures to give meaning to party programs.

As for party cohesion in Congress, the parties have done little to build up the kind of unity within the congressional party that is now so widely desired. Traditionally, congressional candidates are treated as if they were the orphans of the political system, with no truly adequate party mechanism available for the conduct of their campaigns. Enjoying remarkably little national or local party support, congressional candidates have mostly been left to cope with the political hazards of their occupation on their own account. *A basis for party cohesion in Congress will be established as soon as the parties interest themselves sufficiently in their congressional candidates to set up strong and active campaign organizations in the constituencies.* Discipline is less a matter of what the parties do *to* their congressional candidates than what the parties do *for* them.

MORE RESPONSIBLE PARTIES

1. *The need for parties responsible to the public*

Party responsibility means the responsibility of both parties to the general public, as enforced in elections.

Responsibility of the party in power centers on the conduct of the government, usually in terms of policies. The party in power has a responsibility, broadly defined, for the general management of the government, for its manner of getting results, for the results achieved, for the consequences of inaction as well as action, for the intended and unintended outcome of its conduct of public affairs, for all that it plans to do, for all that it might have foreseen, for the leadership it provides, for the acts of all of its agents, and for what it says as well as for what it does.

Party responsibility includes the responsibility of the opposition party, also broadly defined, for the conduct of its opposition, for the management of public discussion, for the development of alternative policies and programs, for the bipartisan policies which it supports, for its failures and successes in developing the issues of public policy, and for its leadership of public opinion. The opposition is as responsible for its record in Congress as is the party in power. It is important that the opposition party be effective but it is equally important that it be responsible, for an irresponsible opposition is dangerous to the whole political system.

Party responsibility to the public, enforced in elections, implies that there be more than one party, for the public can hold a party responsible only if it has a choice. Again, unless the parties identify themselves with programs, the public is unable to make an intelligent choice between them. The public can understand the general management of the government only in terms of policies. When the parties lack the capacity to define their actions in terms of policies, they turn irresponsible because the electoral choice between the parties becomes devoid of meaning.

As a means of achieving responsibility, the clarification of party policy also tends to keep public debate on a more realistic level, restraining the inclination of party spokesmen to make unsubstantiated statements and charges. When party policy is made clear, the result to be expected is a more reasonable and profitable discussion, tied more closely to the record of party action. When there is no clear basis for rating party performance, when party policies cannot be defined in terms of a concrete program, party debate tears itself loose from the facts. Then wild fictions are used to excite the imagination of the public.

2. The need for parties responsible to their members

Party responsibility includes also the responsibility of party leaders to the party membership, as enforced in primaries, caucuses and conventions. To this end the internal processes of the parties must be democratic, the party members must have an opportunity to participate in intraparty business, and the leaders must be accountable to the party. Responsibility demands that the parties concern themselves with the development of good relations between the leaders and the members. Only thus can the parties act as intermediaries between the government and the people. Strengthening the parties involves, therefore, the improvement of the internal democratic processes by which the leaders of the party are kept in contact with the members.

The external and the internal kinds of party responsibility need not conflict. Responsibility of party leaders to party members promotes the clarification of party policy when it means that the leaders find it necessary to explain the policy to the membership. Certainly the lack of unity within the membership cannot be overcome by the fiat of an irresponsible party leadership. A democratic internal procedure can be used not merely to test the strength of the various factions within a party but also to resolve the conflicts. The motives for enlarging the areas of agreement within the parties are persuasive because unity is the condition of success.

Intraparty conflict will be minimized if it is generally recognized that national, state and local party leaders have a common responsibility to the party membership. Intraparty conflict is invited and exaggerated by dogmas that assign to local party leaders an exclusive right to appeal to the party membership in their area.

Occasions may arise in which the parties will find it necessary to apply sanctions against a state or local party organization, especially when that organization is in open rebellion against policies established for the whole party. There are a variety of ways in which recognition may be withdrawn. It is possible to refuse to seat delegates to the National Convention; to drop from the National Committee members representing the dissident state organization; to deny legislative committee assignments to members of Congress sponsored by the disloyal organization; and to appeal directly to the party membership in the state or locality, perhaps even promoting a rival organization. The power to take strong measures is there.

It would be unfortunate, however, if the problem of party unity were thought of as primarily a matter of punishment. Nothing prevents the parties from explaining themselves to their own members. The party members have power to insist that local and state party organizations and leaders cooperate with the party as a whole; all the members need is a better opportunity to find out what party politics is about. The need for sanctions is relatively small when state and local organizations are not treated as the restricted preserve of their immediate leaders. National party leaders ought to have access to party members everywhere as a normal and regular procedure because they share with local party leaders responsibility to the same party membership. It would always be proper for the national party leaders to discuss all party matters with the membership of any state or local party organization. Considering their great prestige, wise and able national party leaders will need very little more than this opportunity.

The political developments of our time place a heavy emphasis on national issues as the basis of party programs. As a result, the party membership is coming to look to the national party leaders for a larger role in intraparty affairs. There is some evidence of growing general agreement within the membership of each party, strong enough to form a basis of party unity, provided the parties maintain close contact with their own supporters.

In particular, *national party leaders have a legitimate interest in the nomination of congressional candidates,* though normally they try hard to avoid the appearance of any intervention. Depending on the circumstances, this interest can be expressed quite sufficiently by seeking a chance to discuss the nomination with the party membership in the congressional district. On the other hand, it should not be assumed that state and local party leaders usually have an interest in congressional nominations antagonistic to the interest of the national leaders in maintaining the general party policy. As a matter of fact, congressional nominations are not considered great prizes by the local party organization as generally as one might think. It is neglect of congressional nominations and elections more than any other factor that weakens party unity in Congress. It should be added, however, that what is said here about intraparty relations with respect to congressional nominations applies also to other party nominations.

III. *THE INADEQUACY OF THE EXISTING PARTY SYSTEM*

The existing party system is inadequately prepared to meet the demands now being made upon it chiefly because its central institutions are not well organized to deal with national questions. The sort of party organization needed today is indirectly suggested by the origin of the traditional party structure. This structure developed in a period in which local interests were dominant and positive governmental action at the national level did not play the role it assumed later.

✦✦✦✦

SOME BASIC PROBLEMS

Party institutions and their operations cannot be divorced from the general conditions that govern the nature of the party system. Before we focus specifically on the deficiencies of existing party institutions, we must account for some of the more important factors that impress themselves upon both major parties.

What are the general features of party organization that have cast up continuing problems?

1. The Federal Basis

The two parties are organized on a federal basis, probably as a natural result of our federal type of government. In Charles E. Merriam's words, "The American party system has its roots in the states. Its regulation and control is conducted almost wholly, although not entirely, by the states acting separately."[1] This means that *the national and state party organizations are largely independent of one another,* each operating within its own sphere, *without* [an] *appreciable common approach to problems of party policy and strategy.*

Such independence has led to frequent and sharp differences between state and national organizations. Antagonisms are illustrated by such terms as national Republicans and Wisconsin Republicans, national Democrats and Dixiecrats. Moreover, state party organizations too often define their interests quite narrowly. This does not merely mean substantial disregard of national needs or matters of national interest, but it also means piecemeal as well as one-sided use of state power and state resources. As John M. Gaus has put it, "In many states—probably in almost all—the party systems are inadequate as instruments for reflecting the need of our citizens for carefully thought-out, alternative programs of public housekeeping."[2]

It is not being argued here that the party system should be cut free from its federal basis. Federalism is not a negative influence in itself; it is equally capable of positive accomplishments in the public interest. Whether it works in the one or the other direction depends in large part on how well the balance of forces within a federal organization accords with the needs of society. In the case of the American party system, *the real issue is not over the federal form of organization but over the right balance of forces within this type of organization.*

On that score, the party system is weighted much more heavily toward the state-local side than is true today of the federal system of government in the United States. The gap produces serious disabilities in government. It needs to be closed, even though obviously our traditions of localism, states' rights and sectionalism will inevitably affect the pace of progress that can be expected.

A corollary of the kind of federalism now expressed in the party system is an excessive measure of internal separatism. The congressional party organization is independent of the national organization, and the House and Senate organizations of the same party are inde-

[1] [Charles E. Merriam, "State Government at Mid-Century," *State Government,* June 1950.]

[2] [John M. Gaus, "The States Are in the Middle," *ibid.*]

pendent of each other. As a result, cooperation between these parts of the national party structure has not been easy to secure.

2. *The Location of Leadership*

In part because of the centrifugal drives that run through the party system, *party organization does not vest leadership of the party as a whole in either a single person or a committee.* The President, by virtue of his conspicuous position and his real as well as symbolic role in public opinion, is commonly considered the leader of his party. If he has a vigorous personality and the disposition to press his views on party policy and strategy, he may become the actual leader during his presidential term. But even the President has no official position within the party organization, and his leadership is often resented and opposed. The presidential nominee of the defeated party is generally recognized as the "titular leader" of his party, yet the very title implies a lack of authority.

The National Chairman is most nearly in the top position, but if he tries to exercise initiative and leadership in matters other than the presidential campaign, his authority is almost certain to be challenged. Ill feeling, rather than harmony of policy and action, is likely to result. In sum, *there is at present no central figure or organ which could claim authority to take up party problems, policies and strategy.*

3. *The Ambiguity of Membership*

The vagueness of formal leadership that prevails at the top has its counterpart in the vagueness of formal membership at the bottom. *No understandings or rules or criteria exist with respect to membership in a party.* The general situation was well put by Senator Borah in a statement made in 1923:

Any man who can carry a Republican primary is a Republican. He might believe in free trade, in unconditional membership in the League of Nations, in states' rights, and in every policy that the Democratic party ever advocated; yet, if he carried his Republican primary, he would be a Republican. He might go to the other extreme and believe in the communistic state, in the dictatorship of the proletariat, in the abolition of private property, and in the extermination of the bourgeoisie; yet, if he carried his Republican primary, he would still be a Republican.

It is obviously difficult, if not impossible, to secure anything like harmony of policy and action within political parties so loosely organized as this. On the other hand, it is easy to see that the voter's political choice when confined to candidates without a common bond in terms of program amounts to no more than taking a chance with an individual candidate. *Those who suggest that elections should deal with personalities but not with programs suggest at the same time that party membership should mean nothing at all.*

SPECIFIC DEFICIENCIES

So much for the most conspicuous consequences that stem from the general features of existing party organization. Now let us consider some more specific aspects pertinent to a reorganization of the national party structure.

1. *National Party Organs*

The National Convention, as at present constituted and operated, is an unwieldy, unrepresentative and less than responsible body.

++++

This lack of balance in representation, together with the peculiar atmosphere within which the Convention operates, makes it very hard for such a body to act in a deliberative and responsible manner. The moral authority of the National Convention to act in the name of the whole party would be greatly strengthened if more care were used to make the convention really representative of the party as a whole.

It can be said equally well of other institutions at the national level that they are not very well suited to carry today's burdens of an effective party system. *The National Committee is seldom a generally influential body and much less a working body.* Indeed, it rarely meets at all.

In *House and Senate,* the *campaign* committee of each party is concerned with aiding in the reelection of members of its chamber. These *committees do not always have a good working relationship with the National Committee.* They do not plan joint election strategy for both chambers and traditionally accept little responsibility for party leadership. Only in the past generation have the parties shown signs of developing a continuous working organization at the national level. *Although their interest in questions of party policy has grown, the national party organs are not so constituted nor so coordinated as to make it simple for them to pay enough attention to these questions.*

2. *Party Platforms*

The growing importance of national issues in American politics puts weight into the formulation of general statements of party policy. Of course, no single statement of party policy can express the whole program of the party in all of its particulars, including questions of timing.

But it is obvious that a serious attempt to define the propositions on which the parties intend to seek the voter's support would serve both party unity and party responsibility.

One of the reasons for the widespread lack of respect for party platforms is that they have seldom been used by the parties to get a mandate from the people. By and large, *alternatives between the parties are defined so badly that it is often difficult to determine what the election has decided even in broadest terms.* Yet unused resources are available to the parties in the democratic process itself if they learn to use a statement of policy as the basis for the election campaign. Platforms acquire authority when they are so used.

The prevailing procedure for the writing and adoption of national party platforms is too hurried and too remote from the process by which actual decisions are made to command the respect of the whole party and the electorate. The drafting of a platform ought to be the work of months, not of a day or two; it ought to be linked closely with the formulation of party policy as a continuing activity. Party policy—in its bricks and straws—is made, applied, explored and tested in congressional and presidential decisions, in the executive departments, in the work of research staffs, in committee hearings, and in congressional debates. No party convention can pull a party program out of the air. *The platform should be the end product of a long search for a working agreement within the party.*

3. Intraparty Democracy

One of the principal functions of the parties—in terms of the concept of party we elaborated in the preceding section—is to extend to the fullest the citizen's participation in public affairs. Measured by this standard, the existing parties are painfully deficient. Direct primary legislation offers opportunities for the creation of a broad base on which to build the party structure, but these opportunities have rarely been fully utilized.

Too little consideration has been given to ways and means of bringing about a constructive relationship between the party and its members. Indeed, any organization really concerned about this relationship does a multitude of things that American parties generally do not do to maintain close contact with the membership. Party membership ought to become a year-round matter, both with constructive activities by the members and with mechanisms by which the party organizations can absorb the benefits of wider political participation.

✦✦✦✦

IV. NEW DEMANDS UPON PARTY LEADERSHIP

THE NATURE OF MODERN PUBLIC POLICY

1. Broad Range of Policy

The expanding responsibilities of modern government have brought about so extensive an interlacing of governmental action with the country's economic and social life that the need for coordinated and coherent programs, legislative as well as administrative, has become paramount. Formulating and executing such general programs involves more than technical knowledge. *In a democracy no general program can be adopted and carried out without wide political support.* Support must be strong enough and stable enough to guard the program as far as possible against such drives as come forth constantly from a multitude of special interests seeking their own ends. This kind of political support can be mobilized on a continuing basis only by stronger parties.

Broad governmental programs need to be built on a foundation of political commitments as written into the programs of adequately organized parties. This is true today also of governmental programs erected on bipartisan backing. In that respect the political requirements to sustain American diplomacy are very different from those of the period before World War I, for example. As Walter Lippmann has recently written of the requirements of bipartisan foreign policy, "It takes two organized parties, each with its recognized leaders in the field of foreign affairs. Today neither party is organized. Neither party has leaders in the field of foreign affairs. In this chaos no Secretary of State can function successfully."[3]

2. Impact on the Public

What is said here about the need for an adequate political base for foreign policy applies equally to such other large sectors of public concern as national defense and economic policy. In each area, the problems are so interrelated that the activities of the government must be integrated over a very wide front. *In a predominantly industrial society, public policy tends to be widely inclusive, involving in its objectives and effects very large segments of the public or even the whole country.*

[3] [Walter Lippmann, New York *Herald Tribune*, March 24, 1950.]

1. *An Historic Trend*

Even if the international scene did not look as it does, *the changes in the nature and scope of public policy* here indicated would press upon the political process. For they *are the result of changes in the social structure and the economy of the United States.* The long-range transformations expressed in industrialization and urbanization and the revolutions in transportation and communication were bound to create a truly national economy and to affect significantly the bases of American politics.

++++

2. *Past and Present Factors*

It is much the same thing to say that *there has been in recent decades a continuing decline of sectionalism,* first noted by Arthur N. Holcombe nearly twenty years ago. Statistical evidence such as is available for the last generation shows that the most significant political trends in the country have been national, not sectional or local. This is not to say that sectionalism is likely to drop to insignificance as a factor in American politics. Here as elsewhere in the political system, change is a matter of degree. The relative decline of the strength of sectional alignments is nevertheless a matter of great consequence. Elections are increasingly won and lost by influences felt throughout the land.

The measurable shift from sectional to national politics cannot fail to have a corresponding effect on party organization and the locus of power within the parties. *Party organization designed to deal with the increasing volume of national issues must give wider range to the national party leadership.*

++++

3. *New Interest Groups in Politics*

The economic and social factors that have reduced the weight of sectionalism have also resulted in the development of a new type of interest groups, built upon large membership. These new interest groups, found principally in the areas of industrial labor and agriculture, are pursuing a novel political strategy. *To a much greater extent than in the past, they operate as if they were auxiliary organizations of one or the other party.* The growing conversion of most of the labor movement to party action is a case in point. Labor organizations now participate energetically in election contests. They register voters, take part in the nominating process, raise campaign funds, issue campaign literature and perform other functions once on the whole reserved for the parties.

Thus the old local monopolies of the regular party organizations have been broken by new large-membership groups. To a very considerable extent the regular party organizations are now so yoked into a partnership with the newcomers that they have lost much of their old freedom of action. The successful political leader in the future is likely to be one who is skillful in maintaining a good working alliance between the older and the newer types of political organization. This applies partly even to conditions today.

The emphasis of the new large-membership organizations is on national rather than sectional issues. What is no less significant, the interests of the membership are not identified with any single product or commodity. Farmers, for instance, cannot hope to prosper in an ailing economy. Workers must measure their pay against the level of prices as well as the value of social security. Hence the large-membership groups are inevitably pushed into consideration of all of the factors that affect the national well-being. How parties stand on programs designed to bring about stability and healthy expansion in the economy as a whole is therefore of great concern to most of the new groups in American politics.

V. THE QUESTION OF CONSTITUTIONAL AMENDMENT

1. A Cabinet System?

It is altogether clear that party responsibility cannot be legislated into being. Not a few Americans have argued, however, that something like the British system of responsible cabinet government would have to be grafted to ours before an effective party system could come about in the United States. Usually this idea takes the form of proposals to amend the Constitution to give the President the right to dissolve Congress and to call a new election at any time, besides certain other changes in the Constitution.

A responsible cabinet system makes the leaders of the majority party in the legislature the heads of the executive departments, *collectively accountable* to their own legislative majority *for the conduct of the government.* Such a relationship prompts close cooperation between the executive and legislative branches. The legislative majority of the cabinet forms a party team which as such can readily be held responsible for its policies. This governmental system is built around the parties, which play the key role in it.

2. *Strong Parties as a Condition*

We do not here need to take a position on the abstract merits of the cabinet system. On the question whether it could be successfully fitted into the American scheme of congressional-presidential government, opinions are widely divided. Even if it were conceded to be desirable *to amend the Constitution in order to create a responsible cabinet system,* it should be plain that this *is not a practicable way of getting more effective parties.* Such an amendment, if it offered likelihood of being adopted at all, would make sense only when the parties have actually demonstrated the strength they now lack. When they show that strength, a constitutional amendment to achieve this end would be unnecessary.

On the other hand, the experience of foreign countries suggests that adoption of the cabinet system does not automatically result in an effective party system. Cabinet systems differ in their results and affect the party system in different ways. Moreover, it is easy to overestimate not only the expected benefits of a constitutional amendment but also the rigidity of the existing constitutional arrangements in the United States. Certainly the roles of the President and Congress are defined by the Constitution in terms that leave both free to cooperate and to rely on the concept of party responsibility.

3. *Adaptation within the Constitution*

The parties can do much to adapt the usages under the Constitution to their purposes. When strong enough, the parties obviously can furnish the President and Congress a political basis of cooperation within the Constitution as it stands today.

Actually the parties have not carefully explored the opportunities they have for more responsible operation under existing constitutional arrangements. It is logical first to find out what can be done under present conditions to invigorate the parties before accepting the conclusion that action has to begin with changing a constitutional system that did not contemplate the growing need for party responsibility when it was set up.

PRESSURE GROUPS

THE ROLE OF LOBBIES
IN A DEMOCRACY

DOCUMENT 12   THE TNEC'S CLASSIC EXPOSÉ

American political power is diffused both institutionally—between the Presidency and Congress, with the judiciary playing a lesser but sometimes vital role—and functionally—with great weight at the state level of party organization. It is therefore not surprising that pressure groups have played an important part in policy determinations. A group seeking support for its projects, or seeking to block the motions of others, can get little help from the Democratic or Republican party as such. It may get its views incorporated in the national platform, but this accomplishment, while heartwarming, has a minimal practical impact. Consequently there has developed what is often called the "fourth branch of government": the lobbies specializing in bringing pressure to bear on legislators, the President, members of regulatory agencies, and administrators. Many former Congressmen have taken positions with these organizations and employ their fund of inside information and range of acquaintanceship to advance the views of their groups.

There are three main schools of thought about lobbying. The first one condemns lobby groups as detrimental to the democratic process. These critics have often alleged that lobbies, armed with prestige and large expense accounts, seduce the legislators from their loyalty to the common good. More recently, lobbies have come under attack not only for leading the legislators astray, but for leading the public itself down the primrose path by the use of devious "Madison Avenue" advertising techniques. Characteristically the supporters of a defeated measure will discover that "sinister lobbyists" rigged their downfall; the rule almost seems to be "You lobby; I represent the Public Interest."

The second school of thought takes a much more benign view of lobby groups. It holds that the absence of pressure indicates that the people are simply not concerned about an issue, that "when a wheel needs grease, it squeaks." It is, after all, a free country, and if the majority wants a piece of legislation passed, there will be plenty of

163

pressure. Spokesmen for this laissez faire group theory therefore deprecate all the furore about "lobbies" and suggest that the denunciations of "unfair pressure" are hurled by bad losers.

The third school of thought argues that the problems that lobbies produce run deeper then either of these other schools might suggest. It starts with the premise that there is nothing inherently dishonest about this practice—it is merely an effective utilization of the Constitutional right of petition. On the other hand, it recognizes that there is more to skillful pressure politics than merely the will to organize. The key question is: Do all vital interests get represented? Or does the battle go by default to those with skill and money, and the time to employ them? Time to build up key political contacts, an experienced organization of lobby cadres, a battery of lawyers, money, and influence in gaining access to public communications are all factors which give some lobby groups disproportionate influence at the expense of others. Advocates of this school note that while only 8 per cent of the nation's work force is currently engaged in agriculture, the great farm lobby, the American Farm Bureau Federation, has rarely been defeated in Congress in the past thirty years. They further emphasize that although 10 per cent of the American population is over sixty-five years old, there is no significant lobby working for medical care for the aged—the Kennedy Administration, for example, worked for the passage of "Medicare" without effective pressure-group allies. Yet "Medicare" was a prominent plank in President Kennedy's election program and allegedly rested on the "will of the people."

However, much of the influence gained by certain lobby groups at the expense of others is a product of the American political system itself. The structure of Congress and the internal dynamics of its politics ensure that any conservative group engaged primarily in holding operations to prevent legislation has an advantage, since it is much simpler to obstruct than to enter legislation on the statute books. For example, the seniority system of committee chairmanships gives an advantage to non-urban conservative Senators and Representatives. And it is doubtful that Senator Harry Byrd of Virginia, Chairman of the Senate Finance Committee, needed prodding from the American Medical Association to trigger his opposition to President Kennedy's "Medicare" program. It is possible that attacks on lobbies confuse the symptom with the malady, blame pressure groups for the workings of the system.

This selection, which bears the New Deal imprimatur, gives a vivid description of the anatomy of lobbying and discusses the functions of lobby groups in a democracy.

The American people are confronted with the problem of who shall control the Government, by what means, and to what ends.

Since the founding of the Republic, the governmental process has been characterized by a struggle for control. With increasing stresses and strains as a result of internal maladjustments and foreign war, the struggle has taken on new and vital significance.

CONTROL VERSUS POWER

Governmental power is qualitatively different from control. Power is a political term, synonymous with authority. Control is dynamic and constantly seeks new methods of limiting or using power. Government may possess power and at the same time wield control, as in a totalitarian state; but ordinarily, in a democracy, power resides in the government, while control is exercised by the various pressure groups, chief of which is business. The extent of the Government's control is limited, not only by the Constitution but by our traditional belief that government should not "compete" with business but should act merely as an umpire in the struggle for control. Only in comparatively recent times, under stress of depression and greatly accelerated technological change, has this traditional belief yielded ground to the idea of increased government activity.

The role of business, on the other hand, has never been static. From the beginning, business has been intent upon wielding economic power and, where necessary, political control for its own purpose. The purpose, moreover, is not solely profit, but includes the exercise of control per se, as an attribute of ownership.

Even today, when the purposeful use of government power for the general welfare is more widely accepted than at any time in our history, government does not begin to approach the fusion of power and will characteristic of business.

THE CONTESTANTS

But economic power and political power are general terms. To understand them it is necessary to determine who uses them, how, for what purposes, and with what results.

FROM: *Investigation of Concentration of Economic Power: Economic Power and Political Pressures,* Monograph Number 26, Temporary National Economic Committee, Seventy-Sixth Congress, Third Session (Washington, D.C., Government Printing Office, 1941), pp. 1–10, 13–19, 47–56.

Government itself is both a form of power and a situs of control. Government in a democracy, however, does not act independently of the electorate; nor does our Federal Government as now constituted proceed in a logical way toward the attainment of carefully thought out and consistent goals.

In the first place, our Government is established on a geographical basis of representation. State, county, and district lines provide an easy way of securing representation, but the assumption that people living in a certain area on the map share, even in a general way, the interests of their neighbors is unjustified, if not actually false. Also, political representation is generally secured through the party system, and as such represents a compromise at the outset. A party platform, adopted to appeal to as large [a] sector of the electorate as possible, cannot follow completely the interests of any group. Lip service, at least, must be paid to the complex of interests represented in the community.

The relatively short time served by public officials is also a limiting factor on the effectiveness of government control. . . .

Philosophically, also, government is amorphous. Within broad limits there are nearly as many philosophies of government as there are men in it, while pressure groups have a tremendous unifying principle in the mere fact of their organization about a certain concept. Congressmen act in a multiple capacity, reflecting at different times a functional, sectional, personal, or partisan viewpoint, but with a few major exceptions, such as the Social Security Act and certain labor legislation, they appear to respond more readily to pressure from business than from other groups. There is probably a far greater difference in ideology between a high-tariff, industrialist Congressman from Massachusetts and a public ownership advocate from the Middle or Far West than there is between two members of the National Association of Manufacturers, or two members of the National Grange. The latter have at least a common economic interest, while the former are probably poles apart on most of the questions which they are called upon to decide.

While the business community may, on occasion, elect "its man" to Congress or to the Presidency, or secure his appointment to a governmental office or to the courts, its indirect influence is of far greater importance. Pressure groups generally find it more satisfactory to influence the votes of legislators in their behalf than to try to elect their own representatives to office.

++++

Economic power is rather widely diffused, although its control is concentrated, as pointed out above. In the struggle for dominance, it is exerted largely through pressure groups—groups organized for the purpose of applying political and economic pressure to secure their own ends. It is these pressure groups with which this study is largely concerned. By far the largest and most important of these groups is to be found in "business," which in this study means the business community, as dominated by the 200 largest nonfinancial and the 50 largest financial corporations, and the employer and trade associations into which it and its satellites are organized. These 250 corporations represent a concentration of economic power in the fields of manufacturing, transportation, electric and gas utilities, and mining, and, to a lesser extent, merchandising, the service industries, and even agriculture.

Another large segment of pressure groups includes the patriotic and service organizations, such as the Daughters of the American Revolution, the American Legion, the Veterans of Foreign Wars, the Navy League, etc.

A third segment includes the reform groups—the Women's Christian Temperance Union, the National Civil Service Reform League, the League of Women Voters, etc.

The farm groups include the National Grange, the American Farm Bureau Federation, and the Farmers' Educational and Cooperative Union, along with minor groups like the Tenants' and Sharecroppers' Union.

There are numerous labor groups, the most powerful being the American Federation of Labor, the Congress of Industrial Organizations, and the various railway brotherhoods.

✦✦✦✦

This enumeration by no means includes all the pressure groups. Some of them spring up for immediate purposes, and when those purposes are achieved disappear. Some of them are organized for purposes other than the wielding of political and economic power, and adopt that function only temporarily. The American Association of University Women is such an organization, which is politically active only on sporadic occasions.

A number of groups organized for the preservation of civil rights, the advancement of democracy, or for purely humanitarian motives, such as the American Civil Liberties Union, the National Association for the Advancement of Colored People, the various committees for the aid of refugees, or for Spain or China, the Red Cross, etc., should also be classified separately. They are normally active only for their own purposes and do not lend themselves readily to alliances with other groups, except to the extent to which their membership is active politically.

There is another contestant in the struggle for power which cannot be ignored, although it is customarily treated by the pressure groups more as an instrument for securing and maintaining their own control than as a rival in the contest. This is the general public. The public is an amorphous mass, largely directionless, often easily swayed, gullible, and easily misled. Nevertheless, it possesses a tremendous potential strength and an enormous determination when it finds a channel for its energies. It would be a mistake to underrate mass opinion, however futile it may seem at any particular moment to try to goad it into effective action in its own behalf.

Mass opinion sets the stage for political action at any particular moment in this country, to a large degree. Gullible as it is, it cannot in ordinary times be pushed beyond a certain point. It is utterly impossible to return to the political conditions of 1800, or 1910, or even 1930, partly because economic conditions have changed and partly because it is impossible to set back the clock of public opinion. The gradual extension of suffrage, unionization, popular control of legislation, extension of social services—all these things are now in the realm of public policy and cannot be removed except by a violent revolution and the use of unexampled force. Even then, most of them would be retained.

Pressure groups attempt to mold public opinion to accomplish their own aims, and at any given moment it seems that government is the result of a compromise between conflicting pressure groups.

✦✦✦✦

METHODS OF CONTROLLING POWER

The methods by which control of power is sought are as varied as the groups which seek it. The role of the general public in the contest may to a large extent be ignored, since the public is generally too formless, too inchoate, to apply pressure at given points for a given purpose, and is largely the passive instrument which both business and government use to strengthen their own arms.

Our purpose is to discover the techniques by which power is directed by conflicting forces toward the attainment of specific goals. The chief contestants in this conflict are business and government. Government, usually in response to external stimuli, seeks to expand its functions, to put itself on an equal footing with business. Business seeks to hold back the rising tide of government activity, struggling to keep itself free from government regulation, so as to pursue its own ends unhampered. Both argue that they work in the interest of the general welfare.

While there has been some interest in this country in favor of government ownership of economic enterprises, it is a philosophy which has never been adopted as a program of action by any large group. The expansion of government activity has been along the lines of providing social services favorable to many groups which would otherwise not be furnished at all, and of regulating economic activity in the public interest.

Business, on the other hand, has fought such regulation and the expansion of social services, and even more bitterly has fought the idea of government ownership. The fight occurs largely in the political arena, but it does not end with the election of Congressmen and Senators. Election is but one phase of the process. The selection of candidates, the drafting of platforms, the party caucus, all function largely in advance of the legislative process. Pressures on Congress while legislating and appropriating, manipulation of law enforcement and administration, and use of the judicial process to achieve individual or group ends, take place during or after the legislative process.

Through the press, public opinion, and pressure groups it is possible to influence the political process. While all three of these factors have played a part in the process since our beginnings as a nation, the extent and consciousness of their use has grown inordinately. They are employed by all contestants in the struggle for control, but reflect the viewpoint of business more accurately than that of others. The press today is not the same kind of factor in the political process that it was in Thomas Jefferson's day. Although the economic basis of politics today is in many respects similar to that outlined by Madison in the Federalist, today's economic pressure groups have advantages which Madison never dreamed of. The revolution in communications, produced by American ingenuity and promoted by American business, makes the press, the radio, and other opinion-forming instruments far more important in the political process than ever before. Both press and radio are, after all, "big business," and even when they possess the highest integrity, they are the prisoners of their own beliefs.

The development of the corporation as a means of control of property necessitates ranking it, too, as an important factor in the political process. By means of the private corporation, ownership of much of American business property has been separated from effective control of that property. Ownership is diffused, at least to some extent; control is concentrated. This development is so recent (it has occurred within the last two decades or so) that its effect on the working of our governmental institutions cannot yet be accurately evaluated. Enough is known, however, to justify the statement that it is warping the basic concepts of our Government. Extending beyond State lines in great national economic empires, business corporations have grown greater than the States which created them. By insisting on the principle of federalism—the division of power between the States and the Federal Government—as a basic tenet in our political philosophy, corporations have been able in large measure to limit the strength of the political power which might control them.

CHARACTERISTICS OF THE STRUGGLE

Among the noteworthy characteristics of the struggle for power between government and business are—

1. The invisibility of most of the action.
2. The continuity of the struggle.
3. Its varying intensity.
4. Its constantly shifting battleground.

INVISIBILITY

Although any legislation under consideration in Congress is spotlighted in the daily news, although the President's activities and the administrative decisions of the various Government agencies are frequently headlined in press and radio, and although court decisions are a matter of widespread public interest, still it is true that a large, and extremely important, part of the governmental process is hidden from the public.

It is a commonplace that the work of Congress is done not in the Senate and House chambers, where the spectators come to watch, but in the committee rooms of the congressional committees. Even this, however, is but a faint indication of the extent to which governmental activity is carried on behind the scenes. The factors which influence legislators are only rarely the opinions of their colleagues, uttered in formal debate in Congress. They are the legislator's own political convictions, his mail from his district or State, the lobbyists who approach him in his office or in the halls of the Capitol, or the witnesses who appear before him in committee. None of these activities is carried on with the publicity devoted to formal congressional action. The callers at the White House rarely are even listed in the papers, although one or two Washington papers make a habit of printing the day's appointments. Still less are callers upon department administrators listed. The trade journal of a certain industry group may mention that its members went to Washington on a mission of benefit to the industry, but the news does not get into the general press. Letters, telegrams, telephone calls, personal visits, and the other contacts between contestants are rarely of enough immediate dramatic content to secure public attention, even if it were not usually made a point to conduct such activities without publicity.

Another strong reason for this invisibility is to be found in the geographical basis of legislative and judicial representation. This organization of government obscures the economic or functional basis for legislative decisions, which are frequently far more compelling than a geographical accident. The political process is invisible also because citizen groups, the most energetic and purposeful of the working forces of government, are completely unprovided for by the written Constitution. Only in the living Constitution are they recognized as having significance along with the formal Government agencies. They function in and through the Government structure, without, however, as a rule suffering from the white light of publicity which surrounds it.

THE SITE OF THE CONFLICT

At what point the brunt of the battle is borne depends on a number of factors, at any particular time. It depends, among other things, on the nature and number of current issues, upon the personnel of the government agencies, Congress, or the Supreme Court, or upon the trend of dominant public opinion.

The first battle of the conflict occurs in the choice of legislators. The second takes place in the legislature itself. If business loses that, it resorts to the administrative agencies charged with the enforcement of the law; if it loses there, or sometimes while it is fighting there, it has recourse to the courts; and if it loses again, the struggle reverts to the legislature, taking the form of an attempt to amend or repeal the law. The forces of propaganda are, of course, in constant use. Business, for instance, first sought to defeat the National Labor Relations Act in Congress. Failing that, a number of trade journals, the publications of the National Association of Manufacturers and the United States Chamber of Commerce recommended that the act be ignored until it was tested in the courts. (At that time, it seemed likely that a favorable court decision could be secured.) When the act was finally declared constitutional, however, the focus of the attack shifted first to the approaching congressional elections, in the hope of amending the act, and then to Congress itself.

Although by no means always favorable, the circumstances determining the site of the struggle usually favor business. Business is less restricted than government in choosing the place to fight. It can fight or not, secure in its conviction that "sixty billion dollars can't be wrong." If it feels itself compelled to fight it can accept the challenge, at the same time starting a back fire elsewhere.

In this connection the business orientation of the newspaper press is a valuable asset. In the nature of things, public opinion is usually well disposed toward business. This is a natural consequence of the popular belief in the virtues of the American system, as understood by the business community. Business is more or less unconsciously assumed to be right. Government is the "prosecutor." But, in addition, newspapers have it in their power materially to influence public opinion on particular issues. When it comes to measuring particular situations of fact against general principles and presenting the comparison as news, newspapers are shapers of opinion as well as purveyors of fact. Editors are aware of this, of course, and many take special precautions to avoid it. With others, editorializing is practiced as a matter of course. And even where editors and publishers are men of the highest integrity, they are owners and managers of big business enterprises, and their papers inevitably reflect, at least to some extent, their economic interest. When organized business deliberately propagandizes the country, using newspaper advertising as one medium, the press is a direct means of channeling business views into the public mind.

Slogans and clichés have a special importance in rendering favorable the circumstances in which business chooses to stand against government. "Inalienable rights," "individual initiative and effort," "private ownership and control" are typical of those used by the National Association of Manufacturers. They are among the essential features of the "American System." They constitute the description of the economy which business prefers, but they seem to hark back to the days before the emergence of the modern corporation as a dominant institution. It stretches the imagination almost to the breaking point, for instance, to regard the operations of Standard Oil of New Jersey as those of an individual in the usually accepted sense of that word.

But the legal profession, at the bidding of business, has been equal to the task. By getting the courts to accept the contention that the corporation possesses a personality separate from those of the individuals acting for it and by getting them also to extend the operation of the Fifth and Fourteenth Amendments to these corporate personalities, lawyers have remade constitutional guarantees in the image of business.

This feat is the best example we have of business control of government. Language used by Thomas Jefferson to state the relationship between citizens and government necessary for the development of the individual personality, has been used by business to attract public support in its effort to avoid regulation. The law, the newspaper press, and the advertising profession have all helped business by spreading this changed conception of the Jeffersonian idea.

✦✦✦✦

CONTESTANTS IN THE STRUGGLE

It is difficult to enumerate the organizations which, together, are the antagonists in the struggle for power. A classification by function, on the basis of government, pressure groups, and the general public, apparently neglects the divergent interests making up the various groups, so that in many cases wider variations in aim, methods, and effectiveness are found within a single group than exists between any of the three groups. The abyss that separates the United States Chamber of Commerce from the Municipal Ownership League, for instance, is far wider and deeper than the separation between the Republicans and the conservative Democrats.

It is probably true that the ranks of the pressure groups shelter some who would prefer to live under a government in which their sole voice was that of individual citizens; and that government agencies and legislative bodies are honeycombed with men and women who feel that business is far better able to wield political control than the politicians. Still it is impossible to classify the interacting forces on a completely adequate basis, and the division here set up has the advantage of emphasizing the energetic, directional approach of pressure groups as against either government or the general public.

Government, of course, includes town, county, and State legislative bodies and administrative agencies, as well as the local courts. The Federal Government's scope of action is so different from the lower levels of government that it must be classified separately, although its general position in the contest is at least partly the same. One of the chief techniques by which pressure groups get and maintain their power is by insisting that a certain function legally belongs to the States, even though it is clear that the State cannot handle it adequately. By insisting that it belongs to the States, they manage to preclude the possibility of any effective action.

Among the pressure groups, business can be divided into two categories—principals and satellites. In the former are included the groups representing business and industry generally, and those representing distinctive parts of American business. In the latter are the professional associations which revolve around business, largely dependent upon it for support.

Chief among the organized groups representing business generally is the Chamber of Commerce of the United States. The outstanding employers' group is the National Association of Manufacturers. It acts not only on its own account, but has also, through the National Industrial Council, been instrumental in coordinating the activities of State industrial associations, local industrial relations organizations, and manufacturing trade associations. Twelve of the country's topnotch corporations keep informed of each other's activities in the industrial relations field through a special conference committee.

In the electric power industry, the Edison Electric Institute, successor to the National Electric Light Association, operates a well-known lobby. Legislative activities of the country's life insurance industry are under the direction of the Association of Life Insurance Presidents. On governmental matters the Association of American Railroads speaks for the railway industry. Iron and steel, petroleum, lumber, coal, [and] copper are represented by the American Iron and Steel Institute, the American Petroleum Institute, the National Lumber Manufacturers' Association, the National Coal Association, and the Copper Institute, respectively. Of special importance, because of the national defense considerations involved in national policy regarding merchant shipping and air transport, are the American Merchant Marine Institute (formerly the American Steamship Owners Association) and the Air Transport Association.

Among industry's satellites, commercial banking presents a united front to government through the American Bankers Association, while the Investment Bankers Association of America functions in the same capacity for investment banking. Although it includes by no means all the country's lawyers, the American Bar Association is the part of the legal profession most closely allied in thought with American business. Through the American Newspaper Publishers Association the country's daily newspapers join their strength for business and against government. National groups in the accounting, engineering, auditing, and advertising professions share the general philosophy of business and shape their public activities accordingly.

The organizations through which laborers, farmers, distributors, and consumers direct their efforts in forming public policy are well known, although they vary considerably in effectiveness. The great bulk of the labor unions are organized into the American Federation of Labor, the Congress of Industrial Organizations, and the railway brotherhoods, although the independent unions are not necessarily inactive in politics. Among the important farm groups are the National Grange, which has been active in politics for 70 years, and the American Farm Bureau Federation and Farmers Educational and Cooperative Union, which have emerged as potent factors in lobbying since the World War. Farmers' membership cooperatives are active politically, working through the American Cooperative Council. Numerous farm commodity producers are organized on a national scale and engage in both National and State politics. The American National Livestock Growers Association is typical of this group. It is particularly difficult to distinguish between such producers' organizations and the pressure groups comprising "business." Their members are, in a sense, farmers, but they have far more in common with the business community than with agricultural groups.

++++

CHARACTERISTICS OF THE CONTESTANTS

In the contest for domination of public policy, four characteristics are of primary importance. They are: length of life, cohesion, visibility, and resources. Length of life, or staying power, is vital because the contest is a continuing one, and an organization which continues to function over a long period of time gathers experience, techniques, and familiarity with the problems which are probably not shared by its opponents.

Cohesion in an organization makes for mutual support, which is invaluable under stress. The more an organization suffers from disunity, or internal dissension, the less is it able to direct its strength toward any particular goal, and the more easily its aims are defeated.

The extent to which the activities of a contestant, whether it is government or a pressure group, are invisible to the general public or to other groups often determines the outcome of a particular maneuver or a whole phase of the battle. A part of the struggle for power is carried on more or less openly, although even then it may be disguised, as propaganda frequently is. Congressional hearings provide another spotlight. The committee meetings in which policies are decided are not open to the public, however, a circumstance which fosters invisibility in political action.

In a conflict between economic and political forces it is inevitable that resources should play an important part. Propaganda is expensive, law suits are expensive, lobbies are expensive. The word "resources" should, of course, include more than money, as there have been occasions when money was of no avail against militant groups who worked with reforming zeal. The record indicates, however, that the side which spends the money usually wins the election.

Business has greater staying power than other pressure groups, or than government, because its constituent units have a longer lease on life. Most private corporations possess perpetual charters. When combined with such resources as those controlled by the 250 largest corporations, these charters enable business to stay in the political game indefinitely. A corporation may, as a result of voluntary or involuntary bankruptcy or merger, lose its identity and with it its charter. But the factors determining a corporation's ability to retain its individuality and thus stay in the political game are far more economic and legal than political. Most of the country's important business units have been in business, and in politics, for decades. Organizations of these business units are equally old. The National Association of Manufacturers was organized in 1895, and the predecessor of the National Industrial Council, the organization through which the lobbying, propaganda, information, and labor relations policies of affiliated local, State, employers', and manufacturing trade associations are coordinated, in 1907.

On the surface it would seem that the power of organized labor, if not of farmers and consumers, to stay in politics would equal that of business, but it is doubtful if this is actually so.

Labor's stamina depends in the first instance on the authority to function, granted in union charters, and, in the second, on the general state of business. Labor union income rises with prosperity and falls with depression. Without resources, labor cannot use effectively the right to function granted them by charter. Also, labor's ability to take an active part in the governing process depends largely on the sympathy of government.

The relative staying power of labor and business is well illustrated by the experience of the National Association of Manufacturers. On three different occasions during the 45 years of its existence it has responded to alleged threats to the security of the American system of free enterprise. The threats were said to come from labor and its bid for Government assistance in its struggle for improved working conditions.

In its first "open shop" drive in 1905 and 1906 the association attempted to break the growing power of organized labor. A similar drive was conducted during the mid-twenties. The third attempt was begun after the legal recognition of labor's right to organize and bargain collectively, in 1933 (a recognition strengthened and made more permanent in the Labor Relations Act of 1935), and it has not yet ceased.

A sympathetic attitude on the part of government toward farm groups is a tremendous factor in their effectiveness. These organizations almost completely lack the legal basis of longevity conferred upon business and labor groups by charter. Farmers' staying power is relatively low, although post-war experience with voluntary organization and recent legislation have improved it. Whether this will be a permanent improvement remains to be seen.

Government clearly lacks the staying power of business. It is subject to changes among its legislators and responsible officials much more frequently than business, and while such changes are inevitable in a representative democracy, they seriously compromise its power to govern. Even lengthening the term of public service to 4, 6, or 8 years, instead of the present 2, 4, and 6 years, would not begin to approach the decades during which businessmen are in office.

One instance of the effect of personnel changes and other shifts over a relatively short period appears in the history of the enforcement of the Federal anti-trust laws. In 1913 Congress placed the enforcement of the Clayton Act in the hands of the Federal Trade Commission. Twenty years later, according to a study made in 1932, enforcement appears to have been effective in the case of "small" but not of "big business." Because of —

the shift in political power within the legislative and executive branches of the Government, and the limitations placed on the Commission by the courts—

the Federal Trade Commission has, according to this study—

been little more than a body for the regulation of the trade practices of small business.[1]

COHESION

Cohesion is a characteristic of great advantage to business. There is some doubt regarding the cohesiveness of all business, large and small,

[1] [T. C. Blaisdell, Jr., *The Federal Trade Commission,* 1932.]

but there is unquestionably a marked degree of "sticking together" in the business community which is of primary importance in the governing process. How important their attachment to a uniformly accepted philosophy is in this respect it is difficult to say. Common observation would indicate that it has considerable weight. In any event, the extent of interlocking in the directorates of the country's leading business units is so great as to result inevitably in a considerable similarity of viewpoint. In 1935, out of 250 corporations (the 200 largest non-financial and the 50 largest financial) 151 companies were interlocked with at least 3 other companies in the group. The assets of these 151 companies amounted to nearly three-fourths of the combined assets of the 250. While it would be easy to exaggerate the importance of this extensive interlocking in the matter of policy formation, it would be a mistake to underrate it, since 59 of the 83 directors who held 4 or more directorates were active in at least 1 of the companies they served. (Active positions include those of board chairman, executive or finance committee members, or executive officers.)

The cohesion resulting from this overlapping is not only economic but political as well. It gives business management a big tactical advantage over business owners, over employees and farmers, and over government itself. Other pressure groups possess the political cohesiveness and single-mindedness of business, but they have not the economic cohesion, in the sense that businessmen all over the country are relatively easy to unite in a single movement. Other pressure groups are smaller, and less well integrated by their organs of communication.

In comparison with business, government appears to be almost completely lacking in cohesion. It can hardly be otherwise. The territorial organization of government is diffuse, particularized, if not atomized. Not even the executive branch is capable of the degree of cohesion possessed by business. It is too large, too diverse in origin and interest, and too lacking in mutual and common concern to be more than very loosely held together by President and Cabinet. Partisan politics inevitably involves some degree of cohesion, at least among the politically-responsible personnel, if the party is to be successful at the polls. But it cannot engender the kind of single-minded purposefulness which business possesses, and which would be so valuable an asset in the contest for power.

As an eminent legislator, later a Cabinet official, once pointed out, "The first law of politics is self-preservation." And any legislator knows that his reelection is primarily his own problem, which he will have to solve by making some compromise with the various groups in his district. A legislator with principles often draws a line beyond which he will not go in compromise; but as representative of a whole district, he cannot in the nature of things achieve the single-mindedness of any one of the pressure groups which tries to influence him.

INVISIBILITY

The invisibility of the struggle was discussed in chapter I. Invisibility, however, is an advantage which accrues largely to business rather than to government. That part of the governmental process which goes on behind the scenes is largely the exertion of pressure on the legislative, administrative, or judicial branches, and the pressure is largely exerted by business.

In greater or less degree, of course, this invisibility is a characteristic of all the private groups which are active in government. It grows out of the longstanding fallacy that government is "public" and pressure groups "private." As a result, government operates under the strong light of publicity, while the other contestants are permitted to conduct their activities as if they were not of public concern.

RESOURCES

Most important of all the factors in favor of business, however, are its resources—not so much because of their size, important as that is, as because of the circumstances surrounding their use. The extraordinary concentration of ownership in the 250 largest corporations, and the even greater concentration of control, enormously increase their mobility and effectiveness.

The ownership and control of these large assets by the business community give point and meaning to the other characteristics of the contestants. They contribute to the comparative longevity of corporations. They also provide a very real basis for the cohesion displayed by the business community in its efforts to maintain the status quo, protect private property, and continue to control business assets, unhampered by public regulation. The darkness surrounding the political activities of nongovernmental groups in the contest is important to business largely because it permits the spending of these huge reserves almost entirely without accounting.

Government expenditures are made out of public revenues, and their use is subject to public scrutiny at all times. Hence, business, as part of the public, is able to challenge and keep to a minimum Government expenditures for propaganda purposes. Government, by means of the taxing power, congressional investigation, and use of antitrust statutes, and so forth, can to some extent limit business' expenditures for propaganda purposes. Compared to the glare of publicity that surrounds Federal expenditures, however, business carries on its activities in a dim and comforting gloom.

++++

POLITICAL PRESSURE GROUPS

The constituent groups into which politically active Americans are divided have as their practical objective the favorable consideration of their respective aims by the legislative, executive, and judicial branches of the Government. We have seen how pressure groups, by soliciting general approval for their aims, raise them to the status of public problems. Also, we have considered the role of these groups in the manufacture of public opinion. It is now appropriate to scrutinize more closely the place of pressure groups in American political life.

Their goal is Government sanction of their continually emerging demands. Those demands are insistent no matter what the form of organization of the group. Trade associations and organizations of professional people press their demands unhindered on the formal agencies of the Government. Similarly, groupings of industrialists and federations of labor and veterans' units insist on consideration of their desires. Peace and patriotic-minded societies likewise impress their programs on the formally-selected officials of the Government. Added together, these citizen groups of varied shape constitute a sizable portion of the American people. And, what is more important, they include practically all the people who recognize the value of official consideration of private interests and are so situated as to command that consideration.

++++

THE LOBBY AND ITS TECHNIQUE

From this broad statement on pressure groups, let us proceed to a closer examination of lobby technique in general.

In their search for governmental favors, national associations of citizens all conform to a pattern which is more or less standardized. They maintain lobbies at Washington, of varying size and resources. The lobby of the United States Chamber of Commerce, for example, is a department of the national headquarters and is maintained on an impressive scale. In contrast is the single lobbyist of the Women's International League for Peace and Freedom.

Some lobbies are permanent, others intermittent or temporary. Important citizen groups organized nationally maintain permanent lobbies. Others maintain intermittent lobbies which have been effective in legislative matters, such as the Fair Trade League, with its objective of retail price fixing. The American Bar Association's special representative in Washington during the fight on President Roosevelt's Supreme Court reorganization proposal is an example of a temporary lobby. At a minimum, each lobby usually includes a legislative agent and a staff of research workers.

It is the lobbyist's job to put on the statute books the bills which embody the aims of his association, or of which it approves, and to keep off the statute books those bills of which it disapproves. Consequently, it is the desire of the typical national association to build a bloc of votes in Congress and then to back it at the right junctures with pressure from the country. The pressure is exerted on neutral or unsympathetic Congressmen by the association's nation-wide membership, as an adjunct of a favorable, or at least not hostile, public mood built up by the association's active propaganda.

The services which a bloc of votes in Congress can render a national association are numerous and valuable. Obviously the most valuable is frankly to represent the citizen group in Congress. Possibly the best known example of such occupational representation by geographically-elected representatives is the farm bloc, which was founded by the Farm Bureau Federation in 1921 and held the balance of power in the Sixty-sixth and Sixty-seventh Congresses. For a group to be able thus to rely on some definite support is always worth a great deal.

In addition to being ready to vote for the group's bills, there are many ways in which a bloc may render service to the group. Sympathetic legislators can watch and influence committee appointments, and can urge committee members to report out bills. Members of the bloc can speak for the group on the floor of the House or Senate. They can introduce bills. Moreover, any member of the bloc can use his franking privilege to send association propaganda through the mails free of postal charge. This propaganda takes the form either of a Member's speech on the piece of legislation in question, or of a prepared statement inserted in the Record through "leave to print." These are all normal and time-honored methods by which sympathetic blocs in Congress can advance the aims of citizen groups.

With several hundred nationally organized citizen groups with agents in Washington, it is obvious that only a relatively small number can gain control of congressional blocs. For representation before Congress, most of the groups must rely primarily on their legislative agents. Even those supported by congressional blocs lean heavily on their lobbyists. In fact, the lobbyist is the key factor in pressure politics. On him rests the responsibility not only of translating his association's legislative program into law as fast as possible, but also of thwarting legislation running counter to that program.

This means that the alert lobbyist must interest himself in a wide variety of subjects on which Congress acts. The objectives of some groups are few and specific, and their lobbyists accordingly need pay but little attention to other legislative proposals. Other groups, however, aim at general objectives, which, to be reached and held, require legislative action in a dozen fields. Outstanding among such groups are those including the Nation's laborers, businessmen, manufacturers; its transport and public utility systems; its bankers, farmers, and professional people. The lobbyists who guard the interests of these groups in Washington must scrutinize carefully a bewildering array of bills. Tax measures and appropriations need close examination. Bills providing for Government reorganization must also be studied.

For almost all these groups the prospects of reaching their objectives are dimmed or brightened by existing and proposed laws dealing with natural resources, transportation facilities, manufacturing, processing, grades and standards, and distribution; with marketing and trading, foreign commerce, banking and credit, and postal operations, quarantine and sanitary measures, and trade practices; with Government purchasing, roads, local tax systems, and education. Almost every one of these subjects, therefore, falls within the scope of the lobbyist's concern. Both his own personal success and that of his association's program depend on his ability to win battles on this many-sided legislative front.

✦✦✦✦

So it is with every citizen group which is organized and operated for purposes of pressure politics. Labor's objective of the American standard of living, the "American system" of the [National] Association of Manufacturers, the "individual initiative" and "free enterprise" of the chamber of commerce, the "free press" of the newspaper publishers, and the "America of the future" of the educators are all examples of general aims with great propaganda value which reach Congress in the form of specific bills and amendments intended to accomplish the purposes of these organizations. The lobbyist or his witnesses explains to

Members of Congress why the attainment of the aim depends upon the enactment of many specific bills and why the general welfare will be promoted by the bills in which he is interested. Part of the lobbyist's job is to make Congress feel that the "public" is back of the bills which his association wants passed. "The men who seek special favors of Congress . . . do not bribe, or give free passes, or pay election expenses; they attempt to make the legislators think that the thing they want is the thing that the public wants."[2] In this process of identifying group interest with public interest the lobbyist occupies the key position.

Congress is importuned for special favors not only by lobbyists who work openly in Washington, but also by pressure exerted from behind the scenes. The pressure reaches a Congressman through telegrams, resolutions, letters, and delegations of constituents, all urging him to vote thus-and-so on a particular bill. The constituents who exert this sort of pressure are not limited to members of the association whose lobbyist directs the campaign. They include also those of many other groups—political clubs, chambers of commerce, young voters' leagues, independent citizens' alliances, etc. Thus a lobbyist mobilizes behind a measure support from a dozen or more different quarters in a congressional district.

Once the decision is made by the officials of the association interested in the bill to "turn the heat on Congress," a number of district organizers tour the country, contacting local organization secretaries, ambitious young lawyers, and professional men, and local celebrities for the purpose of starting the avalanche of letters and telegrams speeding toward the Capitol. Meanwhile, in Washington, the lobbyist is acting as coordinator of the field armies. . . .

. . . The whole strategy of his movements is to stay out of the limelight and to let the voters speak to their Congressmen for him.

On occasion Congressmen are appealed to through this method to vote against a bill because it is "communistic" or "socialistic." In such cases the lobbyist's aim is to have the pressure come to Members of Congress from one or more patriotic organizations. . . .

Devious as well as direct methods are thus employed by lobbyists to influence Congress. To oppose legislation because it is communistic or socialistic and, therefore, un-American, is to take a stand on generalities which is, nevertheless, unassailable, when love of America stands highest in the scale of popular loyalties.

[2] [C. S. Thomas, "My Adventures with the Sugar Lobby," *World's Week,* January 1916.]

The system of representation worked out by pressure groups in this country to supplement the system of geographical representation is co-ordinate with the party system. The presence of groups in Washington—

means that the geographic representation as outlined in the fundamental law of the land has been supplemented by a new and spontaneous and at the same time systematic form of representation based upon various interests of various groups of like-minded people. It means that there has developed in this Government an extra-legal machinery of as integral and of as influential a nature as the system of party government that has long been an essential part of government, though not originally incorporated in the Constitution.[3]

The party system developed in response to two definite needs: First, of a method whereby candidates for manning and operating the governmental machinery might be selected and presented to the electorate; and, second, of a method for choosing between candidates thus selected. Both custom and the Constitution have operated to fix the single-member constituency as the basic unit of representation. This was the system in operation in England in the eighteenth century with which the colonists were familiar.

Moreover, the Constitution designated population as the basis of apportioning the seats in Congress among the several States. Tradition and law were reinforced by the difficulty of communication. Occupational and professional interests were not lacking even during the drafting of the Constitution, yet as a foundation on which to erect the structure of political representation geography seemed the more reasonable. In any event, as the Nation expanded both in area and in population, surveyor's lines were unquestioningly accepted as the method of allocating among the population representation in the legislature.

As long as travel and communication were difficult, representation in Congress on the basis of geography was on the whole fairly satisfactory. Unquestionably, even today, men living side by side in the same vicinity have many common interests. Up to a certain point, the needs growing out of these interests can be met by a legislature elected on the basis of geographical representation. Beyond that point such representation is inadequate.

The machine age has sharpened those interests which are independent of territorial association and has created many new interests. Easy and rapid communication has made men more aware of these new

[3] [E. P. Herring, *Group Representation Before Congress,* 1929.]

interests and has thus facilitated the formation of groups of like-minded individuals. Today, residence in a particular locality is but one of many grounds on which Americans feel a community of interest with others of their fellow citizens. One's vocation, his calling, profession, or occupation, is possibly the most important of these grounds. It can be seen at work in the organization of citizens into trade associations, labor unions, industrial leagues, professional associations. Another important basis is service in defense of the Nation. Patriotism, reform, national defense, and peace are others.

These special-interest groups are not limited by the boundaries of congressional districts. Puzzled by problems beyond their abilities to solve and, turning to the Government for help, they have discovered that the system of representation in Congress makes no provision for them. Two-party government discourages their entrance into politics, thus forcing them into extra-legal channels to achieve their aims in the sphere of legislative activity. The means which they have evolved to do this is the lobby, which thus becomes an instrument not only of opinion forming, but of providing functional, nongeographic interests with representation at Washington.

The decline of the political party as a leader in opinion has been accompanied by the rise of these organized groups of voters. Obviously, the effect of this shift in the relative importance of the party in the political process is important. It has resulted in the virtual domination of politics by the citizen group movement. Both during and after elections the groups hold the key to the explanation of much party behavior. As leaders in the formation of opinion, the parties at election time seek their support more assiduously than that of aggregates of individuals. In election campaigns this means that the real significance of the platform on which party nominees run for election can be found only in the stated or implied desires of the groups supporting the candidates. "The voice which political parties hear now is the voice of groups rather than that of political leaders who profess to speak for the people."[4]

The range of that voice extends to Washington as well. Partisans in Congress and [the] administration also listen to group opinion. Members of Congress are elected by parties but in their votes they tend to respond as a rule more to the voice of groups than to that of the party. . . .

Control of legislation and offices has thus shifted in large measure from the parties to the lobbies and allied organizations.

The real danger of this situation lies not in functional or group

[4] [E. B. Logan, "Lobbying," *Annals*, Supplement, American Academy of Political and Social Science, July 1929.]

representation before Congress, but in the possibility that Congress will be swayed by a pressure out of proportion to the actual number of people in the group, or without regard to the effect of the legislation on the general public. To a certain extent the parties themselves are a check on this dangerous tendency.

At the very point where it might militate against the public interest, the national association is checked by another force, the political party, which theoretically and often in practice works for the national good rather than the welfare of a small special minority.[5]

While this may be too optimistic an appraisal of the situation, it is still true that, without the support of the leaders of the majority party in Congress, citizen groups usually are not able to enforce their demands.

Both parties and groups are active in the shaping of policy. Through nominations of personable candidates, bargains with citizen groups and political factions, and success in elections, the parties play the dominant role in the determination of broad policy. At the same time, the substance of policy both in the beginning and as revised through the years is due more to pressure groups. After all—

most issues are not decided by the parties, but by public opinion. . . . Here the activity of the nonparty groups is of prime significance.[6]

The competition among groups for official approval of their aims is perhaps the outstanding characteristic of the governmental process in America of the twentieth century. To decide who shall win in this competition and what form the victory shall take is the government's continuing assignment.

[5] [E. P. Herring, *op. cit.*]
[6] [C. E. Merriam and H. F. Gosnell, *The American Party System,* 1929.]

DOCUMENT 13   THE SCOPE, THE COSTS, AND THE TECHNIQUES OF LOBBYING

In the spoilsman's bacchanalia, which lasted roughly from the end of the Civil War through the first decades of this century, lobbying techniques were both picturesque and primitive, and few holds were barred. Before the popular election of Senators became common (the Seventeenth Amendment to the Constitution made it mandatory in 1913), state legislatures used to send detailed instructions to their representatives in the upper house. These instructions, of course, reflected the pressures dominant on the state level. On occasion, Congressmen were informed that if they voted wrong, they would be lynched by their constituents, and corruption was endemic on the state level. Henry Demarest Lloyd once observed that the Standard Oil Company did everything but refine the Pennsylvania legislature, and Charles Francis Adams and his brother Henry provided a brilliant, caustic vignette of the New York situation in their Chapters of Erie.

The Washington picture was little better. Between 1866 and 1872, a lobbyist for the Union Pacific Railroad spent $400,000 influencing Congress; over a slightly longer period the Central Pacific Railroad expended almost $2 million. (And the Central Pacific's contact man complained that he was being outbid by Tom Scott of the Pennsylvania Railroad!) While bribery as such was always frowned upon, there was no law which forbade an interest group from "taking care of" its friends. Daniel Webster, while a member of Congress, turned up as a legal consultant to a number of lobbies and did not seem to find the work burdensome, and many other distinguished political figures were on various payrolls. As Collis P. Huntington, who labored for the welfare of the Central Pacific in the 1860's and '70's (and who once came to Washington with $200,000 in a trunk!) put it: "If you have to pay money to have the right thing done, it is only just and fair to do so."

While this flamboyant style of lobbying has long since gone out of fashion under the impact of state and federal laws, large sums are still spent on influencing legislative decisions. This report of the Buchanan Committee, reflecting a generally liberal political position, discusses the nature of the pressure process in contemporary terms.

++++

ON DEFINING LOBBYING

The term "lobbying" has been in common usage for approximately 100 years, and has been given many definitions. In the 1870's and 1880's, "lobbying" meant direct, individual solicitation of legislators, with a strong presumption of corruption attached. The lobbying of the 1880's demanded this kind of definition; the lobbying of today demands

FROM: *General Interim Report,* House Select Committee on Lobbying Activities, House Report Number 3138, Eighty-First Congress, Second Session (Washington, D.C., Government Printing Office, 1950), pp. 5–10, 23–28.

something quite different. Unfortunately, most present-day definitions are both inaccurate and unrealistic; they generally fail to recognize that modern pressure on legislative bodies is rarely corrupt, that it is increasingly indirect, and largely the product of group rather than individual effort. With these limitations, the ordinary definition of lobbying provides an unsatisfactory basis for either congressional inquiry or statutory regulation.

Numerous State laws continue to define lobbying as "personal solicitation not addressed solely to the judgment" of legislators, or as attempts to secure money on the claim or pretense of being able to "improperly influence" them.[1] In other States, definitions of lobbying as "bribery, promise of reward, intimidation, or any other dishonest means" of attempting to influence legislators still remain on the statute books or in State constitutions.[2]

The discussion of lobbying in *Corpus Juris Secundum* is based on an equally narrow view of the subject:

The term "lobbying" has a well-defined meaning in this country, and signifies to address or solicit members of a legislative body in the reception hall or elsewhere with the purpose of influencing their votes. Presentation by argument in a public and legitimate manner of the injurious effect proposed legislation will have on a particular business does not constitute lobbying.

Dictionary definitions are similarly limited in scope. Webster's New International tells us that lobbying is "to address or solicit members of a legislative body in the lobby or elsewhere, as before a committee, with intent to influence legislation." With the passage of the Regulation of Lobbying Act in 1946, numerous groups and persons claimed this kind of definition as their own in an effort to escape full disclosure under the act. The National Association of Manufacturers typically maintained that in passing the act Congress had only intended to reach and include:

. . . activities which seek more directly and specifically to secure the support or opposition of individual Members of Congress toward legislation actually pending in either House. Such an interpretation, in addition to avoiding constitutional questions, is more nearly in accord with the general concept of "lobbying."[3]

The NAM followed this "general concept of lobbying" to its logical conclusion by reporting on only the 1.97 percent of its 4.3 million

---

[1] [*Utah Code.*]
[2] [*Constitution of California.*]
[3] [NAM Statement to the Clerk of the House, April 29, 1948.]

THE ROLE OF LOBBIES IN A DEMOCRACY

dollar budget which the association conceded should be charged to "legislative activities." The association's $2,000,000 public relations program was claimed to be totally unrelated to legislation, and no part of it was reported under the Lobbying Act. Yet this is the same NAM whose president told a Senate committee in 1946 that his organization had spent $395,850, "largely on advertising," in its campaign to abolish OPA.

And so goes the refrain from group after group after group: "Millions for 'education' or 'public enlightenment,' but not 1 cent for lobbying—as we define it." If this committee had followed the lobbyists' definitions of lobbying, we would have had relatively little to investigate.

As noted above, our investigation started with an existing lobbying law on the books. The framers of that statute, The Federal Regulation of Lobbying Act did not use the word "lobbying" anywhere in the act except the title. Instead, they referred to attempts to influence the passage or defeat of legislation for pay or any consideration. Our Committee regards all such attempts as "lobbying" and has generally so used that word during our investigation.

In the final analysis, there are only two practical gauges of lobbying activity—intent and some substantial effort to influence legislation. The means employed are secondary, and any attempt to define lobbying by listing specific methods of influence is inevitably and almost immediately out of date.

These criteria do not define lobbying, but they do set forth the essential conditions without which lobbying does not exist. We feel that these are the only criteria inclusive enough to span the entire present system of pressure politics. They are the only criteria which would have enabled this committee to lay the full facts before Congress and the people.

We firmly believe that, in any inquiry into the process of influencing the passage or defeat of legislation, it is important to utilize a functional approach. Variations in bookkeeping technique or the mere self-serving application of labels by special interest groups should not be permitted to conceal the true nature of their activities. The thing that is most significant in attempts to influence legislation is the expenditure of money, whether it be used for direct contact of legislators, direct communication with legislators, or in efforts to stimulate grass-roots pressure so that members of organizations and members of the general public will communicate with legislators in support of a particular legislative program.

Whether defined narrowly or broadly, lobbying is extremely difficult to measure objectively. The members of this committee [know], as all Members of Congress cannot help but know, that lobbying in the past few years has become more widespread and intensified than at any other time in our history. We recall the Taft-Hartley issue, OPA, rent control, public housing, and a whole host of other recent issues which have been the subjects of terrific pressure campaigns. We knew then as we know now that intense efforts and many millions of dollars were expended in connection with these measures; but these are things which cannot be computed with mathematical precision.

A few useful gages of the extent and cost of lobbying are available, however. Primary among these are the sums reported and registrations made under the Federal Lobbying Act since 1946. The following analysis [see facing page] summarizes the quarterly reports of lobbying contributions and expenditures filed by organizations and groups pursuant to section 305 of the act.

More than $20,000,000 has been reported under another section of the Lobbying Act . . . for the same period. Most of this amount is not included in the figures in the table on page 191.

Seventy-five million dollars for 3½ years of lobbying is a large and impressive sum but it does not begin to reflect all that is actually collected and spent in efforts to influence legislation. Many groups submit only fragmentary reports in which they omit the costs of publications, public relations, and advertising directly related to public issues. The National Association of Home Builders, for example, has not reported the costs of its public relations program which it estimates has aggregated $250,000 in the past few years. Many more groups do not report at all, taking the position that they are exempted by the "principal purpose" clause of the Lobbying Act, or that their agent's registration relieves them of the responsibility of reporting. Witness the fact that the 2,878 quarterly reports were submitted by only 495 groups, a fractional proportion of the permanent national organizations which are vitally interested and continuously active in seeking to shape public policy. In still other cases, a national organization, such as the National Association of Real Estate Boards, or Americans for Democratic Action, will file reports while the State and local adjuncts will not, this despite the fact that legislative operations on the several levels are inseparably meshed. Many other types of nonreporting and partial reporting under the Lobbying Act could be added.

In sum, these reported figures give us a very incomplete picture

QUARTER	NUMBER FILED	ORIGINAL FILINGS[b]	QUARTERLY CON- TRIBUTIONS	QUARTERLY EXPENDITURES
1946: Third	46		$446,049.21	$729,377.81
Fourth	92		1,166,686.41	1,567,903.40
TOTAL	138	99	1,612,735.62	2,297,281.21
1947: First	157		3,724,622.43	1,370,921.92
Second	157		4,563,358.81	2,520,692.48
Third	142		3,066,790.37	1,398,351.77
Fourth	185		3,470,668.65	1,679,930.91
TOTAL	642	152	14,825,440.26	6,969,897.08
1948: First	237		3,334,559.06	1,973,250.85
Second	263		3,469,780.51	1,910,837.41
Third	217		3,920,963.86[a]	1,629,349.06[a]
Fourth	254		7,662,565.59[a]	2,331,231.54[a]
TOTAL	971	146	18,387,869.02	7,844,668.86
1949: First	290		8,896,775.22[a]	2,294,897.38[a]
Second	291		4,541,146.69[a]	2,382,031.63[a]
Third	272		3,162,816.32[a]	2,670,434.60[a]
Fourth	274		3,768,765.84[a]	2,972,307.04[a]
TOTAL	1,127	98	20,369,504.07	10,319,670.65
GRAND TOTAL	2,878	495	55,195,548.97	27,431,517.80

[a] *Includes amounts contributed and expended in previous quarters but not theretofore reported.*
[b] *Groups filing reports for the first time.*

of the realities of lobbying. To accept this picture as complete would be equivalent to saying that no money is gambled on horse races other than that paid through the pari-mutuel windows in the 27 States which have legalized such gambling. If the full truth were ever known, this committee has little doubt that lobbying, in all its ramifications, would prove to be a billion-dollar industry. This figure is not offered in an effort to shock the complacent but as a sober estimate. Consider the costs of letter and telegram campaigns; the thousands of pages of institutional advertising; the purchase and distribution of millions of highly charged books and pamphlets on public issues; the salaries of executives, lawyers, and publicists; the operating budgets of all the thousands of organizations throughout the Nation whose central purpose is to influence what Government does—all of these costs and many more are chargeable to lobbying, whether we like the word or not.

In the same sense that filings under the Lobbying Act grossly understate the number and expenditures of pressure organizations, so too do individual registrations fail to reveal the actual number of persons actively engaged in seeking to influence the governmental process. Over 2,000 persons have registered as lobbyists since 1946, but in many cases these registered lobbyists are merely Washington representatives for national organizations having large, well-paid staffs throughout the country. For example, the CIO national organization has only four registered lobbyists, and the American Medical Association has only seven. Once again Congress and the people are not in full possession of the facts.

Although no exact conclusions are possible as to the number of lobbying organizations and lobbyists, or as to the money which they expend to influence legislation, filings under the Lobbying Act do yield an indication of which groups are mounting the most insistent and well-financed pressure campaigns. This picture varies, of course, from one year to the next, depending somewhat on the issues at stake. In 1949, for example, the American Medical Association led all other registered groups by reporting lobbying expenditures of $1,522,683; but organized business and business-supported groups reported total disbursements of $4,141,480. Of the 35 organizations which reported lobbying expenditures of over $50,000 in 1949, 22 were purely business or trade groups and 2 others derived almost their entire support from corporate or business contributions.

So far as reported expenditures for lobbying are concerned, organized business far outspends other interests. This fact, however understandable, points to a situation which tends to undermine the props on which American thinking about lobbying has traditionally rested. We believe lobbying to be every man's right. But some men are more able to make their rights meaningful than others. In practical terms, this has meant that those interests with the most to spend for protection have proclaimed "lobbying for all men" as an almost sacred article of faith. It is not unlike the elephant shouting "Everybody for himself," as he stomps up and down among the chickens.

The pressure potential of American business is all the more strikingly illustrated by the replies to an inquiry which the committee addressed to approximately 200 corporations, labor unions, and farm groups.

The information contained in these replies is the subject of separate committee reports. The following table is a summary of the corporation respondents' expenditures relating to efforts to influence legislation directly and indirectly during the period January 1, 1947, to May 31, 1950:

NATURE OF EXPENDITURE	NUMBER OF CORPORATIONS LISTING EXPENDITURES	AMOUNT EXPENDED
Travel to Washington	66	$227,256.62
Maintenance of Washington office	7	346,807.65
Distribution of printed matter	65	382,679.77
Printing costs	65	1,811,839.24
Advertising	31	2,013,369.72
Contributions	125	26,941,452.57
Other	37	406,787.27
TOTAL		32,124,835.38

This total dwarfs the $776,466.07 reported under the Lobbying Act by those 37 of the respondents that file reports. The pressure groups continue to receive large contributions, but increasingly the great corporations are mounting their own major lobbying efforts.

MONEY FOR LOBBYING

The late Senator Thaddeus Caraway once stated that 90 percent of the groups represented before Congress were what he called fake organizations, groups which consisted of little more than a letterhead and a promoter busily engaged in lining his own pockets. While this estimate may have been accurate at an earlier time, it is not in accord with the present realities. Soliciting money for lobbying is much more than a device by which a few imaginative opportunists can gull the unwary. Lobbying is an important and usually an honest business, and it is a business which runs on money.

The means by which groups raise funds for lobbying are infinitely varied but there are two general patterns which cover the fund-raising activities of most lobbying organizations. The first might be called "orthodox" solicitation, largely because it conforms to standard practice among the well-established, membership groups. Labor unions, trade or business associations, farm groups, veterans' groups, and professional societies are typical membership groups, that is, groups where membership rests on the basis of occupation, profession, service, or trade. Fund-raising by these organizations is usually simple and straightforward. Membership dues are ordinarily the largest source of funds, and are assessed at the rate of X dollars a year, as they are by most organizations in this category, or they may be assessed according to a standardized sliding scale. The Association of American Railroads, for example, charges dues proportionate to the traffic volume of each member road. Income from subscriptions to house journals and sales of other literature is also a dependable, although usually a modest source of funds.

Frequently, particular legislation demands intensified group effort, and inevitably, more money to sustain it. This is a time for special levies for what the press has called war chests. Thus in 1949, the American Medical Association waged a heavy and generally successful campaign to obtain $25, sometimes not without elements of coercion, from each of its 140,000 members in order to support an all-out drive against national health insurance. This kind of tactic is unusual; most groups approach their members without threats. The National Association of Real Estate Boards, for example, uses its local organizations as collection agencies for its special assessments. In a letter dated December 17, 1948, the association's president-elect wrote to presidents of member boards:

We need to know now if your board will support the Realtors' Washington Committee by sending money or by sending in its pledge immediately in an amount equal to $5 per active member. *How your board raises this money is its own affair.* [Emphasis supplied.][4]

Actually, most groups do not have to use direct pressure in obtaining funds for the group's lobbying activities, for in most cases the members do not have to be sold on the job that the group is doing for them. They believe in the group and they identify themselves with the group's purposes, even though they have taken no great part in formulating them. Most members do not have to be pressured for contributions; they give freely and enthusiastically not only of their money but often of their time and effort as well. Once a group has convinced its members, raising money is fairly simple.

Membership dues form only a small part, if any, of the funds raised by another type of lobbying organization—the "leagues," "foundations," and "committees," which have multiplied so rapidly in the past decade. These groups almost universally profess the loftiest of motives,

[4] [*Housing Lobby,* Hearings, Buchanan Committee.]

THE ROLE OF LOBBIES IN A DEMOCRACY

entirely dissociated from the mundane business of lobbying. They "educate," or "preserve the Constitution," or preach "the fundamentals of the American way of life." In the process, they obtain millions of dollars from sources other than membership dues.

++++

TECHNIQUES OF LOBBYING

Lobbying is as natural to our kind of government as breathing is to the human organism, and it is almost equally complex. Part of this complexity springs from the fact that there are no significant interests in our society—economic, social, or ideological—which do not in one way or another seek something from government. With so many conflicting voices clamoring to be heard, the only means of securing a full hearing has been to constantly find new techniques by which your views can be presented more effectively than your competitor's. The demands of vigorous competition have thus made lobbying an exacting and an ever-evolving profession. The encyclopedia of lobbying practices needs frequent supplements to keep it up to date.

And they had best be cumulative supplements; for while lobbying techniques are continually being streamlined, the old stand bys of pressure tactics are only slowly relinquished. New methods are added but old ones are not dropped. For example, direct contacting of legislators, the critical component of any traditional definition of lobbying, is still a common practice. Individuals and groups very properly seek to apprise legislators directly of their views on public issues. The variations on this old practice are, of course, endless.

Some groups make their views known by letters, telegrams, and phone calls. Others depend largely on personal contact with Members of Congress, and still others think that they can best serve their cause by organizing delegations for marches on the Capitol. The Civil Rights Congress has often used this last approach and has on numerous occasions sponsored mass train trips to Washington for the purpose of what its officers call "speaking on . . . legislation."

Members of Congress are used to being sought out in their offices, in their homes, in the corridors of the office buildings and of the Capitol, in the cloakrooms and restaurants, on the floor of the Chamber itself. They expect and welcome letters, telegrams, and telephone calls from constituents and from those outside their districts as well. In an age where the actions of Congress directly affect the lives of so many, legislators depend on these communications in a very real and immediate way. They are both the pipelines and the lifelines of our kind of representative government.

But such statements and comments are not always as spontaneous, original, or genuine as they appear. Some tend to degrade the right of petition into a solemn-cynical game of blind man's buff, a test of wits between the lobbyist and the legislator. Representative Clarence Brown remarked jocularly during an early hearing that he could smell such inspired pressure letters without opening the envelopes; but it is not always easy to separate the real expression of opinion from the contrived one. Consider, for example, the following letter sent by the National Association of Real Estate Boards to realtors throughout the Nation:

Suggested paragraphs for use in letter to Congressman (Note.—Be sure to change form and ideas into your own words, rearrange, omit some parts, and add personal experiences):

DEAR ————:

We have both heard a lot of complaints about rent control and OPA generally. . . .

Recently I met with some of our good friends, including ———— ————, and we discussed what best should be done to correct the injustices being practiced in the name of controlling rents.

Our decision was to start here in (city) ———— a movement to force the OPA Administrator to allow adjustment in rents of at least 15 percent. This should be done this fall in order to give all of us plenty of time to arrange the adjustments. I am taking this up with (name of friend) ———— of (another city) ———— also and may discuss it with others to see whether we might spread the movement over the country.

Before doing that, however, I want to ask you if you will (sponsor) (support) such an amendment to the price-control law. If you will do so, I will try to get such a movement started in other sections immediately.

Here are some of the reasons why I think this should be done—and they apply only to rents:

(State in your own words some of the "15 facts" which you think will appeal to him most.)

I am asking others of the group to write you about this, and I will telephone you later, as we are anxious to start the movement with your help.

(Signed) ———— ————.[5]

Most other lobby groups also encourage their members to contact Members of Congress on pending legislation, and suggestions on what to say and how to say it are frequently provided. But usually time is too short for detailed planning of this kind. The group that is pressed

[5] [*Ibid.*]

for time can only ask its supporters to make themselves heard. This statement in a letter of June 7, 1948, from Nathan E. Cowan, legislative director of the CIO, to the presidents of all CIO international unions and to State industrial councils, is typical of this approach:

Telegraph or, if possible, telephone your Congressman urging that he be on hand if the bill comes [up] for a vote. Demand that no weakening amendments be added during debate.[6]

The National Association of Real Estate Boards, however, has systematized all means of direct contact between its members and legislators more completely than any other group appearing before this committee. This group conducts letter and telegram campaigns. It also prepares, sometimes on request, specific letters which local members transmit to their Senators and Representatives. The association has developed through its local member boards remarkably extensive lists of congressional "contacts," persons who are expected to wield particular influence with the Representative or Senator from the district or State concerned. There is, among others, a list of "special contacts" for the House Banking and Currency Committee; another for the Senate Banking and Currency Committee; a third for the House Rules Committee; and a fourth which is labeled "Key Senate Phone Contacts." When a pressure campaign reaches the critical stage, when a final ounce of effort may be the margin between success or failure, the "contact" swings into action. The expectation is, of course, that the "contact's" political, business, or personal acquaintance with the Member of Congress—and it is on this basis that he is selected as contact—will enable him to make a decisive impression on the Member's thinking. Six to seven hundred of these contacts make up the membership of what the National Association of Real Estate Boards calls the enlarged committee of the Realtors' Washington Committee, which handles and directs much of the lobbying for the association. Herbert U. Nelson, National Association of Real Estate Boards executive vice president, describes the work of the enlarged committee as follows:

The specific objective and activity of the enlarged committee, when called upon, is to wire or write their Senators or Representatives regarding any critical matters which may arise from time to time that seriously affect the real-estate industry and where quick action is required. Only those who have shown a willingness or desire to render support in this manner, or who are closely acquainted or have personal contact with Members of Congress, have been appointed on the enlarged committee.[7]

[6] [*Ibid.*]   [7] [*Ibid.*]

There is, of course, nothing essentially new in this approach except the degree of careful organization and planning which the National Association of Real Estate Boards applies to it. Every pressure group worthy of the name has recognized since at least 1910 that the sheer volume of letters and wires from home is apt to have some influence on congressional decisions. They have also recognized, however, that volume alone is apt to raise congressional suspicion. Hence, the National Association of Real Estate Board's careful selection of contacts, usually men of substance within their communities, men whose views are likely to command maximum respect. For example in a letter dated April 10, 1947, the executive secretary of the Dayton Real Estate Board wrote to Calvin K. Snyder of the Realtors' Washington Committee:

DEAR MR. SNYDER:

Reference is made to your letter of April 3, 1947, relative to realtors in Dayton who might carry weight with Senator Taft.

Some of these are as follows:

Sidney Eisenberger, prominent in town, has entree with Taft. Address: 729 Grand Avenue, Dayton 6, Ohio.

Ernest Steiner, former State senator, prominent Republican, Shriner, realtor, 607 Winters Building, Dayton 2, Ohio.

Allen Becher, well known realtor; experienced in legislative matters, 1107 U. B. Building, Dayton 2, Ohio.

Paul Schenck; real estate board president; president of the board of education, 709 Gas and Electric Building, Dayton 2, Ohio.

Please let this office know whenever we may be of service to your committee.

Sincerely yours,
THE DAYTON REAL ESTATE BOARD,
James J. Spatz, *Executive Secretary*.[8]

The following letter to Lee F. Johnson, executive vice president of the National Housing Conference, from a Florida member shows that other groups also operate on much the same basis:

THE HOUSING AUTHORITY OF THE CITY OF LAKELAND,
Lakeland, Fla., June 21, 1949.

Mr. LEE F. JOHNSON,
Executive vice president, National Housing Conference, Inc.,
Washington, D.C.

DEAR MR. JOHNSON:

You will be interested to know that I have secured strong telegrams each of which was addressed to Hon. J. Hardin Peterson, Congressman from [the] First Florida District urging him to support H. R. 4009. As I told you in Wash-

8 [*Ibid.*]

ington when there a few weeks ago I had the assurance of Congressman Peterson that he would support this measure but just wanted him to know that the leading citizens of Lakeland, his home town, were in favor of this measure. For your information I am giving you the names of the people sending telegrams as well as their vocation and avocation.

E. B. (Smokie) Sutton, mayor commissioner, city of Lakeland, general contractor.

George J. Tolson, commissioner, city of Lakeland, railroad union leader.

L. Guerry Dobbins, commissioner, city of Lakeland, gasoline and oil dealer.

C. V. McClurg, president, Peoples Savings Bank, large property owner and civic leader.

J. W. Cordell, president, Florida National Bank.

Thomas W. Bryant, attorney and large property owner, Florida State representative (former).

Judge A. R. Carver, attorney, large property owner and civic leader.

Fred T. Benford, merchant, director, First Federal Savings & Loan.

Homer E. Hooks, president, junior chamber [of] commerce, advertising executive.

Levie D. Smith, president, Lakeland Chamber of Commerce; past president, Lakeland Board Realtors, realtor and property owner.

Tom B. Marler, president, Lakeland Board Realtors, realtor and civic leader.

Dr. Herman Watson, outstanding physician and surgeon, owner, Watson Clinic, large property owner.

John Templin, lumberman, general contractor and builder, director, chamber of commerce.

I feel that these 12 men are probably the most outstanding men in Lakeland and each of them is definitely in favor of slum clearance and additional public housing for Lakeland.

I trust this information will be of some value to you and with very best wishes, I am,

Cordially yours,
Earle M. Willis.[9]

Such support for any measure could understandably exert some influence. Quality as well as quantity pays in pressure politics.

In the days when lobbying meant little more than unabashed bribery, committees of Congress were the favorite focus of the old lobby barons. Then as now, crucial decisions were made in committee, and men having entree to them could quietly make the necessary arrangements. The committees are even more important in the modern legislative process, but with the institution in 1911 of open hearings on all major legislation the possibilities of easy influence diminished. The lobbyist who appears formally before committees today is generally obliged to argue on the merits. Despite public scrutiny and the watch-

[9] [*Ibid.*]

fulness of competitors, however, some misrepresentation is still possible. In a letter dated January 17, 1949, to Herbert U. Nelson, of the National Association of Real Estate Boards, Art Barrett of Detroit had an interesting suggestion along these lines:

My thinking is simply this: I believe our case opposing the extension of rent control would be helped tremendously if we could parade in a few small property owners from around the country, a little bedraggled and run-down-at-the-heels-looking, who could get their story over to Congress that the small man who owns a little property is taking one hell of a beating. . . .[10]

This sort of stagecraft fully developed could turn the congressional process into a masquerade ball.

Although the techniques of direct contact with Members and committees are as old as lobbying itself, they can still be of service to the modern pressure group in the presentation of its point of view. New twists have to be added to keep the old methods useful, but they continue to be of importance in the over-all lobbying picture. Not only do these techniques allow groups and individuals to present their views but they also provide the means by which valuable and perhaps otherwise unavailable information can be brought to the Congress' attention. This intelligence function of lobbying is likewise not new, but it does assume special importance in an era of complex and wide-ranging legislation. The pressure group is, of course, quite likely to exaggerate its research and informational activities. The National Association of Manufacturers typically maintains, for instance, that at least 80 percent of its operations are of this character. Although such claims bear close scrutiny, it is nevertheless true that most well-established pressure bodies take their informational work quite seriously.

Facts are seldom presented for their own sake, or without having been carefully selected for maximum impact. But where a full hearing is available for all interested groups, we can rely on competitive watchfulness and public scrutiny as partial safeguards against misrepresentation of the facts by any one group.

The service function in lobbying takes many different forms. When representatives of organized groups appear before committees of Congress, for example, they are not only presenting their own case but they are also providing Members of Congress with one of the essential raw materials of legislative action. By the same token, the drafting of bills and amendments to bills, the preparation of speeches and other materials for Members, the submission to Members of detailed memoranda on bill-handling tactics—all of these are means by which lobby

[10] [*Ibid.*]

groups service the legislative process and at the same time further their own ends.

In addition to these services rendered to Members of Congress in their official capacities, lobbying organizations often perform favors of a more personal sort. Three generations ago, when standards of congressional morality were less exacting than they are today, the lobbyist could favor the Member in ways which strike the modern mind as crude. The lobbyist of the 1880's was a bountiful host, a social guide, a financial confidant, and a free-handed companion at the gaming table. But times change, and, while the theme of personal attentiveness still runs through modern pressure tactics, the forms which it takes have changed. Formal dinners for Members of Congress and, in addition to these, more casual and intimate gatherings, remain part of the lobby group's stock in trade. But apart from these vestiges of the old "social lobby," the personal service aspects of lobbying have been considerably revamped. Today, the resourceful pressure group may seek to serve themselves as well as Members of Congress by arranging remunerative speaking or writing engagements for them, or by such friendly acts as helping the new Member to secure housing in Washington.

The relationships between Members of Congress and groups interested in legislation are infinitely varied. Many Members have spoken before such groups, frequently for no remuneration whatsoever. In other cases, Members have arranged for groups to reproduce their writings on public issues. One Member, for example, has regularly written a weekly Washington column which has been distributed by a group filing reports under the Lobbying Act. He has received no pay for this writing, but he has received "research expenses" which have ranged from $250 to $500 per month. Obviously, those groups which cannot work on equally close terms with Members are left at a considerable disadvantage.

There is a final long-standing lobbying technique which, without any modernization at all, has become increasingly prevalent during the past 40 years. We refer to the use of the franking privilege for mass mailings of printed matter.

It is unlawful for Congressmen or Government officials to lend the frank or "permit its use by any committee, organization, or association. . . . " Furthermore the Criminal Code provides for a fine of $300 in the case of any person who "makes use of any official envelope . . . to avoid the payment of postage. . . ." Yet the Committee for Constitutional Government obtains mass distribution of various materials through the use of congressional franks in the following manner.

A Member inserts in the Congressional Record an article or speech that may or may not have been furnished him by the committee. It is reproduced by the Government Printing Office much less expensively than at commercial rates. The printing is paid for by the Member, who in turn is reimbursed by E. A. Rumely's group. The matter is mailed in bulk, sometimes already stuffed and sealed in franked envelopes, to the Committee for Constitutional Government in New York, where it is stored. At the moment deemed most timely and convenient for the committee, the individual envelopes are addressed and mailed postage-free under the congressional frank.

Some Members have not used their best judgment in allowing the employment of their frank by lobbying organizations. We think that franked mailings to a Member's constituency, by himself and for himself, are useful and entirely proper. But some Members in allowing the extraordinary if not indiscriminate use of their frank by lobby groups, have failed to abide by this or any comparable standard. When one organization, the Committee for Constitutional Government, admits to having distributed 8 to 10 million franked releases in the past 4 years, it is assuming a privileged status to which it is not entitled. The frank is not properly used as a veiled subsidy to any group, whatever its views may be. Close to 2½ million pieces of franked material of one Member of Congress were obtained by this one organization alone in a single year for distribution postage-free at the taxpayers' expense. This same organization publicly advocates Government economy.

THE LOBBYING ACT OF 1946

DOCUMENT 14 THE LAW AND ITS LOOPHOLES

In 1946, as part of a general attempt to reorganize its activities, Congress enacted the Lobbying Act. This measure was based on the "exposure" principle (Document 9 suggested another application of this technique) rather than on any positive effort to regulate pressure groups; legislators felt that public exposure of the whole pressure process would enable the people to be aware of any disequilibrium that might develop and to retaliate massively. In short, if it became apparent that the trade unions or the National Association of Manufacturers were employing outrageous pressure tactics, the American people's sense of fair play would be aroused, and the culprit would be punished in the "court of public opinion."

Since that time a large mass of data has accumulated in the offices of the Congressional clerks, but loopholes in the Lobbying Act make most of it valueless. In the 1870's, lobbyists used to come to Washington with a carpetbag full of currency and engage in simple bribery, but this sort of knavery has long since been relegated to the outer margins of politics. However, a lobby may report $5,000 as an expense for a dinner party for concerned Senators, for example, but it may not report a multimillion-dollar public relations campaign that pressed its position on the public without being "directly" calculated (as the Act has been interpreted) to influence the course of legislation. In addition, there is no special provision for enforcement of the Act. The Clerk of the House and the Secretary of the Senate file the reports without verification of their contents, and only in extraordinary cases (perhaps initiated by a remark in Drew Pearson's caustic column in the Washington Post) is there any further investigation of their veracity. In short, the fact that most pressure groups have dutifully registered their "legislative representatives" and provided a précis of their expense accounts does not—as George B. Galloway points out in this selection—tell the full story.

I. *LEGISLATIVE HISTORY*
OF THE FEDERAL LOBBYING ACT

The Lobbying Act was enacted as title III of the Legislative Reorganization Act of 1946, which was reported to Congress by the Joint Committee on the Organization of Congress. The Senate and House reports accompanying the bill were identical with respect to title III. Both declared that the Lobbying Act applies

chiefly to three distinct classes of so-called lobbyists:

First: Those who do not visit the Capitol but initiate propaganda from all over the country, in the form of letters and telegrams, many of which have been based entirely upon misinformation as to facts. This class of persons and organizations will be required, under the title, not to cease or curtail their activities in any respect, but merely to disclose the sources of their collections and methods [by] which they are disbursed.

Second: The second class of lobbyists are those who are employed to come to the Capitol under the false impression that they exert some powerful influence over Members of Congress. These individuals spend their time in Washington presumably exerting some mysterious influence with respect to the legislation in which their employers are interested, but carefully conceal from Members of Congress whom they happen to contact the purpose of their presence. The title in no wise prohibits or curtails their activities. It merely requires that they shall register and disclose the sources and purposes of their employment and the amount of their compensation.

Third: There is a third class of entirely honest and respectable representatives of business, professional, and philanthropic organizations who come to Washington openly and frankly to express their views for or against legislation, many of whom serve a useful and perfectly legitimate purpose in expressing the views and interpretations of their employers with respect to legislation which concerns them. They will likewise be required to register and state their compensation and the sources of their employment. . . .[1]

Both the Senate and House reports accompanying the bill state that the act ". . . does not apply to organizations formed for other purposes whose efforts to influence legislation are merely incidental to the purposes for which formed."[2] . . . In the Senate discussion preceding enactment, Senator Hawkes asked Senator La Follette, chairman of the joint committee in charge of the bill, for an explanation of the

FROM: "A Report on the Operation of Title III of the Legislative Reorganization Act of 1946," George B. Galloway, *Final Report,* Special Committee to Investigate Political Activities, Lobbying and Campaign Contributions, Senate Report Number 395, Eighty-Fifth Congress, First Session (Washington, D.C., Government Printing Office, 1957), pp. 189–200.

[1] [Senate Report 1400, Seventy-Ninth Congress, Second Session.]
[2] [*Ibid.*]

THE LOBBYING ACT OF 1946

"principal purpose" requirement. In particular, Senator Hawkes sought assurance that multipurposed organizations like the United States Chamber of Commerce would not be subject to the act. Senator La Follette refused to give such assurance, stating:

So far as any organizations or individuals are concerned, I will say to the Senator from New Jersey, it will depend on the type and character of activity which they undertake, . . . I cannot tell the Senator whether they will come under the act. It will depend on the type of activity in which they engage, so far as legislation is concerned. . . . *It* [the act] *affects all individuals and organizations alike if they engage in a covered activity.* [Italics added by Galloway.] . . .[3]

II. *THE EXTENT OF LOBBYING*

The Federal Regulation of Lobbying Act provides in section 308 (a) that

any person who shall engage himself for pay or for any consideration for the purpose of attempting to influence the passage or defeat of any legislation by the Congress of the United States shall, before doing anything in furtherance of such object, register with the Clerk of the House of Representatives and the Secretary of the Senate. . . .

Section 308 (b) provides that all information required to be filed with the Clerk of the House and Secretary of the Senate shall be compiled by them, acting jointly, and shall be printed in the Congressional Record. Their quarterly report of the registrations have been published in the Congressional Record for 10 years, beginning with the issue of January 3, 1947. A weekly listing of lobby registrations is presented by Congressional Quarterly News Features in the section on "Pressures on Congress" of its Weekly Report, and summary tabulations in its annual Almanac.

From the effective date of the lobby law down through July 30, 1956, 4,382 persons and organizations registered as lobbyists. Exclusive of duplications, total registrations over this period down through July 27, 1956, were 3,273. Of this total, 2,794 registrants were individuals, 147 were law and public-relations firms, and 332 were classified as organizations.

1947 was the peak year when there were 731 registrations. 1952 marked the lowest record when only 204 lobbyists registered. These figures represent many duplications of individuals and groups who have registered more than once over the decade. The annual figures, as compiled by Congressional Quarterly, are as follows:

[3] [*Congressional Record.*]

YEAR	NUMBER
1946 (last 4 months)	222
1947	731
1948	447
1949	599
1950	430
1951	342
1952	204
1953	296
1954	413
1955	383
1956 (through July 30)	315
TOTAL	4,382

An analysis of registrations during the 80th Congress, the first full Congress during which the lobby law was in operation, was made by the Legislative Reference Service. This analysis classified the registrations by type of organization. Of the 25 types of organization, it was found that 667 registered during 1947, and 725 during 1948, compared with more than 1,800 organizations that maintained Washington offices at that time.

Of the 315 additions to the lobby lists during the second session of the 84th Congress, 191 were new registrants who had not filed before. Of the 191, 131 were individuals, 19 were law and public relations firms, and 41 were organizations.

Congressional Quarterly breaks down its compilation of lobby registrations into eight group categories: business, farm, labor, professional, veterans and military, citizen groups, foreign groups, and individuals. According to this classification the 329 persons and organizations that registered under the lobby law during the first session of the 84th Congress, through August 2, 1955, represented the following groups:

REGISTRATIONS DURING 1955, CLASSIFIED BY GROUPS

Business	199	Veterans, etc.	5
Farm	19	Citizens	27
Labor	20	Foreign	11
Professional	5	Individuals	43
		TOTAL	329

These figures show that 60 percent of the registrants during 1955 were lobbyists for business groups.

REGISTRATIONS DURING 80TH CONGRESS, CLASSIFIED BY THE TYPE OF ORGANIZATION

TYPE OF ORGANIZATION	TOTAL NUMBER OF ORGANIZATIONS	NUMBER ACTUALLY REGISTERING	
		1947	1948
Agriculture	51	31	26
Business: General	78	29	39
Citizen organizations:			
Civil and political	115	53	57
Economic	38	9	7
Education	34	7	10
Financial	49	24	22
Food and beverage	96	44	48
Health	28	3	6
International	58	10	14
Labor:			
Government employees	30	21	18
Private	104	54	49
Lumber and forest products	30	10	7
Official (governmental)	113	8	14
Oil, gas, and metal products	107	46	57
Power and communications	41	22	23
Printing and publishing	34	6	8
Professional	117	14	12
Real estate: Building and construction	45	14	12
Religious	42	10	10
Tax groups	42	23	30
Textiles and apparel	34	15	12
Trade groups: Miscellaneous	129	56	61
Transportation:			
Air	17	5	10
Highways	34	8	14
Rail	96	60	57
Water	30	12	20
Veterans and military	53	21	22
Welfare	28	16	15
Women's organizations	30	14	13
Individuals	107	22	31
TOTAL	1,807	667	725

No exact conclusions can be reached as to the actual number of lobbyists and lobbying organizations. Probably there are many more lobbyists than the registration lists reveal. As the Buchanan committee remarked, "filings under the Lobbying Act grossly understate the number and expenditures of pressure organizations; so too do individual registrations fail to reveal the actual number of persons actively engaged in seeking to influence the governmental process."[4] . . .

III. *THE COST OF LOBBYING*

In accordance with the Federal Regulation of Lobbying Act of 1946, all groups whose principal purpose is to influence legislation are required to register and file quarterly reports of their receipts and expenditures with the Clerk of the House of Representatives. Analysis of these quarterly reports for the first 4 years of the act's operation showed a grand total of $71.8 million in contributions and $34 million in reported expenditures. . . . In response to a Buchanan committee questionnaire, 173 large corporations reported that they had spent $32.1 million over a 3½-year period for lobbying activities. . . . "These figures," remarked Chairman Buchanan, "reflect a significant picture of tremendous amounts of time and money being expended by pressure groups and pressure interests throughout the country in seeking to influence actions by Congress." Many groups submit only fragmentary reports of their expenditures and many others do not report at all. "If the full truth were ever known," said the committee in its general interim report, "this committee has little doubt that lobbying, in all its ramifications, would prove to be a billion-dollar industry."[5]

In its catalog of costs the Buchanan committee included "the costs of letter and telegram campaigns; the thousands of pages of institutional advertising; the purchase and distribution of millions of highly charged books and pamphlets on public issues; the salaries of executives, lawyers, and publicists; the operating budgets of all the thousands of organizations throughout the Nation whose central purpose is to influence what Government does. . . ."[6] An added economic cost of lobbying is money spent by political interest groups in the form of campaign contributions to the major political parties, as well as in the form of grassroots propaganda.

Money for lobbying is raised or derived from membership dues, special assessments for particular legislative programs, and large con-

4 [*General Interim Report,* 1950.]
5 [*Ibid.*]   6 [*Ibid.*]

tributions. The latter source has been especially relied upon to finance the circulation of literature bearing on public issues. For example, the Committee for Constitutional Government accepts contributions of $490 or less for the distribution of books and pamphlets. Over a 7-year period this committee distributed 82 million booklets and other items of literature designed to influence legislation, much of it under congressional franks. . . .

The lobby-spending picture varies from year to year and from group to group, depending on the issues at stake. An analysis of spending by categories shows that business accounts for by far the largest amount spent. For example, a Congressional Quarterly compilation of the financial reports of 225 organizations in 1954 showed the following expenditure breakdown:

TYPE OF GROUP	REPORTING	AMOUNT SPENT
Business	132	$2,289,538.71
Labor	21	656,149.09
Citizens	38	615,582.61
Farm	14	411,629.27
Professional	15	195,437.46
Military and veterans	5	117,821.09
TOTAL	225	4,286,158.23

Source: *Congressional Quarterly Almanac, 1955, p. 679.*

Total lobby spending over the past decade has been computed by Congressional Quarterly on an annual basis as follows:

YEAR	AMOUNT	YEAR	AMOUNT
1947	$5,191,856	1953	4,445,841
1948	6,763,480	1954	4,286,158
1949	7,969,710	1955	4,365,843
1950	10,505,204	1956	3,787,734
1951	8,771,097		
1952	4,823,981	TOTAL	60,708,904

Source: *Congressional Quarterly Weekly Report, vol. XV, No. 10, March 8, 1957, p. 309.*

It will be seen from the above table that 1950 was the peak year, and that the 1956 figure was the lowest since the passage of the lobby law. The apparent downward trend of recent years is attributed to changes in methods of reporting lobby expenditures since the Supreme

Court decision in the *Harriss* case narrowed the legal definition of lobbying. It seems safe to say that the amounts actually spent by all individuals and organizations seeking to influence legislation are considerably in excess of the reported totals. Uncertainty concerning the coverage provisions of the lobby law has given rise to a wide variety of methods of reporting receipts and expenditures.

The itemized expenditures given in the reports are for public relations, wages, salaries, fees, printing, office overhead, telephone and telegraph, travel, food, lodging, entertainment, etc. By far the largest single item is wages, salaries, fees, etc.

The number of lobbies spending considerable amounts and the 10 lobbies which reportedly have spent the most in influencing legislation since 1950 are [represented in the following charts.]

In 1951, 23 groups reported spending more than $100,000:

LOBBY	AMOUNT SPENT, 1951[a]
1. American Farm Bureau Federation	$878,813.14[b]
2. Committee for Constitutional Government	773,957.59[c]
3. American Medical Association	450,372.57
4. National Association of Electric Companies	434,325.91[b]
5. National Association for Advancement of Colored People	335,591.49[b]
6. Trucking Industry National Defense Committee	249,882.56
7. Association of American Railroads	237,809.89
8. United World Federalists	207,285.82[c]
9. The Proprietary Association	193,805.97[b]
10. National Milk Producers Federation	185,315.78[b]

[a] *Congressional Quarterly Almanac, vol. VIII, 1952, p. 432.*
[b] *All purposes, including legislative.*
[c] *Said only "part" of this sum was legislative.*

In 1952, 24 groups reported spending more than $50,000:

LOBBY	AMOUNT SPENT, 1952[a]
1. National Association of Electric Companies	$477,941.74
2. American Medical Association	309,514.93
3. Association of American Railroads	235,977.74
4. National Milk Producers Federation	219,837.26
5. National Association of Real Estate Boards	127,893.65
6. Colorado River Association	111,538.15
7. National Economic Council, Inc.	106,464.66
8. The American Legion, national headquarters	106,235.09
9. American Federation of Labor	105,537.20
10. National Federation of Post Office Clerks	97,869.16

[a] *Congressional Quarterly Almanac, vol. IX, 1953, p. 579.*

In 1953, 20 groups reported spending more than $50,000:

LOBBY	AMOUNT SPENT, 1953[a]
1. National Association of Electric Companies	$547,789.32
2. Association of American Railroads	235,727.73
3. National Milk Producers Federation	233,557.84
4. American Federation of Labor	123,608.43
5. National Association of Real Estate Boards	122,368.46
6. National Economic Council, Inc.	116,477.90
7. American Medical Association	106,624.90
8. Southern States Industrial Council	105,106.65
9. American Farm Bureau Federation	102,403.06
10. Chamber of Commerce, United States	90,988.05

[a] *Congressional Quarterly Almanac, vol. X, 1954, p. 673.*
[b] *Amount for 3 quarters only.*

In 1954, 23 lobby groups reported spending more than $50,000:

LOBBY	AMOUNT SPENT, 1954[a]
1. National Milk Producers Federation	$185,496.13
2. Association of American Railroads	185,379.55
3. National Federation of Post Office Clerks	146,012.75
4. American Federation of Labor	125,996.16
5. Congress of Industrial Organizations	120,119.09
6. American Farm Bureau Federation	112,408.00
7. National Association of Electric Companies	110,537.14
8. Southern States Industrial Council	99,805.88
9. Farmers Educational and Cooperative Union of America	85,762.49
10. National Rural Electric Cooperative Association	83,325.92

[a] *Congressional Quarterly Almanac, vol. XI, 1955, p. 679.*

In 1955, 26 lobby groups reported spending more than $50,000:

LOBBY	AMOUNT SPENT, 1955[a]
1. National Association of Electric Companies	$114,835.55
2. American Federation of Labor	114,079.74
3. American Farm Bureau Federation	113,610.00
4. Congress of Industrial Organizations	111,787.50
5. Association of American Railroads	104,806.26
6. Southern States Industrial Council	100,244.64
7. United States-Cuban Sugar Council	99,275.70
8. National Association of Real Estate Boards	93,801.89[b]
9. American Legion	91,794.18
10. National Federation of Post Office Clerks	90,551.68

[a] *Congressional Quarterly Weekly Report, vol. XIV, No. 6, Feb. 10, 1956,*
p. 137.
[b] *3 quarters' spending only.*

In 1956, 18 lobby groups reported spending more than $50,000:

LOBBY	AMOUNT SPENT, 1956[a]
1. AFL-CIO	$145,181.91
2. Association of American Railroads	124,585.00
3. American Farm Bureau Federation	115,507.00
4. Southern States Industrial Council	104,104.85
5. National Farmers Union, Farmers Educational and Cooperative Union of America	86,212.94
6. American Trucking Associations, Inc.	85,918.47
7. National Federation of Post Office Clerks	85,849.63
8. U.S. Savings and Loan League	76,122.11
9. National Housing Conference	68,268.04
10. American Legion	64,703.56[b]

[a] *Congressional Quarterly Weekly Report, vol. XV, No. 10, Mar. 8, 1957, p. 311.*
[b] *3 quarters' spending only.*

IV. *ALLEGED DEFECTS OF LOBBY LAW*

✦✦✦✦

Writers in the law reviews and learned journals assert that the lobby law has disclosed certain weaknesses in its operation. According to the critics of the act, experience under it indicates that it is defective as to—

1. Coverage.
2. Information required.
3. Publicity given.
4. Administration.
5. Enforcement.

As to coverage, it is alleged (a) that use of the words "principal" and "principally" in section 307 is subject to various interpretations and has restricted the persons to whom the act applies; and (b) that the act does not require the registration of lobbying before Federal executive departments and agencies, whose administrative decisions and interpretations may have wide repercussions.

As to information required, the act fails to require (what the La Follette-Monroney Committee recommended) that registration statements include information as to the size of groups that lobbyists claim to represent, how the membership decides its lobbying policy, and by what right the lobbyist speaks for the group.

As to publicity, critics say that inadequate publicity is given by the act to pressure group activities; that quarterly publication of certain information in the Congressional Record is too limited; and that financial statements, containing most important information, are not even given the limited circulation of the Record.

As to administration, it is said that the registration statements are filed upon receipt but are not analyzed. Neither the Clerk of the House nor the Secretary of the Senate has the administrative facilities to analyze relevant information submitted under the lobby law, make pertinent abstracts from it, adopt an efficient classification and indexing system, or tabulate and summarize the information filed by registrants.

As to enforcement, the act makes no provision for a special enforcement agency to investigate the accuracy of the statements filed and the compliance of those to whom the act applies. The Department of Justice, which enforces the criminal provisions, is in a different branch of the Government and its facilities for investigation are already overtaxed. And no appropriation is made specifically for enforcement of the act.

V. PROPOSED CHANGES IN LOBBY LAW

The La Follette-Monroney Committee was led by testimony it heard, as well as by its own independent studies, to believe that the registration of the representatives of organized groups would "enable Congress better to evaluate and determine evidence, data, or communications from organized groups seeking to influence legislation action" and thus avoid the distortion of public opinion. The joint committee believed that inclusion of a lobby title in the Legislative Reorganization Act would strengthen the Congress by "enabling it better to meet its responsibilities under the Constitution." To turn the spotlight of publicity on lobbying activities and expenditures would be a big step forward, they felt. After the lobby law had been in operation for a few years, it was hoped that experience would reveal any defects which could be corrected by amending and strengthening the act. . . .

How should the lobby law be amended so as to correct the weaknesses revealed by its operation? A variety of answers has been given to this question in the discussions of the past decade.

As to coverage, it has been suggested that the act be amended:

a. By eliminating the words "principally to aid, or the principal purpose of which person is to aid" in section 307. If the object of the act is to publicize efforts to influence legislation, it is argued, then all substantial efforts should be publicized, regardless of whether they are the "principal" activity of an individual or an organization or the "principal" purpose of contributions.

b. By including all organizations which spend more than a specified sum—say $1,000—to influence legislation. Smaller expenditures, it is argued, do not justify the effort of reporting or of enforcing the act. The law is not concerned with trifles.

c. By including within the law all those subject to the narrow provisions of the Corrupt Practices Act, instead of exempting them as the present act does. . . .

d. By making the act broad enough to cover all organizations which mold public opinion in any way, directly or indirectly, and by givng the enforcement agency authority to exempt those which it finds to be outside the pressure group category, e.g., genuine educational societies. This would extend the coverage of the act to include "lobbying at the grassroots" by local branches of national organizations which seek to influence legislation indirectly.

e. By requiring the registration of all persons who lobby before ex-executive departments and agencies. Most observers are agreed that efforts to influence administrative policies and decisions should be included in the coverage of the Lobby Act. This requirement might help to restrain the activities of the "5-percenters" and others who have been the subject of congressional investigations.

As to information required, it has been suggested that the act be amended:

By requiring registration statements to include data on the bona fide membership of an organization and the methods of determining its stand on legislation. Such a requirement would enable Congress and the public to judge the character of a group and would help to expose "fake lobbies."

As to publicity, it has been suggested that the acts be amended:

a. By making it absolutely clear that the public and press may inspect all lobby registrations and reports at any time within 3 days after they are filed; that inspection of such documents means they can be studied, and copied, in part or in full, and that the information obtained may be published as desired.

b. By providing for the quickest and widest possible circulation in a simplified and intelligible form of the information revealed on registration statements and financial reports, including distribution to press and radio services. Information compiled from reports of expenditures, now published quarterly in the Congressional Record, often comes too late to spotlight attempts to sway Congress on pending legislation. If registrations could be publicized at weekly or monthly intervals, as is the practice in some States, the identity, backing, and objectives of lobbyists could be known soon after their activities begin.

As to administration and enforcement, it has been suggested that the act be amended:

a. By establishing a special enforcement agency in the Department of Justice with power to suspend or revoke lobbyists' certificates of registration, to hold hearings on complaints, to investigate the accuracy of statements filed and report violations of the law, to examine periodically the administration of the law, and to recommend revisions. Alternatively, the administration of the act could be entrusted to an independent agency in the legislative branch of the Government, modeled on the General Accounting Office.

b. By creating a standing joint congressional committee to supervise the work of this enforcement agency.

✦✦✦✦

VI. SUMMARY

Although there had been several previous attempts to regulate lobbying by Federal law, the Federal Lobbying Act of 1946 was the first measure of its kind to be enacted. It was adopted as title III of the Legislative Reorganization Act of that year. Not the immediate result of a congressional investigation of lobbying activities, it followed a recommendation in the final report of the La Follette-Monroney committee. It was only briefly debated and not amended on the floor, but its passage represented congressional recognition of a longstanding need for legislation on the subject.

Despite incomplete data the registration statements and financial reports filed under the lobby law reveal that lobbying in recent years has become more extensive and expensive than at any other time in our history. Issues of price control, public housing and rent control, labor regulation, natural-gas regulation, and many others have been the subjects of intensive pressure campaigns in the past decade. As of July 30, 1956, a total of 4,382 persons and groups had registered under the lobby law; their reports showed that they had spent almost $60 million since the law's enactment. However, many groups have submitted only fragmentary reports, and many others have not reported at all, taking the position that they are exempted by the "principal purpose" clause of the act, or that their agent's registration relieved them of the responsibility of reporting.

Many types of pressure, both direct and indirect, are brought to bear upon the legislative and executive branches of the National Government in an effort to influence governmental decisions. They include both direct communication with Congress and executive departments and "lobbying at the grassroots" with a view to influencing public opinion and through it legislative and administrative action. The modern techniques of interest groups in the legislative process include direct contact with legislators, avalanches of letters and telegrams, group alliances and logrolling, the use of committees and committee hearings, congressional investigations, pamphleteering, editorial advertising, etc.

The constitutionality of the lobby law has been challenged in the courts, but in the latest of a series of court decisions, on June 7, 1954, the United States Supreme Court, by a 5-to-3 vote, upheld the key registration and coverage provisions of the Lobbying Act. This decision came in the case of the *United States* v. *Harriss* (347 U.S. 612), in which the controversial penalty provisions of the act were not at issue.

While the 1946 lobby law was regarded as a step in the right direction, its vague and ambiguous language has given rise to many interpretive difficulties stressed in the court decisions. The defects in the act have in turn stimulated many proposed changes to meet the standards for a criminal statute. The basic aim of the act is to publicize lobbying activities so that Congress can identify these pressures and be guided thereby in making its decisions. But the act has failed to achieve this basic purpose because the information reported by lobbyists is not analyzed and evaluated in a systematic manner so that it can be effectively utilized. The general consensus seems to be that Congress should amend or replace the present act with a workable law administered by an independent agency and effectively enforced by the Department of Justice.

THE CASE HISTORY
OF A LOBBY

THE HARRIS–
FULBRIGHT
NATURAL GAS ACT

This case history is a classic instance of a lobby overplaying its extremely strong hand. The natural gas producers began their fight against regulation by the Federal Power Commission in the 1940's. The FPC had held that the interstate activities of the gas companies fell within Commission jurisdiction, notably with regard to rate regulation. The gas lobby went to work and succeeded in blocking President Truman's reappointment of FPC Chairman Leland Olds by trumping up fictitious charges of pro-Communism; subsequently the FPC reversed its previous decision and excluded the companies from regulatory coverage of their distributive activities.

At this point, tremendous urban pressure built up, particularly in the Midwest, to prevent the companies from escaping the scope of regulation; the mayors of large cities and urban Senators and Congressmen protested the "giveaway," and the state of Wisconsin took the matter to the federal courts. After prolonged litigation, the Supreme Court overruled the Federal Power Commission; the Justices informed that reluctant body of regulators that the gas lines were subject to its authority. Only an act of Congress could save the companies, and they now devoted their attention to that forum. The Harris-Fulbright bill (sponsored by two distinguished Democratic members of the "conservative coalition") would have exempted the gas producers once again from FPC authority and allowed them to raise rates.

After heavy debate in both Houses, where liberals fought the proposal with great vigor, the bill passed and was sent to the White House. President Eisenhower had previously stated his approval, and the issue seemed closed. But suddenly in the Senate a quiet, inconspicuous man, Senator Case of South Dakota—who had favored the bill—arose in fury and announced that the gas interests had tried to bribe him. The gas lobby snatched defeat from the jaws of victory: President Eisenhower refused to sign the legislation, and a Senate *investigation was launched which turned up the following information on the work of the natural gas lobby.*

ACTIVITIES TO INFLUENCE HARRIS-FULBRIGHT BILL TO AMEND NATURAL GAS ACT

The Harris-Fulbright bill to amend the Natural Gas Act . . . was undoubtedly one of the most controversial pieces of legislation in recent years. The bill was passed by both Houses of Congress but vetoed by President Eisenhower.

It will be helpful to our discussion to refer briefly to the background of the Harris-Fulbright bill.

On June 7, 1954, the Supreme Court rendered its decision in *Phillips* v. *Wisconsin* (347 U.S. 673), by which it held that natural gas producers were subject to regulation by the Federal Power Commission under the Natural Gas Act. The decision had a profound effect on the oil and gas industry. There was, first, the natural reluctance of any industry to be regulated; second, the fear that regulation of gas producers might lead to regulation of the oil and other industries.

The chief object of the Harris-Fulbright bill was to exempt natural gas producers from regulation by the Federal Power Commission under the Natural Gas Act . . . . In vetoing the bill, the President stated that he was "in accord with its basic objectives" but felt impelled to impose the veto because of certain activities described by him thus:

Since the passage of this bill a body of evidence has accumulated indicating that private persons, apparently representing only a very small segment of a great and vital industry, have been seeking to further their own interests by highly questionable activities. These include efforts that I deem to be so arrogant and so much in defiance of acceptable standards of propriety as to risk creating doubt among the American people concerning the integrity of governmental processes.

Legally constituted agencies of Government are now engaged in investigating this situation. These investigations cannot be concluded before the expiration of the 10-day period within which the President must act upon the legislation under the Constitution.

I believe I would not be discharging my own duty were I to approve this legislation before the activities in question have been fully investigated by

FROM: *Final Report,* Special Committee to Investigate Political Activities, Lobbying and Campaign Contributions, Senate Report Number 395, Eighty-Fifth Congress, First Session (Washington, D.C., Government Printing Office, 1957), pp. 9–17, 57–58.

the Congress and the Department of Justice. To do so under such conditions could well create long-term apprehension in the minds of the American people. It would be a disservice both to the people and to their Congress. Accordingly, I return H. R. 6645 without my approval.

In view of the President's statements in his veto message, the committee specifically asked the President of the United States, the Director of the Bureau of the Budget, and the Attorney General for any facts or information in their possession concerning the subjects the committee was created to investigate. No evidence was made available to the committee by the executive branch of the Government.

The first inquiry was directed to the Director of the Bureau of the Budget. The Director of the Bureau replied that he had no information as to what facts were known to the President prior to the veto message, other than what had already been made public through the press and radio. Upon receipt of the reply of the Budget Bureau, the committee addressed a letter inquiry to the President, asking that the body of evidence referred to in the veto message be made available to the committee. The Assistant to the President, Sherman Adams, replied for the President. Mr. Adams stated that the President had—

reached his decision on the bill after considering information of questionable activities which came to him through many channels. All of this information was turned over to the Department of Justice . . . any request concerning this matter should be made to the Department of Justice.

Accordingly, a request was directed to the Attorney General. William P. Rogers, Deputy Attorney General, replied. He stated that some information had been made public through the hearings of the George committee, and that an indictment had been returned charging violations of law by Neff, Patman, and the Superior Oil Co. He therefore felt, he said, that it would be inappropriate to make files available prior to the completion of the trial. Subsequent inquiries failed to produce additional information.

On February 6, 1956, 11 days prior to the Presidential veto message, the Senate had passed Senate Resolution 205, creating a select committee "to investigate the circumstances involving an alleged improper attempt through political contributions to influence the vote of the junior Senator from South Dakota, Mr. Case, in connection with the Senate's consideration of the bill, S. 1853, the natural gas bill."

That committee met February 7, 1956, and selected the President pro tempore of the Senate, Mr. George, as chairman, and former President pro tempore of the Senate, Mr. Bridges, as secretary. That committee's hearings began before the Presidential veto message, and continued to March 5, 1956. The George committee reported its findings to the Senate April 7, 1956.

Following a Federal grand jury investigation in the District of Columbia, indictments were returned July 24, 1956, against Superior Oil Co., Neff, and Patman. Thereafter, the defendants entered guilty pleas. Fines of $10,000 on Superior Oil Co. and $2,500 each on Neff and Patman were imposed by the court.

Commencement of Senate action to investigate lobbying on the natural gas bill antedated the Presidential veto. The George committee investigation was limited to the Neff-Patman incident, while the resolution creating the special committee to investigate political activities, lobbying and campaign contributions covered a wider area of inquiry.

The special committee, therefore, conducted an extensive inquiry into activities relating to the Harris-Fulbright bill and the techniques employed to influence action on the bill.

TESTIMONY FROM SUPPORTERS
OF HARRIS-FULBRIGHT BILL

Immediately after the Phillips decision, the natural-gas industry began to organize a broad national campaign seeking to nullify, by congressional action, the Supreme Court decision in the Phillips case. Later, when their campaign was underway, a counter effort was launched by local public utilities, labor unions, and other groups which opposed the oil industry's effort.

From the time the Harris-Fulbright bill was first introduced until its passage by both Houses of Congress, there was a continuous stream of letters to Members of Congress from all over the country either in support of or opposition to the bill, as well as numerous personal contacts with Members of Congress.

Testimony was elicited at public hearings of our committee from the following organizations and groups supporting the Harris-Fulbright bill: Natural Gas and Oil Resources Committee, General Gas Committee, and Joint Committee of Consumers and Small Producers.

Major oil companies whose activities in support of the bill were the subject of public hearings were: Gulf Oil Corp., Humble Oil & Refining Co., Shell Oil Co., Standard Oil Company of California, and Standard Oil Company of Indiana.

Testimony was also received from opponents of the bill. . . .

THE CASE HISTORY OF A LOBBY

The Natural Gas and Oil Resources Committee (hereafter "NGO") was formally organized on October 20, 1954, by a cross section of the oil and gas industry. The officers were:

Chairman: Leonard F. McCollum (president of Continental Oil Co.).

Vice chairman: Paul Kayser; resigned in June 1955 (president of El Paso Natural Gas Co.).

Treasurer: J. C. Donnell II (president of Ohio Oil Co.).

Executive director: Baird H. Markham (retired; formerly with American Petroleum Institute).

The avowed objective of NGO was to formulate and execute a long-range public information program, national in scope, to inform the public concerning the business of exploring for and producing natural gas, the harmful effects of Federal regulation, and the benefits of an unregulated industry; also, to counter representations made by organized groups which allegedly distorted the role of the industry.

The testimony of Leonard F. McCollum, chairman of NGO, on legislative aspects of the campaign conducted by NGO, was in part as follows . . . :

MR. FAY (chief counsel to the special committee): Would you say that it was correct or incorrect to conclude that one of the ultimate aims was to influence legislation which would exempt gas producers from regulation or control?

++++

MR. MCCOLLUM: You said one of the ultimate aims. Now, I can answer your question this way: In the record is a statement of the Natural Gas and Oil Resources Committee, a statement of purpose, which . . . stated that . . . this committee . . . was a long-range information and education committee.

++++

Certainly if the public were informed on a subject as we understood it . . . one thing ultimately could be legislation of some form or the other.

++++

To answer your question, yes; it is conceivable that one of the results would be legislation.

MR. FAY: That was one of the results desired by the objectives and purposes of NGO?

MR. MCCOLLUM: One of the purposes was to inform the public and, if you will read my statement here, out of that they would realize the harmful effects of excessive Federal regulation, and if the public realized that, we are convinced necessary action will take place.

✦✦✦✦

THE CHAIRMAN (Senator McClellan): And one of its purposes was, in fact, primarily its chief purpose was, to influence legislation by informing the public and trying to persuade the public to your point of view; isn't that correct?

MR. MCCOLLUM: One of its purposes.

THE CHAIRMAN: Was that not its principal purpose? I am not saying that there is anything wrong with it.

✦✦✦✦

MR. MCCOLLUM: I would like to answer it was not the principal purpose.

THE CHAIRMAN: What was the principal purpose?

MR. MCCOLLUM: The principal purpose was to have an educated and informed public, so that the public would act, and one of the results would be legislation, not only against this Federal regulation but also that it would be an informed public, that we are under the threat of price controls, and they think we are making too much money and we don't think so. We have the problem of conservation, and we don't have an informed public. We know some of us contend and have fought for more widespread dissemination of information concerning the American petroleum and gas industry.

MR. CHAIRMAN: Let us see if we understand each other. The effect of your testimony is that these other purposes that you have just related were worthy objectives that would justify the forming of the organization, the committee, even though there had not been a decision such as the Phillips case. The other reasons you have given would have justified, in your belief, the creation of this character of a committee and prompted this character of program, public relations program, and public information program; is that correct?

MR. MCCOLLUM: Yes; that is correct, and you will find the record on several meetings where I, among others, have contended we should do this.

THE CHAIRMAN: Prior to the Phillips decision?

MR. MCCOLLUM: Yes, sir.

THE CHAIRMAN: But the Phillips decision actually set it in motion?

MR. MCCOLLUM: It kicked it off.

THE CHAIRMAN: And caused it to be created.

MR. MCCOLLUM: It hastened its creation; yes, sir. It hastened it.

The operations of NGO were financed by contributions based on a formula keyed to production. Contributions aggregating $1,950,000 were received from over 1,000 contributors. About 80 percent of the contributions, amounting to $1,646,500, came from the following 26 firms in the oil and gas industry:

Humble Oil & Refining Co.	$175,000
Texas Co.	153,000
Shell Oil Co.	138,000
Standard Oil Company of California	119,000
Socony-Vacuum Oil Co.	114,000
Standard Oil & Gas Co.	112,500
Gulf Oil Corp.	111,000
Phillips Petroleum Co.	81,000
Continental Oil Co.	57,000
Cities Service Petroleum, Inc.	56,000
Sinclair Oil Corp.	53,000
Sun Oil Co.	53,000
Atlantic Refining Co.	52,500
Union Oil Company of California	50,000
Ohio Oil Co.	47,000
Tidewater Associated Oil Co.	44,000
Amerada Petroleum Corp.	38,000
Pure Oil Co.	34,500
Sunray Oil Corp.	34,000
Skelly Oil Co.	33,000
Carter Oil Co.	25,000
Seaboard Oil Co.	14,500
El Paso Natural Gas Co.	14,050
Chicago Corp.	13,000
Richfield Oil Corp.	12,500
Honolulu Oil Co.	12,000

NGO did not register under the Federal Regulation of Lobbying Act, since it was stated that it was engaged solely in conducting an information and education program, without any direct legislative contact work. That conclusion was based on the legal opinion of its attorneys.

At the outset of its work, NGO retained the public relations firm of Hill & Knowlton, Inc., to furnish an outline of a complete program of operations.

One of the first steps taken under the guidance of Hill & Knowlton was the retention of Opinion Research Corp. to conduct a survey of thought leaders (editors, teachers, clergymen, professional people, businessmen, and farm leaders) on matters pertaining to the gas industry, at a cost of $10,000. Said firm interviewed 561 persons and submitted a comprehensive report of its work and findings.

Under the broad program outlined by Hill & Knowlton, NGO set up 15 regional districts throughout the country, with a regional chairman for each district. A chairman was also selected for each State. In addition, chairmen were also chosen for county areas and other local levels, personnel for which were furnished by the oil and gas companies.

The campaign to mold public opinion involved all media of communication, including newspaper and magazine advertisements, radio and television programs, films, speeches, and wide dissemination of numerous pieces of literature.

Elaborate kits were prepared by NGO for distribution to its representatives throughout the country, containing, among other things, material for newspaper editors, press releases, speeches tailored to various types of audiences, interviews, and scripts for radio-television broadcasts.

By September 1, 1955, it was estimated by NGO that it had distributed over 5 million pieces of literature; that its representatives had delivered thousands of talks and made thousands of contacts with editors of daily and weekly newspapers and organizations such as chambers of commerce; that about 500 radio broadcasts had been made by its representatives; and that extensive exhibition had been made around the country of a film distributed by NGO entitled "You, the People."

The manpower which enabled NGO to carry out its extensive program nationally was furnished by various firms in the industry without charge. The part-time services of approximately 3,000 men were thus donated to NGO. Such services were rendered while these men were engaged in their regular employment in the industry.

The expenses of NGO from October 1954 until March 31, 1956 amounted to $1,753,513.70. . . . The sum of $798,304.59 had been expended for newspaper and magazine advertising and $499,181.77 was spent for printed materials. The remaining sum, amounting to something less than $500,000, went to pay for administration expenses ($234,732.62), national publicity ($87,032.89), Hill & Knowlton, Inc. ($85,160), and lesser items.

The greater part of the disbursements were channeled through Hill & Knowlton, Inc., which paid for NGO's advertising, printed material and other items, and then was reimbursed by NGO. In addition to its fees of $85,160 mentioned earlier, Hill & Knowlton, Inc., made charges for staff time under an agreed schedule of rates, which are included in the expenses described above.

++++

One of the perplexing problems before the committee was whether to recommend that activities such as were conducted by NGO should be brought within provisions of any legislative activity disclosure act.

The testimony of Hines H. Baker, president of Humble Oil & Refining Co., one of the Nation's largest companies in the industry, sharpened not only the activities of NGO in relation to another group soon to be discussed (General Gas Committee) but also brought out relevant tax features. His testimony was, in part . . . :

THE CHAIRMAN: (Senator McClellan): What other expense did your company go to?

MR. BAKER: We contributed to the budget of the General Gas Committee.

THE CHAIRMAN: What was your contribution to that?

MR. BAKER: About $3,500 in that area.

THE CHAIRMAN: And to the Natural Gas and Oil Resources Committee? . . .

MR. BAKER: We contributed in 2 years to that committee $175,000.

THE CHAIRMAN: Were both of those contributions charged as operating expenses of the company in one category or another?

MR. BAKER: For income tax purposes?

THE CHAIRMAN: Yes.

MR. BAKER: The contribution to the Natural Gas and Oil Resources Committee was charged, but the other was not. The contribution to the General Gas Committee was not so charged.

+ + + +

THE CHAIRMAN: . . . There has been some issue raised here as to whether it is proper or improper to charge it, and the law is rather hazy on it at the present time. . . . I think it is something that will have to be resolved.

+ + + +

THE CHAIRMAN: What was the distinction or differentiation between the Natural Gas and Oil Resources Committee and the General Gas Committee that you felt a contribution to the former was a perfectly deductible expense, whereas the one to the General Gas Committee was not? . . .

MR. BAKER: The General Gas Committee arose out of the effort within the industry to unify all of the various elements in the industry on some common objective with reference to the enactment of legislation to overcome the effects of the Phillips decision, that is, to free the producer of oil and gas from FPC regulation and control.

+ + + +

The NGORC had a distinct purpose, and that was to present to the American public at the grassroots a better understanding of the natural-gas industry. . . .

The industry generally apparently followed the same course on tax phases, namely, to treat contributions to NGO as a regular operating expense and thus charged off for income-tax purposes, and to refrain from treating contributions to General Gas Committee as an operating expense, with no tax benefit thereon.

The following testimony of McCollum on tax phases is pertinent . . . :

SENATOR ANDERSON: The Treasury paid 52 percent in the beginning of this campaign, the Treasury of the United States put in 52 percent of the money right there. I assume that you are not exempt from the 52-percent corporate tax?

MR. McCOLLUM: We are not.

✛✛✛✛

SENATOR ANDERSON: Now, this certainly is either the promotion or defeat of legislation, or it is the exploitation of propaganda other than trade advertising. You are not advertising Continental Oil products in any way. How could you deduct it from gross income?

MR. McCOLLUM: Senator, your assumption is that we are lobbying.

SENATOR ANDERSON: Oh, no; I am leaving out the lobbying, and I am taking your statement at face value, that it is not lobbying. But the promotion or defeat of legislation—if you don't come under lobbying, you certainly come under that, and if you don't come under that, you get caught by the third category, the exploitation of propaganda other than trade advertising.

✛✛✛✛

MR. McCOLLUM: I tried to make it crystal clear this morning that this was a broad, national, long-range educational campaign.

SENATOR ANDERSON: But it was not conducted by your people as trade advertising . . . .

✛✛✛✛

SENATOR ANDERSON: Now, similarly, money which you spent for the promotion or defeat of legislation, and certainly some of this was designed to help pass the gas bill, or if not, it is the exploitation of propaganda other than trade advertising, and that is not deductible.

MR. McCOLLUM: I don't agree to that, Senator.

SENATOR ANDERSON: You don't agree?

MR. McCOLLUM: No.

✛✛✛✛

SENATOR ANDERSON: If you treated that as business expense and it is not— if it was designed to promote or defeat legislation, or was an exploitation of propaganda other than trade advertising, it should not be charged to business expense.

MR. McCOLLUM: It wasn't for that purpose. Here is the recited purpose of it.

SENATOR ANDERSON: Well, now, are we asked to believe that the purpose of this organization was not for the promotion or defeat of legislation or, failing that, for the exploitation of propaganda other than trade advertising?

MR. McCOLLUM: Yes, sir; you are asked to believe that and that is what the legal opinion shows we did.

SENATOR ANDERSON: You thought this was trade advertising that you were putting out here?

MR. MCCOLLUM: No; long-range educational information to acquaint the people with the facts concerning the production of natural gas.

SENATOR ANDERSON: Well, it is interesting.

++++

SPURIOUS TELEGRAM CAMPAIGNS

Two organized campaigns to influence senatorial vote through the use of spurious telegrams were the subject of public hearings before the committee. One campaign occurred in Minnesota; the other in Massachusetts. These campaigns involved different pieces of legislation, were sponsored by different principals, and were wholly unrelated to each other.

THE MINNESOTA CAMPAIGN
(Summary of Testimony)

In January 1956, particularly around the 12th and 13th of the month, Senator Edward J. Thye (Minnesota) received some 900 telegrams from Minnesota regarding the Harris-Fulbright bill to amend the Natural Gas Act. With few exceptions, the telegrams urged passage of the bill.

None of the telegrams came from Minneapolis or St. Paul, the two largest cities in Minnesota. Regardless of the size of the community, no more than 3 or 4 telegrams, usually 3, were sent from each. In all, approximately 300 communities in the State were allegedly the sources of the telegrams.

Several types of messages were used. With some variations, they were basically the same. It was not uncommon for the three telegrams from each community to have been sent not only on the same day but at exactly the same time. In some instances telegrams from 3 to 6 communities were all filed at one central point, an indication that some-one was collecting the telegrams.

The telegram campaign originated with and was supervised by representatives of Standard Oil Co. (Indiana), which firm bore the expenses of the telegrams.

An investigation and spot-check showed that many telegrams were sent without the knowledge or authority of the purported senders. The printed testimony shows in detail the mechanics employed in running the campaign.

Each level of personnel employed by Standard Oil Co. (Indiana) in

Minnesota, or dealing with its products, was utilized in rounding up prospects' names for the sending of telegrams from some 300 communities in the State, including division managers and the State network of regional salesmen and bulk agents on more local levels.

William C. Kniefel, northwest regional manager for Standard Oil Co. (Indiana), with headquarters in Minneapolis, testified that the campaign arose out of a meeting of Minnesota representatives of the company, which Joseph Markusich of the company's home office in Chicago attended. The subject was the Harris-Fulbright bill. Markusich advised the group that a plan to have the company pay for the telegrams was satisfactory to the company.

It was decided to concentrate attention on Senator Thye, according to Kniefel, because Senator Humphrey had publicly stated his vigorous opposition to the bill, whereas Senator Thye had not publicly declared his position on the bill.

H. J. Hilliard, manager of the Twin Cities division, and A. K. Reed, manager of the Duluth division, next in line to Kniefel, were among those who attended the meeting, and put the campaign into operation through some 402 bulk-station agents, 41 bulk-station salesmen, and other employees and agents.

One of the representatives of Standard Oil Co. (Indiana) who testified before the committee, admitted that he was responsible for the sending of 30 of the spurious telegrams.

Each representative who paid for telegrams sent during the campaign noted them on his expense sheet, for which he was reimbursed by the company.

According to Kniefel, the spurious nature of the telegrams was not discovered until some 7 or 8 months later, after the matter became the subject of investigation by the committee, at which time the home office expressed its disapproval of the entire program, allegedly having been ignorant of the same.

The cost of the telegrams amounted to about $1,500, the expense being ultimately borne by the company. The advice of Markusich at the January meeting was stated to have been given without authority or knowledge of the home office.

✦✦✦✦

DEMOCRACY'S DILEMMA

DOCUMENT 16 **THE BUCHANAN COMMITTEE'S CONCLUSIONS**

Do lobbies pervert the "public interest"? Or are they legitimate and necessary instruments for its definition and implementation? One tradition in political theory, which finds its inspiration in the stark and compelling logic of Plato's Republic, suggests that only when men are stripped of their selfishness, their sense of self-interest, can the common good truly be discerned. The eighteenth-century French philosopher Jean-Jacques Rousseau reformulated the Platonic notion in terms of the "General Will" and argued that pressure groups must be eliminated in the healthy community since they institutionalize selfishness and deflect the people from the needs of the society as a whole.

The American tradition, however, began with a different set of assumptions that were brilliantly expounded by James Madison in the tenth and fifty-first Federalist papers. The only operational definition of the "common good," Madison contended, is the residue that remains after groups have advanced their private views, struggled with their opponents, and achieved a synthesis: a compromise or a consensus. The legislature thus becomes an arena in which representatives of various interests fight, bargain, and reach at least temporary agreement.

However, in recent years, this Madisonian concept of the function of interest groups has been called into question. The growing international importance of the United States during the twentieth century has led serious commentators such as Walter Lippmann and George F. Kennan to express concern over the role of pressure groups in the conduct of foreign policy—emphasizing the essentially Socratic view that the management of foreign affairs is a delicate task that must be left to experts. They suggest that the average citizen is roughly as well equipped to advise a surgeon on a heart operation as he is to express a view, for example, on our government's policy vis-à-vis Cuba.

229

Even more fundamental is the question of whether the Madisonian model still adequately reflects American political realities. Underlying this Madisonian position is the assumption of equality of access—the right and ability of all interests to get into the arena and struggle for their goals. This report of the Buchanan Committee suggests that inequalities of access may be undermining the democratic character of the group-bargaining process.

PRACTICAL CAUSES OF LOBBYING

For all the high gloss with which discussions of lobbying are usually adorned, it remains a very practical problem with a number of very practical causes. First among these is our long and splendid tradition of free association. Americans are free to band together as they choose, subject only to the requirements of public safety. This tradition, compounded with the high degree of group consciousness and organization typical of any modern industrial society, has provided the raw materials from which our present system of lobbying has been built.

The tools with which this system was built were the constitutional guarantees of political freedom, especially the right of petition, of which lobbying is usually regarded as the most important expression.

The conditions in which a highly developed system of pressure politics could flourish were provided by two other unique features of our governmental arrangements. First, our political parties have grown progressively more loosely controlled and undisciplined. Pressure groups thrive on the inability or unwillingness of political parties to exercise the powers of government which they have lawfully gained at the polls. The advantages of this situation to the lobby group are obvious: lack of cohesion in the parties enables well-organized private interests to secure some of the advantages of political power without having to submit to the democratic electoral process by which this power is usually attained.

The necessarily complex structure of our Government, with its separation of powers, checks and balances, and bicameral legislature, has also contributed to the growth of lobbying. Complex government inevitably means government with bottlenecks at which pressure can be quietly and effectively applied. Thus the great pressure campaigns of recent years have relied heavily on the tactics of attrition and delay at

FROM: *General Interim Report,* House Select Committee on Lobbying Activities, House Report Number 3138, Eighty-First Congress, Second Session (Washington, D.C., Government Printing Office, 1950), pp. 62–67.

DEMOCRACY'S DILEMMA

every critical spot in the legislative process. The prevention of governmental action, and this is the aim of many lobbies, is relatively easy under these circumstances.

Finally, lobbying has reached its present proportions because our Government has always been sensitive to private demands. One successful piece of special pleading bred another and the entire system developed gradually but with irresistible momentum.

THEORY OF LOBBYING

While these practical causes are paramount, there are several theoretical considerations which underlie the present high level of lobbying activity. We lack and have always lacked any established theory as to the proper relationship and balance between private power and the power of government. Lacking such an established theory, we have rested our thinking about lobbying on two premises: first, that lobbying is not a problem of who is to exercise political power, but is, rather, a matter of expressly granted individual rights; and, second, that lobbying is no problem in a free society because one interest can be depended upon to "cancel out" another. This process of cancellation and compromise, it is said, should produce responsible public policy.

As to the first premise, the right of petition is cited as both the cause and justification of lobbying, and rightly so. Organized groups of interested citizens have an important informational and representative role to play in our kind of government. Citizens can and should exercise their right of petition individually and through organized groups. Without this constitutionally guaranteed right of petition, our kind of free government could not exist. But we often fail to recognize that while lobbying is a necessary right which should not in any way be restricted or abridged, it is a right which is not exercised for itself alone. People and groups seek to influence legislative policy because they hope to gain thereby and not because they want to keep their rights from becoming flabby for want of exercise.

So it is that, in their public utterances, lobbyists show the utmost attachment to constitutional rights. Privately, however, they often admit that rights to them are only a means to an end and not an end in themselves. As one of the most expert of them said, ". . . organized power is the only thing that government can take into account."[1]

It is also a bitter paradox that the right of petition, one of the highest rights which democracy can bestow on a free people, is sometimes

[1] [*Housing Lobby,* Hearings, Buchanan Committee.]

put to its most effective use by persons who are far from devoted to the principles of democracy. "I do not believe in democracy. I think it stinks,"[2] wrote Herbert U. Nelson, of the National Association of Real Estate Boards. Yet Mr. Nelson's organization was and is spending hundreds of thousands of dollars for lobbying, something which can only be done in a democracy such as ours.

The second major premise, that one interest will cancel out another, has been a staple of American political thinking since James Madison wrote his Federalist Paper No. 10. Unfortunately, Madison's prophecy has never matured; instead of canceling out, the pressures on Government have become cumulative. We referred earlier to the growing joint effort in lobbying, the long-run tendency of which is to break down the barriers against private domination of State power. Even if pressure groups did compete instead of joining forces, the advantage in lobbying would always lie with those interests which were best organized, best financed, and had the easiest access to mass media of communication. Organized business has always gained the most from lobbying because it has had the best organization, the most money, and the readiest access to publicity. It has had, in addition, the great advantage of seeking generally to prevent rather than encourage action by broadly based popular government. Given the strategic bottlenecks of our legislative procedure, it is far easier to obstruct than it is to create.

Could responsible public policy result from this theoretical canceling of group interests? It is not likely. While this process seems neat and automatic, it simply does not operate as it is supposed to. Even if it did, it would represent a degrading conception of democratic politics in which the highest function of government would be to yield to the strongest pressure. Absolute responsiveness to group interests is one thing, but truly responsible representative government is quite another.

All these questions inhere in the traditional American approach to lobbying. We raise them only to indicate that while lobbying is natural in our system, and should not be curbed, the outer limits beyond which lobbying is an offense against the welfare of the whole community have not begun to be charted.

THE COSTS OF LOBBYING

We seldom stop to consider the legislative costs of lobbying, perhaps because it is difficult to say when a measure is the product of lobbying and when it is an accurate reflection of real public need. Still 150 years

[2] [Ibid.]

of congressional history provide dozens of clear cases in which well-organized pressures have been instrumental in the enactment of ill-considered, inequitable, or vastly unpopular legislation. In many other cases, private pressures have been responsible for the defeat, delay, or emasculation of measures having overwhelming public support. With Congress daily assuming new and complex responsibilities, the dangers of increased pressure on the legislative process are very real.

What might be called the social costs of lobbying are even more serious, although just as seldom recognized. Our leadership in a troubled world demands clear thought and common effort; but can we maintain this leadership in the face of the social tension, the group conflict, the "me first" attitude of which mass lobbying is both a cause and a symptom? The lobby-as-usual philosophy which prevailed in some quarters during World War II should serve as a grim reminder that even the deadliest of national perils does not put an end to selfish interest. As we enter the new world crisis, this experience is both a sobering lesson and an ugly portent.

The lobbying situation is basically a reflection of the state of our economy. As the management of this economy has drifted into fewer and fewer hands, so too has pressure on the legislative front been sharply intensified. The giant concentrations of corporate wealth which the Temporary National Economic Committee found to dominate the prewar economy have developed since at an accelerated pace. It is inevitable that such great concentrations of economic power should seek to extend their power to the political field as well, and we count this fact as one of the most serious problems which large-scale lobbying poses for our kind of easygoing institutional structure. Economic power provides one of the essential raw materials for successful pressure politics; the greater the power, the larger are the possibilities of success. And so to the extent that some groups are better endowed than others, there is a disparity in the pressure which these groups can exert on the policy-making process. As we said earlier, "lobbying for all" may be a sacred right but it is a right which some men can make more meaningful than others. It is said, for example, that the individual consumer and the billion-dollar corporation have equal rights before the law, but are they equal before the lawmakers?

This, then, is the problem: the great political imbalance between tightly organized economic power blocs, such as big labor, big business, and big agriculture, and more casually organized interests and a loosely patterned state. This imbalance is reflected in lobbying activities as it is in other aspects of our national life.

We also count as "social costs" of lobbying the ideological conflict

and public confusion which has already begun to result from the growing use of a charged public opinion as an instrument of pressure. Men
need slogans, catch-phrases, and generalizations to reduce their experience to understandable terms. But these slogans should not be a substitute for thought; when they are, men have lost the first part of their
ability to govern themselves. Yet this is precisely what the pressure
groups and their public relations experts are about. Organizations seeking to protect a privileged status for their members at the expense of
the general welfare of all Americans use terms like "socialism," "stat-
ism," and "welfare state" to forestall rational analysis of legislative
proposals which they oppose. We are prepared to risk our national existence against totalitarianism, yet there are those among us who live
by the totalitarian principle of the great distortion, endlessly repeated.
Political freedom cannot live in an atmosphere of such hysterical over-
simplification.

There are finally the economic costs of lobbying to be considered,
and these are staggering. The costs of 150 years of relentless raiding
of the Public Treasury are beyond estimate, but we do know that the
present demands of the great interests total far more than the Nation
can afford. The people must also bear the costs of lobbying as well
as pay for its end results. It is ultimately the people who pay for the
big front and the high-pressure campaigns that the pressure boys put
forward. They pay Mr. Rumely's commissions on all receipts of the
Committee for Constitutional Government; they pay for the National
Association of Home Builders' round-robin telephone conferences; they
pay Mr. Purcell L. Smith the $65,000 salary which he draws as Wash-
ington representative for the private utilities; they pay the $2,000,000
which the American Medical Association has spent in its effort to defeat national health insurance. Pressure groups are quite free-handed
with both their own and with other peoples' money. The circle of
lobbying is endless, and endlessly expensive.

THE ALTERNATIVES

We have sought to express above our conviction that the present
system of pressure politics has assumed extraordinary proportions. We
have also tried to show that this system must continue to expand, and
that this expansion may challenge the existence of representative government as we have known it. What is to be done? The constitutional
right of petition must be preserved, and no restriction should be imposed on legitimate lobbying.

234   DEMOCRACY'S DILEMMA

A number of approaches to the problem have been suggested. Some of the more important of these are discussed below.

1. It has been suggested, seldom with any clear outline for practical implementation, that Government should support those important interests which do not have adequate resources so that they can contend on an equal basis with better-financed groups. This approach might help solve the problem of the present imbalance between various groups, but it would ultimately result in more rather than less pressure on policy making; we are not persuaded that this would be desirable. There is, in addition, the difficulty of selecting some reasonable criteria on which such support could be based.

2. Suggestions are frequently made that organized groups be given some formal place in the policy-making process. We already achieve something of this kind in the advisory councils to numerous administrative bodies and in the invitations extended to interested groups to appear before congressional committees on most major legislation. But we do not believe it would be wise to go beyond these steps. Again, there is a problem of choosing the criteria on which formal group representation should be based. In this respect, the experience of various European countries with official economic councils is not very encouraging. Would this not also be yielding to pressures rather than coping with them? Popular, geographic representation is basic in our system of government.

3. Streamline the legislative and administrative process, for pressures thrive on Government when it becomes too complex for ordinary citizens to understand. This may point to at least a partial answer, and the Legislative Reorganization Act of 1946 and the work of the Hoover Commission indicate that useful first steps have already been taken in this direction. There still remains, of course, a considerable need for further improvements.

4. We need stronger political parties and party discipline. This is basic. Much of the current onus placed on partisanship in politics overlooks the fact that if the parties don't accept responsibility the pressure groups will move in by default. Lobbying is no serious problem in a society where the parties can make up their minds and live up to their commitments. A stronger sense of party cohesion may be difficult to achieve in the United States, for most Americans seem to like their parties as they are. Ultimately, however, responsible parties are an essential requisite of responsible government.

5. We need more information on lobbying and lobbyists. This, at the moment, is the most feasible approach. Every group has the right to present its case, but at the same time Congress and the public have a

right to know who they are, what they are doing, how much they are spending, and where the money is coming from—in a word, full disclosure of the relevant facts. Such disclosure is thoroughly in accord with our system and principles and has already received legislative recognition in the Regulation of Lobbying Act. What is needed is that this act be equipped to fulfill more effectively the purposes for which it was designed. . . . The act as it stands is a workable and valid piece of legislation. Our recommendations will be designed to eliminate some of the misconstructions that have hampered the operation of the act. The act does not seek to regulate but to inform. It works on the simple premise that Congress and the public have the right to full information on those who actively attempt to influence the decisions of government.

No one of these approaches alone is equal to the magnitude of the problem we face; but together, they are the first steps which must be taken if special interest groups are not to ride roughshod over a public interest which may often be inarticulate.

There is a final catalyst which can cement these various approaches together into a solid and meaningful program. Prof. Stephen K. Bailey expressed it splendidly when he testified before the committee:

This is not a job for visionaries, although vision is needed; it is not a job for the calculating mind, although intelligence is needed; it is not a job for pressure groups, although the interest of every segment of our society must be weighed in the formulation of national and international policy. It is basically a job for people like yourself who know and understand the complexities and cross currents of political and economic pressures, but who are in a rare position to exercise moral judgments in the public interest over the conflicting claims of private groups.

Such moral judgments constitute the real answer to the existence of lobbyists. No registration law, no listing of connections and salaries in the Congressional Record, no system of party responsibility, by itself, can scratch the surface of the problem of controlling pressure politics. In the long run, a civilized morality is the sole key to the survival of democracy. . . .[3]

[3] [*The Role of Lobbying in Representative Self-Government,* Hearings, Buchanan Committee.]

STUDY QUESTIONS

1. What political considerations are there in the United States that contribute to the impotence of the national party committees?

2. What arguments can be advanced in support of the present system of nominating Presidential candidates? What alternative techniques could be utilized and what would their advantages and disadvantages be?

3. What role do party platforms play in the internal equilibriums of the Democratic and Republican Presidential coalitions?

4. Why have state legislatures not modified the distribution of electoral votes by use of the district system or by proportional allocation of votes to the parties according to their percentages of the popular vote?

5. It has been argued on one hand that limitation of campaign expenditures would contribute to a more democratic electoral system, and on the other that such limitation would interfere with the freedom of Americans who wish to support the candidates of their choice. Discuss the issues involved and develop a position of your own based on either of the two polar arguments above or any intermediate view that you endorse.

6. Discuss the statement that the real line of division in Congress is between urban and non-urban factions rather than between Democrats and Republicans. Are there other major lines of division?

7. What alternatives are there to the seniority system as a method of attaining committee positions and authority in the House and Senate? What difficulties do these alternatives present? Why is seniority maintained as the general ladder to power?

8. It has been suggested that the adoption of the British party system of centrally disciplined parties would create more problems in the United States than it would solve. Examine the advantages and disadvantages of such a project.

9. Is there such a thing as the "public interest"? If there is, how does one ascertain it? If not, is democratic government merely institutionalized selfishness?

10. It has been argued that if the people want something, they will organize to get it. If not, there is no point in worrying about the "unrepresented"—their inertia is their problem. Discuss efforts to regulate lobbying in the light of this proposition.

SELECTED
BIBLIOGRAPHY

BINKLEY, Wilfred E., *American Political Parties* (New York, Knopf, 1945).

BONE, Hugh A., and Austin Ranney, *Politics and Voters* (New York, McGraw-Hill, 1963).

BURNS, James MacGregor, *The Deadlock of Democracy: Four-Party Politics in America* (Englewood Cliffs, N.J., Prentice-Hall, 1963).

KEY, V. O., Jr., *Politics, Parties, and Pressure Groups* (New York, Crowell, 1958).

———, *Public Opinion and American Democracy* (New York, Knopf, 1962).

McKEAN, Dayton, *Party and Pressure Politics* (Boston, Houghton Mifflin, 1949).

ROCHE, John P., and Murray S. Stedman, Jr., *The Dynamics of Democratic Government* (New York, McGraw-Hill, 1954).

SCHATTSCHNEIDER, E. E., *Party Government* (New York, Farrar and Rinehart, 1942).

———, *The Semisovereign People* (New York, Holt, Rinehart and Winston, 1961).

TRUMAN, David, *The Governmental Process* (New York, Knopf, 1951).

WHITE, Theodore H., *The Making of the President, 1960* (New York, Atheneum, 1961).

RANNEY, Austin, and Willmoore Kendall, *Democracy and the American Party System* (New York, Harcourt, Brace & World, 1956).

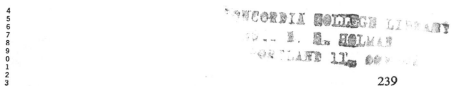
239